ILLUSTRATED
HISTORY OF
BASEBALL

ILLUSTRATED HISTORY OF
BASEBALL

BY ROBERT SMITH

MADISON SQUARE PRESS
Grosset & Dunlap
Publishers • New York

This book is dedicated to my friend
General Matthew B. Ridgway
(U.S.A., ret.), Soldier, Statesman, Sportsman,
and a true national hero.

Acknowledgment

Let me offer public thanks to a number of friends who helped me gather, verify, and record the facts on which this narrative is based. They include: Hank Bauer, Jim Bunning, Stan Coveleski, Frank Crosetti, Joe Dugan, Elston Howard, Waite Hoyt, Mickey Mantle, Tim McAuliffe, Marvin Miller, Red Reeder, Joe Reichler, Tom Rooney, Seymour Siwoff, Bob Turley, Gene Woodling, the late Lee Allen, and the late George Weiss.

Picture Credits

JOHN E. BIEVER: 282 (bottom)

VERNON J. BIEVER: 210, 215

BOSTON PUBLIC LIBRARY: 69, 72, 87 (bottom), 88, 89, 90–91, 92, 121

BROWN BROTHERS: 14, 20–21, 26, 48, 64–65, 78, 83, 87 (top), 94, 103, 108–109, 110, 114, 148, 202, 203

FRANK CROSETTI: 145, 242, 261

CULVER PICTURES, INC.: 17, 18–19, 25, 28–29, 32, 36, 38, 42–43, 45, 46–47, 51, 52, 56, 60–61, 75, 84–85, 97, 100, 107, 112, 115, 119, 122, 125, 128, 141, 158, 169, 184, 187, 188, 194

DAN GOSHTIGIAN: 280, 284

LOUIS REQUENA: 166, 170, 172, 175, 207, 213, 220 (bottom), 225, 226, 232, 244, 245, 248, 251, 254, 256, 291 (bottom)

WILLIAM TAGUE: 234, 252

UNITED PRESS INTERNATIONAL: 137, 150, 155 (top), 163, 182, 214, 216, 258, 264, 266, 268, 272, 275, 278, 286, 287, 288, 291 (top

WIDE WORLD PHOTOS: 116, 117, 130, 131, 134, 138, 144, 152, 155 (bottom), 157, 159, 176, 177, 178–179, 191, 196–197, 198, 201, 208, 220, 228–229, 320–231, 239, 262, 282 (top), 292

Jacket illustrations:
FRONT—Photo of Walter Johnson, Brown Brothers.
          Photo of Reggie Jackson, Malcolm Emmons.
BACK—Schoolboy baseball players, 1887.
          Culver Pictures, Inc.

Contents

ILLUSTRATED HISTORY OF
BASEBALL

Early Days

WHEN baseball began it was no more complicated than a game of tag. A boy—or girl: Both sexes played the game—used a small straight stick that was wielded in one hand to strike at a ball, tossed into the air by himself or served him by a playmate. If he struck it off, no matter what direction it carried, he then scampered for the safety of a base. If the ball was recovered and he was hit by it before reaching the base, he was "out," and another "striker" moved in. There were no sides, no scoring, no foul lines, no good pitches or bad. It was one child against the mob, with all his playmates scattered about, ready to retrieve the ball and hit him with it as he ran for

the base. If he hit the ball far, he might make it to the base and back.

Being hit out by the ball was not likely to do damage, for the ball, which might be just a leather sphere stuffed with cloth, was no more lethal than a bag of beans. Yet from out of this simpleminded pastime grew the National Game of the United States—a game that has made some men rich, driven others to drink, turned whole cities upside down, and even lured a U.S. Senator from the councils of his country to come rule over the organized version.

Once the game had been imported to America, it began to grow rougher, wilder, faster, and far more complex.

The playing of sides had begun in the mother country, where the rule (to keep sides taking turns with the bat) was "one out, all out." Such a rule was required, because it took a great deal of breathless footwork and swift accurate throwing to recover a batted ball and hit a moving runner with it. And there was no other way of putting a striker out. There were no real "positions" in the early forms of the game. There was the striker and sometimes a bowler—or pitcher. All the rest of the party were "scouts," who scattered themselves all over the playing area, wherever a batted ball might land.

This helter-skelter form of the game, which had been called rounders in England, became known as town ball in the American Colonies, it being habitually played on a day like Election Day or Town Meeting Day, when all the habitants would be turned out in the same place, with time to play games. It was also called burn ball, sting ball, or soak ball, after its most interesting feature—the whacking of the ball against a runner's hide. It could still involve all the grown or half-grown males in a town, because there was no limit to the number of scouts allowed to scramble for the chance to cut down a runner in full flight by soaking him with the ball.

The ball became harder in the Colonies, where young men, particularly in the rural areas, were privy to the delight of taking and giving hard blows. The harder the ball, the more exciting the game, for fear of a bruising wallop on the backside lent speed to every runner's feet. Sides eventually were required to keep the game in bounds—to provide strikers enough to move a runner beyond the first base and to add zest to the competition by counting scores.

Gradually the game fell into more formalized patterns, with each section of the country evolving its own private design. The Massachusetts Game, which its partisans held was the most demanding and the most rewarding version, was played throughout New England. This form of the game lasted until well past the middle of the nineteenth century and seemed destined to grow into the accepted style for the nation.

In the Massachusetts Game, there was an official pattern for the arrangement of bases—a quadrangle with a post, for a base, at each corner. The posts were 60 feet apart. The home base was not the spot where the striker stood, for obviously he could not hit from a post. Instead he stood inside a four-foot square equidistant between first and home base, facing overhand throws from the server or bowler 35 feet away. The bowler and the catcher were required to change places every three innings, and the striker could stand up there until he found a ball he liked. If he hit the ball he could be put out by being plugged with it anytime he was not in contact with one of the bases. Once he was out, his whole side was out. The game was played for 100 runs, and the first team reaching that score in even innings was counted the winner. There could be from 10 to 14 players on a side, but only the thrower and the catcher were assigned positions. The first intercollegiate baseball game, made much of in official baseball history, was not baseball at all but this Massachusetts Game. When the scorer of that game recorded that a player had been "hit out" off third base, he meant

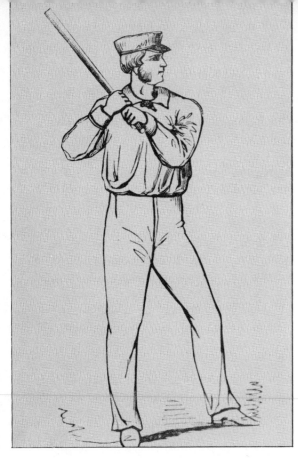

The striker, or batter, in the early versions of baseball (usually called Town Ball), used a stick not much larger than the billy club children used to use in rounders — the British ancestor of the game.

In Town Ball, as in the Massachusetts Game, the ball was not pitched, but thrown overhand. A "square pitch," that is, an underhand toss, was a feature of the New York Game, invented by Alexander Cartwright.

The catcher, also called "behind" in early versions of baseball, stood far enough behind the striker's position so that he had no difficulty in taking the throws barehanded.

Bases, in the earliest versions of the game (including the one Abner Doubleday was supposed to have invented), were often posts rather than bags.

he had indeed been hit, so that he felt it.

There was still another game in Philadelphia, which was far closer to what baseball eventually became. In 1833 the Olympics Base Ball Club of Philadelphia were playing a game that used a "diamond square" design for the base arrangement, with an iron plate—home base—at which the striker stood. In the Philadelphia version the base runner could be put out by being tagged with the ball or by getting the ball to the base ahead of him.

This politer method of disposing of an enemy on the baselines apparently was better suited to gentle young men who liked to play the game in their good clothes. In 1845, when sting ball, soak ball, burn ball, and the Massachu-

setts Game were still heartily enjoyed throughout the small nation, Alexander Joy Cartwright, a member of a group of well-to-do New York City youths who habitually met several afternoons a week to play some sort of ball game, worked out on paper, with the help of a friend named Wadsworth, a new game that had no plugging in it, used the Philadelphia design, and assigned players to regular positions.

Cartwright's game had some of the features of catapult ball—another goal game involving a ball, fashioned after the ancient game of cricket. Catapult ball required no bowler or pitcher. The ball was originally set on the end of a board, seesaw fashion, and propelled into the distance by a blow by foot or fist on the high end of the board. While

players undertook to retrieve the ball and set it back at "home," the striker would see how many times he could race back and forth between home and a base before the ball was returned. Eventually this game too was played with a bowler, who simply served the ball to the striker until a serve suitable to the striker came up. The striker achieved safety and counted a score when he grounded his bat (which he carried with him) in the "crease" or "hole" marking the striking position. This was the "one-hole catapult" or "one-hole cat" that became "one 'ole cat" and then "one old cat," or "one-o-cat," known to all our grandfathers. When it was played with two strikers and two holes, it was, of course, "two-hole cat."

Cartwright borrowed the "base circle" (really a square) from the Philadelphia Game and enlarged it. He kept the one-hole-cat feature of putting a man out by simply getting the ball to the base ahead of him. But he used the pitcher and catcher of Town Ball and the Massachusetts Game and did not require the striker to carry his bat along but used only the home base as a striker's point. (There were also a "pitcher's point," some 45 feet away from home and a "catcher's point," which originally was 40 feet or more the other side of home. Until late in the nineteenth century the men chosen to pitch and catch were often listed as "in the points.") In the Cartwright version the pitcher threw underhand.

Despite what the legend at the

The Knickerbockers and the Excelsiors were acknowledged, in the 1850s, the most expert practitioners of the New York Game. Dr. Jones, in the top hat and frock coat, eventually organized the first national baseball tour—by the Washington (D.C.) Nationals. Harry Wright created the first admittedly professional baseball club, the Cincinnati Red Stockings of 1869.

The Red Stockings of 1869 included Harry Wright (front row, center), Harry's brother George (back row, second from left), and Asa Brainard (front row, second from right), the best pitcher in the land.

Baseball Hall of Fame may say, Cartwright did not suggest the nine-inning game. His game was to be played until one side or another, in even innings, had scored 21 or more "aces." An ace was scored each time a runner crossed the home base. There were no strikes or balls, but balls that landed outside the baselines were foul. And a runner could be put out by the ball getting to the first base ahead of him or by tagging him, with the ball in the hand, if he was off a base.

In this game, hitting was important —indeed, it was practically the whole game. But it was almost impossible to avoid getting a hit, because the ball was made largely of India rubber, and the striker could hold his position at the plate until the bowler served him a ball to his liking. If a man waited too long for a pitch that suited him, he might be hooted at by his own teammates, but he was not penalized. Every man was entitled to "his hit." If the ball, after being hit, was caught on the bounce (or on the fly) by an opponent, the striker was out. This rule applied even if the ball merely ticked the bat and went into the hands of the catcher on one bounce.

It took no skill to be a pitcher, for it was deemed unsportsmanlike to use wiles of any sort to keep a striker from making his hit. A bowler (or pitcher) who tried to deceive a batter would be looked upon much as would a golfer today who tried to distract an opponent by making loud noises or waving his arms as the opponent was teeing off. In Cartwright's game, which was soon called the New York Game, all the pitcher was supposed to do was toss up the ball so the striker could wallop it.

Individual skills were not made much of to begin with in this game. Anyone in full possession of his major faculties could pitch, and almost anyone could eventually hit the ball with the bat. Speed on the bases was of some account, although the ball usually bounded so far and so fast that the first base could be taken without strain. Stealing bases was not countenanced, and the use of dodging or sliding to avoid a tag was deemed a cowardly deed. Even strong language was ruled out of the New York Game as first played by Cartwright's playmates, who called themselves the Knickerbocker Club. A man who used a big, big D in the heat of the action was fined 25 cents. And so was a man who failed to show up for practice.

Among the young gentlemen of Murray Hill who first played the game, it was not thought necessary to bind the performers with a whole decalogue of regulations to keep them from taking mean advantage of each other. Strikers were expected to strike as heartily as their strength allowed. Fielders were supposed to deal with whatever balls came into their territory and not to poach upon the territory of others. Pitchers were supposed to deliver hittable pitches; fielders, who never even thought of wearing protective gloves, were supposed to retrieve wide pitches and foul hits and get them back into play as swiftly as possible.

Men who could field ground balls with dexterity or catch fly balls on the bounce without dropping them were considered the best players of this Knickerbocker version of baseball. But none earned any special fame. The game was all for fun, and every club member was expected to have a go at it. Outsiders—that is, nonmembers of the club and those ineligible for membership, from lacking the means or social position—were not welcome even to watch the play. If spectators did gather, they were expected to behave with as much decorum as the players themselves. And the players performed in white cricket flannels and straw hats.

Nothing the original Knickerbockers could do, however, could keep the lesser breeds from imitating them. When the Knicks began to play match games with clubs of their own standing, they took their games across the Hudson River to the bucolic reaches of Hoboken, New Jersey, where lay the Elysian Fields, the site of many cricket contests. Young Irishmen and impecunious Dutchmen, who could no more have aspired to membership in the Knickerbocker Club or its like than they could have lectured on the binomial theorem, saw the teams in action there and soon caught on to how the game was played, it being not too unlike the soak ball they were accustomed to playing on New York's wide and unpeopled West Side dumps. It was from among these outlanders that the first crack players were developed, although a few grew out of the athletic staffs of the clubs themselves.

For these doughty young men, not unlike the Frenchman who thought the purpose of a fox hunt was to run a sword through the fox, assumed that the purpose of a baseball game was to win it, and they set out to accomplish that aim through stratagems that would bedevil rulemakers throughout the next five decades.

First of all, they observed that it was possible to deceive a batter by flinging the ball at top speed toward the home base, so that the best he could do was top it or pop it up. Then they learned —or at least one ingenious young Irishman named Dickey Pearce, from Brooklyn, discovered—that it was possible to throw the entire enemy team into turmoil by not hitting the ball hard at all, just tapping it so it would land in fair territory and roll away, out of reach of the distant catcher. These merry young men also took to running from one base to another when a soft pitch was wobbling to the plate, forcing the poor catcher to stand close behind the striker if he was going to have any chance of throwing a runner out.

As a result of the elemental changes these men made, plus the adoption of the Philadelphia nine-inning rule, the game of baseball suddenly became swift, thrilling, and tightly contested, one in which men could take or give a bruise and where daring, muscular strength, and sharpness of eye and hand were rewarded with victory. Within a very few years the New York Game had taken over the whole city, and there were a dozen or more clubs that could field teams who played with dash and skill.

The gentlemen's clubs, which were not immune to the impulse to finish first, began to recruit numbers of un-gentlemanly players to represent them on the baseball diamond—awarding them jobs, or make-believe jobs, in some plant or emporium controlled by a wealthy member, to enable them to play as amateurs. But even with all the major clubs—the Knickerbockers, the Excelsiors, the Atlantics, the Eagles, the Gothams, the Putnams, and the Charter Oaks—fielding baseball nines

made up of young men whose hands were soiled with the dirt of the forge or ditch or quarry—there still persisted in each club a "muffin" nine, consisting of members who played just for the joy of tossing the ball about. And in the middle of the nineteenth century nearly every major city had organized baseball nines that counted in the hundreds, with every profession—from cops to schoolteachers, and including the men who delivered the milk—boasting a baseball team with its own colors.

Colors were as important to baseball as they were to horse racing, which, when baseball was taking hold, was the number one spectator sport in the land. In the midcentury baseball caps were multicolored, like jockey caps, and might vary from position to position as much as from club to club. Some clubs set far more store by their uniforms than by their play. More than one baseball club outfitted itself in the ballooning-trouser style of Colonel Ellsworth's Zouaves, along with braided jackets and fezzes, and tried to play ball in such attire. And nearly all, when visiting a club for a match game in another town, paraded in decorated carriages, with a marching band, both before the game and after. There were team songs, a bountiful refreshment tent near the third base line, and organized merriment after a game in which the home club set out to overwhelm its opponents with the generosity and variety of its food and wines—and even its "fine ice cream."

One aspect of the sport that derived directly from its gentlemanly antecedents was the gambling. Betting was open and almost universal, with sometimes even the umpire getting a wager down on one of the clubs in the game he was calling. There was only one umpire in a baseball match game throughout the game's first several decades, even after it had become openly professional. In the early days the umpire was a gentleman in a top hat, with a stool to perch on, who took his stance off to the right of home plate, sometimes a great deal farther away than the catcher, and who did not move up "under the bat" until there were runners on base. But the umpire did not need to crouch under the bat in the beginning, for he was not called upon to decide on balls and strikes. A batter could stay at bat as long as he pleased, to begin with. And even after baseball had got its growth, the umpire did not begin to call strikes until after he had gruffly warned a dilatory batter that he had received a "good pitch!"

There were, of course, no admitted professionals in the amateur game that flowered just before and immediately after the Civil War. One club even carried a rule on its books providing for a stiff fine for a member who accepted money to play ball. But there were only a few score of really able players of the New York Game in the whole land, and the big athletic clubs, moved by pride as much as the urge to win wagers, scrambled after them as earnestly as professional coaches today scramble after quarterbacks.

Of the early experts, who, regardless of rules, played for pay or at least were awarded no-show jobs at high salaries, the best-known of his day—the late 1850s and early 1860s—was James Creighton, a young pitcher for the Brooklyn Excelsiors, who was lured from one club to another through promise of better pay. Creighton seems to have been the first to discover that an underhand pitch did not need to be a

toss, and that speed could be supplied by cocking the wrist and giving the ball a last-minute flick. Creighton's "lifting speed"—the ball, starting about shoe-top high, came zooming up and up until it seemed to explode past the batter's face—was the marvel of its day, considered illegal by some, but unhittable just the same. Creighton died in 1863 from an injury sustained on the diamond, apparently a ruptured bladder, following the strain of running out a home run. The game's first martyr, he was honored by mourners throughout New York City.

Other heroes of the 1860s, when the New York Game ran away from its original sponsors, were mostly men who could field bouncing balls with dexterity or gather in long hits and throws on the fly. (The Knickerbockers, early in their career, began to insist on the "fly game," when most clubs still adhered to the traditional catch-on-the-first-bounce rule. This assured the Knickerbockers of only game and experienced opponents.)

Peter O'Brien, black-bearded shortstop of the Brooklyn Atlantics, was one of the best known players in baseball country, which stretched from New York City and its immediate suburbs to towns up the Hudson to which the early clubs could conveniently travel. But three of his teammates finally outreached him in fame. Dickey Pearce, who succeeded O'Brien as shortstop, was not only among the best at this difficult position (the shortstop had to cover all the ground between the pitcher's point and the baselines), but he was an innovator at bat.

Whether Dickey, a stumpy but handsome Irishman with a luxuriant moustache, invented or just accidentally dis-

Baseball, in the 1850s, inspired many a dance-tune. The uniforms, featuring a linen shirt with dickey-bosom, a collar and tie, long flannel trousers and high shoes, were not designed for rough-and-tumble play. Bats were long and skinny, similar to some of today's softball bats, and the ball was about the size of a modern softball.

The Atlantics of Brooklyn became Champions of America after they defeated the Excelsiors, 15 to 14 in 1860. Cleverest of them all was little Dickey Pearce, third from left. Steadiest was Old Reliable Joe Start, fourth from left, most famous first baseman in the East. Peter O'Brien, the whiskered gentleman in the center, captained the club, and before Pearce came along, had played shortstop. Jack Chapman, who stands at O'Brien's left shoulder, played left field and was known as "Death to Flying Things."

covered the bunt, it is now too late to determine. But he remained for a long time its ablest practitioner, and he is acknowledged the inventor of the fair-foul hit—a devilish device that drove catchers and pitchers into frenzies of profanity. All Dickey used to do was tap a pitch in such a way that it struck in fair territory and then rolled off over the foul line, sometimes so deep among the spectators that it would take two or three minutes to recover it—minutes Dickey would use to rack up as many bases as his limber legs could cover. The rules in the early days called any hit fair if it *landed* inside the baselines

or their extensions, and Dickey's bunts surely landed fair, even if they wound up under a carriage somewhere. Eventually the rulemakers called such ground balls foul, if they left fair ground before passing beyond a base. But it was years before they could even put a few limits on the bunt. As late as the 1890s, the thefty crew from Baltimore was using bunts to wear out pitchers with. And Cap Anson, one of the century's mightiest basemen, was trying to ridicule it out of existence by calling it "the baby act."

Joe Start, first baseman of the Atlantics, was called "Old Reliable" because he seldom dropped a throw. Nowadays a first baseman who drops any throws at all could be called "Old Stonefingers." But in those barehand days, just before and after the Civil War, catching hard-thrown balls all afternoon with no glove on was a task for a doughty fellow indeed. Joe was the personal hero of young Mike Kelly, who became perhaps the most famous ballplayer of the 1880s, largely through his fame as the man always ready to slide. Young Mike, playing for amateur clubs in Washington, D. C., where his soldier father was stationed, and later for a team of kids in Paterson, New Jersey, tried to imitate Joe Start in dress and in batting style. But Mike became a catcher and an outfielder rather than a first baseman, for he was too fast-moving a man to be anchored at one base.

The most famous Atlantic outfielder was young Jack Chapman, a lean, horse-faced fellow, tallest on the team, whose curly hair and dark moustache drew most female eyes on or off the field. Jack, for his skill at catching balls on the fly—one of the most vital skills of his day—was called, in the stilted catchphrase of that tight-buttoned era, "Death to Flying Things."

But even when the Atlantics were defying the whole world to come take their measure, most of the nation was still playing woolier brands of baseball than the New York Game. In some places there might be 10 fielders on a side, and you could still find—in the back reaches of the eastern and southern states—teams that played the game with posts for bases and scored outs by slamming the ball hard at a moving enemy. Even early in the twentieth century, Rube Waddell, newly come to organized baseball, forgot himself one day and picked a runner off first base by felling him with the ball. "That's *out,* where I come from!" Rube explained.

By the time the Brooklyn Atlantics were ready to meet the great Cincinnati Red Stockings—the first club to admit they were paying their players in cash—for the championship of the baseball world, spectators had begun to crowd right on to the field of play. One Brooklynite, forebear no doubt of the breed that would thrive in the borough for nearly the next century, helped settle the championship business by leaping right on to the back of Atlantic outfielder Cal McVey while he was trying to gather in a fly ball.

The techniques of baseball remained elementary throughout this era. The professionals, such as George Wright, Andy Leonard, and Asa Brainard—all members of the famous Cincinnati Red Stockings (named after the stockings a young lady named Margaret Truman made for them by hand)—prided themselves on their dexterity with the ball. Leonard and Wright especially would amaze and excite spectators before a game by doing tricks with the ball such as a schoolboy today would find commonplace—tossing the ball high and catching it in one hand, bouncing it off the inside of the elbow and catching it, and flicking it from behind one's back —over the head or shoulder—and grabbing it before it struck the ground. George also set spectators to shouting in a game by his weasel-like ability to avoid a tag on the baselines, by dodging, reversing direction, faking, ducking, and wriggling away. Runners in the 1860s and 1870s were slow to take up sliding, although Bob Addy of the

This is the Excelsior Club that first carried the New York Game up the Hudson in 1860 to play amateur clubs in upstate cities. Their fearsome pitcher, known for his ''lifting speed,'' was Jim Creighton, who holds the ball in his hand. The ball by this time had been made smaller and bats much longer.

Forest City nine of Rockford, Illinois, frequently made spectators laugh and opponents curse by slipping to his duff to slide into a base under a tag, with dust spurting high. Bob's act was largely thought a clownish one, and many hard-core ''kranks'' (the old-time name for fan) deplored it openly and often, as tending to turn the grand game into a hippodrome or something less lovely.

The style of the game generally was rather like a modern softball game played by men not thoroughly schooled in it. The ball was oversized. It was delivered underhand to the bat. Occasionally it was so alive with rubber that it would bound higher than a man's head upon striking the outfield turf. And sometimes it was so mushy that a hitter could hardly drive it out of the infield. Bats were far from uniform in size. Some parts of the nation still played their version of baseball with bats that looked like sawed-off broomsticks. Bats in the East might be longer than a man's leg.

Most infielders played with a foot on the base they were covering, wandering away from it only to pursue a ground ball. The first baseman sometimes would stand in foul territory, the better to deal with fair-foul bunts. Only the shortstop would range far and wide, covering the open space between the pitcher's lines or point and the baselines. Inasmuch as the pitcher stood only 40 feet away from home plate, there was a wide area to cover, between first and second and between second and third. George Wright, curly-haired, happy-faced, with gleaming white teeth, was one of the first shortstops to play ''position'' on batters, even going behind the baseline sometimes to make it harder for a batter to get a ''daisy-cutter'' through to the outfield. In the event of a foul fly, the shortstop might even hurry in and crouch by the catcher (or by whichever player was trying to make the catch) to be ready to grab the ball should it bounce out of the other man's hands, as it too often did.

There were sports publications— such as *Mercury* and *Spirit of the Times*—that gave coverage to baseball. But boxing, cricket, horse racing, cock fighting, croquet, and rowing were likely to command more space. The first writer to give himself over exclusively to the new game, or to its New York version, was a bearded gentleman of British origin named Henry Chadwick. Chadwick, who had played the game in Washington, D.C., as a member of a loosely organized club called the Nationals (they played on the White Lot, opposite the White House, on the spot where softball games are sometimes played today), devoted himself so wholeheartedly to baseball that he was known to most kranks and players in the late nineteenth and early twentieth century as the Father of Baseball. Even A. G. Spalding, who practically invented the modern organization of the professional game, often referred to him as Father Chadwick. It is in many ways typical of Organized Baseball that Chadwick, who certainly had as much to do with popularizing the game as any man who ever lived, received very little solid reward from the men who controlled the game and owned the clubs. Even in death Chadwick has been memorialized less than Abner Doubleday, whose claim to the fatherhood of baseball, made long after Doubleday's death, is about as solid as my Uncle Joe's.

Chadwick ended his days living on a tiny pension from the National League, forced to write—in bitter contravention of his principles—reports of ball games played on Sundays. Even when death was close the poor old man, barely able to sustain himself and his wife on the meager pension and stingy space rates paid by publications, continued to write out, in his cramped, patient script in green or purple ink, play-by-play accounts of the big league games. In his best day, Chadwick had been one of the ultimate authorities on baseball rules and their interpretation, had helped revise the rules, and had written many a handbook on how to play the game. He was editor of *Beadle's Dime Baseball Player* (the "Spalding Guide" of the day) and of other regular publications that codified the rules and recorded the season's doings on diamonds in every city.

In Chadwick's time there were already hundreds of baseball clubs throughout the land, with a dozen or more, organized and uniformed, in every major city. But it took a visit from one of the top clubs to illustrate how the game should be played and to excite new young men to try it.

It was considered a special accomplishment to catch batted balls on the fly; nines that were willing to play "the fly game" were deemed especially redoubtable. If a "pretty hit," one that

sailed high into the heavens, was taken by an outfielder before it could touch the turf, there would be screams of delight. When the New York Mutuals, Boss Tweed's club—originally sponsored by the Mutual (volunteer) Fire Company—played the Cincinnati Red Stockings (made up largely of professionals recruited from Eastern nines), the kranks and writers commented wonderingly on the fact that "not a single fly catch was dropped!"—not even an incredibly high cloud-scraper delivered by Harry Wright. Nowadays even a high school outfielder who lets such a fly ball drop wants to go hide behind the scoreboard. But in the Sixties and Seventies there were hundreds of paid baseball players who had never learned to catch a ball, except with the hands held together like an open clamshell. When a lad named Jerry Fruin came from New York to St. Louis to scratch out a baseball diamond in the dirt in a lot that was to become Lafayette Park, he had to teach his playmates the "Eastern trick" of letting the hands give with a thrown ball, so as to be sure it would not bounce free.

The players on the Mutual and Red Stocking teams were the most skilled in the land, and the game they played, on June 15, 1869, was acknowledged the finest ever seen. The score (4 to 2 in favor of the Red Stockings) was so incredibly low that followers kept repeating it to each other. A score in that day might add up to more than a hundred. When the Red Stockings beat their hometown rivals, the Buckeyes, in a match game of baseball, the score was 103 to 8. (The Buckeyes disbanded after that game.) And less skilled clubs were not the least abashed to report scores of 111 to 98. When the Chicago club, after the ball had been slightly deadened, was actually kept scoreless in a game, a shutout became known as a "Chicago." For a long time afterward, sportswriters would report that this or that team had been "Chicagoed" by its rival.

The Red Stockings are famed now as the first professional baseball club. They were not the first aggregation of paid players—merely the first nine that admitted out loud they were taking regular salaries for playing baseball. Harry Wright had long been irritated by the hypocrisy of setting up imitation jobs for ballplayers brought in from far and wide to create a nine; Chadwick, too, had insisted almost from the start that the frank hiring of players (at a "moderate" salary) would help rid the game of some of its evil influences, notably the acceptance of a few dollars to throw a game to the home club, to accommodate local bettors.

Before the Red Stockings were organized, the rival club in Cincinnati, the Buckeyes, had been paying their players steady wages. Most of the great names of early baseball—Al Reach, Harry and George Wright, Al Spalding, Dickey Pearce, Bob Ferguson, and Cal McVey—depended on baseball for their living, even though they might have told the census taker they had other occupations. (Spalding and George Wright were "clerks," while Harry was a "jeweler." Spalding's salary, however, was about ten times what the other clerks in his shop were paid. And George Wright, when he played in Washington, gave a vacant lot as his business address.) Big Al Reach, who played first base for the original Philadelphia Athletics, never made any secret of his willingness to play "for

the top dollar." Al, like Jim Creighton, had started to play baseball with the amateur clubs in Brooklyn and finally starred for the Eckfords—a club organized by a shipbuilder and scorned by many clubs in the New York area as being peopled by "greasy mechanics," that is, men who worked about the shipyards or pretended to. The Athletics lured Al Reach away from the Eckfords by openly offering him a weekly salary.

The National Association of Base Ball Players, formed in 1857, nevertheless still insisted that it was strictly an amateur association. In 1865 at the very time that the Forest Cities of Rockford, Illinois, was paying seventeen-year-old Al Spalding $40 a week to be a four-dollar-a-week grocery clerk, the Empire Club had to drop James Roder from its roster because he accepted money to play. Club members, like modern college alumni, often rewarded athletes with gifts, prizes, or bonuses, and they did so largely for the glory of the club. Gate receipts were of no concern to the original amateur clubs. Indeed admission charges had first been introduced to cut down on the attendance at match games. When the Nationals took their baseball team beyond the Alleghenies on the first "national" tour, the team refused any share of gate receipts and would not accept more than a free lunch from any of the hosts.

But before 1869, the game of New York baseball, hardly more than twenty years old, had begun to draw crowds in the thousands in all parts of the nation. The Knickerbockers, believing that the game belonged to them, had been reluctant to form a "national" association. Indeed when the association began, it included only the clubs

Games with a bat and ball were played in England in the fourteenth century. The figures at the top are engaged in club ball, with a young lady about to toss a ball for the gentleman to wallop with a ragged club. In the center picture, one player is about to toss an enormous ball into the air to strike it off with a long paddle. This game was called "fung-o" in Scotland. The figures at the bottom are using a catapult to toss the ball up to be struck off with a paddle. This game was the grandfather of catapult-ball or cat-ball, which became one-hole cat and finally one-o-cat.

in the New York area and not all of those. There was, however, no restraining the youth of the land. Baseball was one of the finest games in the world to play and one of the simplest to learn and find room for.

Of course the dressed-up version of the game became fairly complex compared to the vacant-lot version. In the organized form, home plate was a solid iron disk, like a manhole cover, and bases were squares of thinly stuffed canvas, spiked to the ground. Sometimes the foul lines were engraved with the help of a horse and a bull-tongue plow. The balls were made of two pieces of horsehide carefully sewn over a stuffing that consisted of a large pellet of India rubber, swathed in wool. The bats, long and heavy, were made of hardwood, thick in the handle and wider at the business end. Some crafty strikers (until the practice was outlawed) preferred to flatten their bats on one side so they could more carefully place fair-foul hits. (Kids occasionally played the game with old cricket bats.)

The Cincinnati Red Stockings, to

show off the garments from which they took their name, were the first to appear on the diamond in short pants, a style that was promptly adopted everywhere, so that more than ever the game seemed like a kids' game persisted in by adult men. And grown men everywhere engaged in it. It was possible in those days (the Sixties and Seventies) to buy a set of baseball spikes that could be attached to dress shoes, so that a man could ready himself to take part in a game in a few seconds and go right from ballpark to office.

The National Association of Base Ball Players soon became national. Even before the Civil War was to spread the baseball gospel throughout the opposing armies, there had been clubs on the Pacific Coast, in the South, and throughout the Midwest. And right after the war the touring clubs were to find skilled opponents in nearly every quarter.

The tour of the Nationals was ruined, according to Colonel Frank Jones of the War Department, who helped organize it, by a skinny, long-legged teen-age pitcher for the Rockford, Illinois, Forest Cities. The Nationals took on this small-town club as a warm-up before playing the big-time club in Chicago, the Excelsiors. (In Chicago, the Rockford Forest Cities were called "the country boys.") But Rockford took the game from the Nationals 29 to 23, and everyone agreed that it was the kid pitcher who made the difference. His name, Albert Goodwill Spalding, still appears on the baseballs used by the National League, for like a number of the game's other early heroes, Spalding went into the sporting goods business. He managed to wangle the contract to supply all the balls to the League,

which he himself had a hand in organizing. Al Reach of the Athletics also made baseballs for a living when he grew too old to play. His name and facsimile signature appear on the balls used by the American League. The balls are identical, made by the same manufacturer to the same specifications. Only the signatures are different. The Spalding organization quietly absorbed the Reach company early in its career. George and Harry Wright, the other big names of baseball's beginnings, also sold sporting goods. Harry was partner in Wright and Mahn, which was accused of making "mushy baseballs" and did not stay long in business. George's firm, Wright and Ditson, was still doing business in Boston years after George's death at the age of ninety. (And they, too, had been taken over, without publicity, by Spalding.)

Admission charges (of ten cents or more) were made regularly in the 1860s, and some amateur clubs divided the receipts among the players on a cooperative basis. A few of the old-time amateurs deplored this practice of charging people to come look at the game, and some resigned from their clubs in protest. But the gate receipts (at first deemed the property of the man who owned the field or put the fence around it) grew so rapidly, even before the game's post-Civil War explosion, that men soon were able to abandon regular chores and devote their full time to organizing or managing teams that played baseball. By the late 1860s the major clubs were counting total seasonal receipts in the tens of thousands.

By this time the game had changed so radically that there was no knowing it. Perhaps the first major change was the effort of the pitcher to keep the batter from getting "his hit." This was followed by efforts on the part of the batters to outwit the defense, through the bunt, the fair-foul hit, or by merely refusing to swing at pitches that did not suit their tastes. There had been earnest efforts all along the way to shame ballplayers out of resorting to such tactics. In 1874 writers reporting the baseball game between Harvard and Yale spoke scornfully of the Yale pitcher's ignorance or lack of sporting blood: He delivered the ball to the plate with a sort of sweeping sidearm throw that was not a pitch at all and merely meant to provide him an unfair advantage.

But unfair advantages were being sought all along the line by politicians, by gamblers, and by ballplayers alike. It became necessary first of all to give the umpire power to start calling "strikes" on a batter, even when he had not struck. (McKeever of the Mutuals once watched fifty pitches go by before he offered at one.)

But then to keep matters in balance, the pitcher also had to be prevented from delaying the game by deliberately keeping the ball away from the batter. If the umpire felt that the pitcher's efforts to avoid the plate were deliberate, he could start calling "wides" —and three wides were enough to give the batter the first base free. Such matters as a runner's passing another on the baseline, catching the ball in the cap instead of the bare hands, and deliberately letting a fly ball drop to create a force play all had to be dealt with one at a time, either by changing the rules or adding new rules to cope with them.

But it was one thing to write a rule and quite another to see it obeyed. With only one umpire on the field, who sometimes had to turn his back to a base runner or a fielder to see some other part of the play, all sorts of skullduggery was perpetrated. Sometimes a runner would not bother to touch all the bases on his way home. And sometimes a player would distract the umpire so a mate could catch a fly ball in his cap.

Or players learned in the rules might take advantage of careless phrasings, as when a pitcher would push a mate aside so *he* could catch a foul fly. On such a fly, the rule said, the base runner was immune from being tagged out until "after the ball had settled in the hands of the pitcher." What the rulemakers intended was that the ball should be tossed back to the pitcher in his position before fair play could resume. But they forgot to say it that way and crafty characters like Al Spalding were quick to take advantage, by leaving the pitcher's point to catch such a fly and then quickly tagging the runner out. The ball *had* settled in the pitcher's hands!

Nearly every team in the land carried a clubhouse lawyer who knew enough about the written rules to invent a dozen ways to get around them. To enforce the use of the "square pitch," or underhand toss, instead of the brutal throw by the pitcher, the rules set forth that the ball must be delivered with the hand "below the belt," so some pitchers began to wear their belts under their armpits. When Cornelius McGillicuddy of East Brookfield, Massachusetts, known all his life as Connie Mack, was a lanky catcher with Pittsburgh, he took special advantage of the rule that put a batter out if a foul tip, or tick, was caught on the fly. ("A tick and a ketch," young players learned to tell themselves, "will always fetch.") Connie, like most catchers of the late Seventies, wore fingerless kid gloves to ease the bruising on his hands and give him a better grip on the ball. Connie learned to skip his gloved hands together in such a way as to reproduce the sound of a ball ticking the bat. Then he would catch the ball and look to the umpire who, often as not, would declare the batter out.

Infield play in early professional baseball remained relatively static, even though George Wright and a few others had long been "playing position" on batters by shifting left or right, shallow or deep, according to the skills and habits of the man at bat. On many clubs there was not much made of adapting the player to the position. Inasmuch as basemen usually played with one foot on the base and ranged only a few feet this way or that, with hardly any coordination of play among the defenders on other bases, a man could just as well play second base as third, be he tall or short, left-handed or right-handed, fast on his feet or slow.

Before the introduction of gloves and catcher's mask, protective equipment consisted sometimes of no more than a wide rubber band worn by the catcher over his mouth to reduce the incidence of fat lips and loosened teeth. The first to wear gloves were the catcher and pitcher, who used dress gloves with the fingers cut off as much to counteract the spin of the ball as to protect the flesh.

With all the ballplayers in short pants, the uniforms were distinguished usually by the color of the stockings. Besides the Red Stockings in Cincinnati (they shifted to Boston in 1871), there were the White Stockings of Chicago, the Blues in Hartford, and eventually the Browns in St. Louis. A wide leather belt was standard, and usually the belt buckle, worn at the side, displayed the club emblem—an Old English "E" for 'Empire Club' or a "B" for Boston. The letter also appeared on the dickey bosom of the player's blouse.

For a long time players wore neckties on the field, and some took pride in their clean collars. (Wes Fisler, an outfielder-infielder of the original Philadelphia Athletics, who played in the 1860s, was long known as "the icicle" for his coolness on the diamond. He usually finished nine innings without soiling or rumpling the new paper collar he had put on at the start of the game.) Baseball shoes came over the ankles, and some had spikes as sharp as those on track shoes. Before the coming of short pants, players often tucked their trousers into the tops of their shoes. And even when the pros were wearing their little-boy britches, coming just below the knees, or sometimes tightened above it and blousing down over the knee, many amateur clubs still clung to cricket-style uniforms with long flannel pants.

For many years substitutes could not be used in a baseball game. If a pitcher had to be changed because the batters were making too free with him, the relief man was brought in from right field, where he always played until needed on the pitcher's point. The used-up pitcher then repaired to the outfield and stayed in the game. If a man suffered a disabling injury *during* the game, he might be replaced. But if he was taken ill the night before, looked too long upon the wine when it was red, or just missed the horse-drawn omnibus, the club would have to take the field without him.

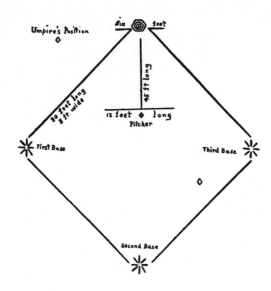

Umpire's Position
◊

Six   feet

45 ft long

90 feet long
3 ft wide

12 feet ◊ long
Pitcher

First Base ✳

Third Base ✳

◊

Second Base
✳

Right ◊ Field

Left ◊ Field

Centre ◆ Field

The New York Game in the 1850s placed the pitcher 45 feet from the striker, who stood at the home base. (In the Massachusetts Game, the striker stood between the home base and the first base.) The catcher stood about the same distance the other side of the striker, and the umpire placed his stool where he could judge "wides" and also make decisions at the bases.

The order of batting was haphazard and unscientific. "First bats" was thought to be an advantage—as it surely was in a game like Town Ball, in which the first side up might stay at bat all afternoon and part of the next morning, to count scores in the hundreds. It was usually decided by the toss of a coin, or even by the flip of a stone that had been spat on, with one of the captains calling heads or tails, or wet or dry. The winner of the toss almost always decided to put his team up first. It took more than a decade of competition to teach ballplayers the advantages of coming to bat last in a game that required even innings, as baseball did.

Men went to bat usually in the order of their importance on the club, with the captain coming first. Or they might bat the way they did in one-hole cat, with catcher leading off, pitcher coming second, and right fielder last in line. One of the first to suggest the use of science of a sort to arrange a batting order was Henry Chadwick. It was best, said old Henry, to place a weak hitter between two strong ones. One must never, he averred, have three strong strikers coming up in a row. Nor did it ever occur to him that the best striker should stand anywhere but first in the order.

Field strategy developed slowly, along with the growth of the idea that the pitcher's job was not merely to serve balls to the striker but to try to put him out. When a strong pitcher was on the points, basemen were advised to play close in, the way they might play today when a play is expected at the plate. If the pitcher had less speed ("medium-paced"), then basemen were urged to lay back and allow the shortstop to cover second base. By this time the pitcher was enclosed within a box to keep him from charging up to the delivery point from a spot ten yards behind. To invite him to take part in covering bases would have been deemed a sort of sacrilege.

Not much thought was given either to the proper method for hitting a pitched ball with a bat. Every man had his own style, as each man carried the sort of bat he liked best. Some bats in the Sixties and into the Seventies were true "wagon tongues" that required a man's strength to heft. The striker ordinarily just whaled away at a pitch from whatever pose it pleased him to take. It was not unusual for a batter to face the pitcher squarely or to point his bat forward like a "charged bayonet" before the pitch came down. (Even in the early 1900s when Christy Mathewson started to play baseball for pay, he held his bat cross-handed at the plate.)

Because there was no rule against passing the runner ahead of you on the baselines or even one requiring runners to stay on the baselines, the early base runners and sliders developed tricks and show-off stunts to take advantage of these lacks. Mike Kelly, the most famous slider of all, taught his teammates who preceded him to the plate to stop quickly and allow him to dive through their straddled legs to tag the plate first. And once in an exhibition game when one of his long hits became lost in the deep outfield grass, Mike solemnly made a tour around each outfielder as he proceeded around the bases toward home.

Before the Kellys and the Nolans and the McGillicuddys entered the game, ballplayers—except for a few stray Irishmen such as Peter O'Brien and Dickey Pearce—mostly were the Anglo-Saxon, Dutch, and French names of middle-class America: There were Spalding and Wright and Barnes and Brainard; Polhemus, Jones, Zettlein, and Creighton; Waterman, Pabor, Cummings, Shelly, Holden, Ketchum, Fisler, Reach, Kissam, De Best, Chapman, Eggler, Addy, Cuthbert, Gould, Allison, Mills, Wolters, Walker, Simmons, Hastings, Barker, and Cone. Many of these men initially were manual workers, but none were spawned in the city slums or had toiled in the silk mills or the shoe factories that soon drove young fellows to the ball diamond to seek an easier way to make a dollar.

Mike Kelly perhaps did most to teach ballplayers how to slide and use deceit. (He once ended a game in the evening gloom by pretending to catch a ball that really sailed far over his head.) Edward Nolan demonstrated the value of fearsome speed in delivering the ball to the plate. Deacon McGuire was only one of a group of intrepid catchers who caught up close, defying black eyes, broken fingers, and split lips. (A catcher named Dockney once caught a game while wearing stitches in some fresh knife cuts acquired in a barroom discussion the night before. When a fast ball broke the stitches, he kept on catching with the blood pouring down his chest, soaking his shirt and pants.)

Eventually the National Association of Base Ball Players gave way to the National Association of Professional Baseball Players. Their membership was indeed a far different breed of cat from the long-trousered and soft-spoken young men who a few years earlier had formed the association. These were men who, alas, made no bones about their devotion to the high dollar; they were sometimes openly addicted to drink, and from having been long short of cash, were far from immune to the lure of an easy few pieces of silver. As a result, while the Game continued to thrive in ever new environs—on the prairies, in the bursting cities, in factory towns, and in farm villages—the professional version fell on evil times indeed, when one team after another had to disband or seek new playgrounds. Baseball for a time, while a great game to play, lost favor as a spectacle. But there were always a few places where great games were played and where men and boys, and even a few women, paid to watch.

Reds and
Browns and Whites

IN the new organization of Professional Baseball Players, which constituted the major league of its day, the Boston Red Stockings were supreme. They played their games in Boston's South End, on a field purchased from the Hammet family, where Walpole Street ran into the roadbed of the Boston & Providence Railroad. There was a fence around the park—as there needed to be now that the game lived on admission fees—and there was a small grandstand with wooden benches that held up to 500 customers.

For the most part the players lived close to the park and walked out there through the pleasant open streets on game and practice days, sometimes car-rying their bats and often followed by wide-eyed worshiping boys. A. G. Spalding, no longer just the kid who had beat the Nationals but now a fleshed-out strapping, long-armed young man—and the greatest pitcher of his day—took rooms at the southern end of Washington Street (which had been Orange Street when the city was new, the longest street in town). Spald-ing roomed with Cal McVey of In-dianapolis, who had played right field for the Red Stockings in Cincinnati, and Roscoe Barnes, the game's greatest fair-foul hitter, who had been Spald-ing's teammate in Chicago. Although some of their mates were timid about admitting they were no longer amateurs upon arrival in Boston, these three proudly gave the census taker their occupation as baseball player. Harry Wright, captain of the team, at first set out to pretend he was still a "jeweler." And George Wright, the batting and fielding star, opened a shop on Eliot Street where he sold "cigars and base-balls," what time he was not destroy-ing baseballs at the park. George made his home in Savin Hill, then one of the choicest residential sections. Most of the others lived within a few blocks of where Spalding, Barnes, and McVey had hung their hats.

They all thus became one with the town, neighbors to most of their fans, and as much a part of the South End scene as were the famous Chickering Piano factory and the Reformatory for Penitent Females. There was a horse-drawn railroad that brought spectators from distant sections, but mostly on game days the kranks walked in from Roxbury and even from South Boston to cheer their new champions.

For four consecutive seasons the Boston boys came in first. One season they never lost a home game. And invariably Al Spalding did the pitching, tossing the ball up tirelessly day after day and seldom meeting a crew that could lick him. From 1872 until 1876 Spalding won more than two thirds of his games every season. And he usually pitched at least 40 games in a cam-paign. In 1875, however, he pitched 70 and lost only 18. This was, inciden-tally, the most games that the Boston Red Stockings ever played in one sea-son before the founding of the National League.

It was not just the skill of Spalding, Barnes, Wright, and the big catcher Jim White (who had caught for the other Forest City team, the one in Cleveland) that made the Reds great. It was also their reputation for clean behavior and avoidance of any truck with gamblers, or "pool sellers." Drink and gambling, which would eventually spell the doom of the association, were open and notorious. At championship games in some of the cities, and notably in New York, whiskey sellers, like the soda pop sellers of a later day, traveled among the crowd peddling their bottles out of baskets. Professional gamblers openly shouted their odds and took bets for hours before the game began. Some-times the odds would be posted on a board beneath which the pool sel-lers would retail their slips. And it was not at all unusual to see a gambler hand-ing money to a uniformed ballplayer before the game began, money that the ballplayer would shamelessly count right there in public before tucking it into his pocket and going out to take care that the other team won.

Sportswriters in many cities through the early Seventies and even later often called for an end to baseball in their town, for it had become far less lovely a spectacle than cock fighting or bare-knuckled fighting, and it was often as phony as modern-day professional wrestling matches, a mere hippodrom-ing with the outcome all agreed in advance among players and umpires. Certain of the traveling teams even brought their own umpire with them and insisted that he judge all the play. One newspaper writer urged the home team one day to fold up and go home if they could not play a square game. A St. Louis paper declared that the pub-lic had seen enough of the noisome spectacles crooked ballplayers put on. And a paper in Buffalo suggested that its own heroes might do well to schedule an early game with the Keeley Institute, a plant devoted to drying out and curing confirmed alcoholics.

With the association clubs playing only from 45 to 85 games a season, they did not, of course, encompass all of baseball, either as a sport or a spectacle. Nor was the professional game really a business, inasmuch as admission fees could not support much more than a few salaries and the ground rent. The usual admission fee was 25 to 50 cents, still a considerable sum to a working man and one that he was not likely to lay out for amusement more than once or twice a week. A few clubs, despite scanty income, committed themselves, in a scramble to sign a few top players, to salaries they could not sustain. And one of the better clubs, the Hartford Dark Blues, could not draw custom enough in Hartford and had to play their "home" games in Brooklyn, N.Y.

Outside of Boston there were players aplenty who were ready to sell a ball game to any gambler who could come up with the price. Nor were club owners themselves immune, what with the scanty collection of quarters and half dollars they were gathering at the gate. The New York Mutuals, or "Mutes," that collection of nonworking civic employees, carried in their outfield a fellow named Dick Higham, who won national notoriety in later years as the first (and only) umpire ever caught accepting a bribe. The Mutuals also found room on their payroll for a shortstop named Thomas Devyr, who had been accused of taking money to fix a game and had never, in some people's eyes, been properly cleared. The Mutes also listed on their roster a man named Ed Duffy, who had been the supposed

promoter of that fix; Duffy was not deemed fit company for honest young men. Another player named in the same scandal was William Wansley, who after sitting out a season or two, came back into the game without a black mark against him. And there were few more bare-faced fixers than the man who owned the Lansingburgh Haymakers, State Senator John Morrissey, later part owner of the racetrack at Saratoga. Morrissey's club won or lost as he directed. And when it could not beat the Cincinnati Red Stockings in 1869, the team just walked off the field so that John would not have to pay off.

Open professionalism was supposed to be the cure for game fixing. But professionalism had been reasonably open for years, despite spasmodic efforts to discipline men who took money to play or clubs who paid them. Eventually the Amateur Association had thrown up its hands and admitted that *some* of its members played the game for more than love. But even then, the gamblers found any number of players willing to add to their take by playing less than their best.

The Association of Professional Baseball Players also suffered because only a few of its clubs were able to complete their schedules every season. The Chicago White Stockings went out of business for two seasons—1871 and 1872—because of the Great Fire, which broke out on the very day the White Stockings were scheduled to play the Rockford Forest Cities. New clubs joined the association each year as old ones dropped out, until only three were left that had lasted from the start: the Philadelphia Athletics, the Boston Reds, and the New York Mutuals.

By 1884 Harry Wright, having built championship clubs in Cincinnati and Boston, was leading another in Providence, Rhode Island. Brother George was still the best shortstop around. Radbourne, the pitcher, an Illinois boy, became the Old Hoss when he pitched 72 complete games for this club and led them to the championship. Joe Start was the Old Reliable at first base. John Montgomery Ward, pitcher and shortstop, became the leader of the first players' union, the Players' Brotherhood, which staged the strike of 1890.

By the Seventies professional baseball had grown more swift and skillful. Not all basemen had learned to range away from their bases to play position on the batters, and not all outfielders had learned to shift, but most of them had and the shortstop particularly had begun to specialize in grabbing hard ground balls on either side of the diamond. And other men began to specialize in regular positions, depending on their size, speed, and strength of arm; most of the long-legged fellows sought jobs in the outfield, and scurrying, sure-handed boys looked for work on the bases.

Among the amateurs, of course, the old-fashioned style clung for several more years, and fathers still taught their sons—regardless of what they might see on the professional diamond—that they should keep one foot on their base until the ball was hit and they knew where it was going, while even paid players in the back reaches of the country continued to catch balls with their wrists together. Some amateur, or muffin nines, continued to shun the "fly game" as one too likely to put a man's fingers out of joint and disqualify him for a week from pushing a pen. (The pros had dropped the "out on the first bounce" rule in 1864.)

This is not to say that the quality of play on all the professional nines was of the first order. Catchers still appeared in the 1870s who could not throw all the way to second base on the fly. Easy flies were often muffed in the outfield, and spinning foul pops often escaped the base hands of an infielder. Indeed, in a game in Boston in 1871, when George Wright, crouching beside Cal McVey, grabbed a foul pop-up that had bounced out of Cal's hands, the spec-tators set up a roar such as a modern crowd might offer a home run.

But the game was faster than ever. Runners were dodging and sliding as never before. Infielders raced out on the grass to relay throws to the plate. And the catcher, safe behind the new bird-cage mask, invented by a Harvard man named Thayer, invariably took his position close behind the plate.

While Henry Chadwick still seemed to long for a return to the old Knickerbocker spirit when men played as much for glory as for gold, and when "brute strength" in pitcher or batter was of less worth than craft and self-control, the other "fathers" of the game, Harry Wright and A. G. Spalding, were hard at work improving it and spreading its gospel. And Jim O'Rourke, the Boston first baseman, who was known as "the Orator" for his skill with the telling phrase was fighting the good fight on behalf of the uniformed player.

Old Harry, who did not like to be called the Father of Professional Baseball because it made him "feel old," freely answered inquiries from everywhere about laying out diamonds, charging admission, and recruiting players. He also offered earnest advice on conditioning and diet (rare roast beef was the ticket, said Harry).

Al Spalding, itching at the dismal prospects for an ambitious young man in professional baseball, and just having completed a triumphant baseball tour of Canada, conceived the idea in 1873 of taking a baseball team over to England to demonstrate what the Americans had cooked up out of rounders crossed with cricket. He managed to raise wind enough among the game's wealthy promoters to ship himself over as advance man to England, where he found

Truthful Jeems Mutrie (in the derby) named this 1883 New York club the Giants. Biggest and toughest was number 13 (at Mutrie's left hand), first baseman Roger Connor. Best loved by the fans was the catcher Buck Ewing. Longest known to fame was the invincible pitcher, Tim Keefe, number 2.

remarkably few sportsmen interested in sponsoring an exhibition of America's National Game. Whereupon, with the agility for which he was noted, Spalding quickly changed his pitch by offering to bring over a set of American ballplayers to meet the local heroes in *cricket* matches. That was a gray horse of a very different hue. The fathers of the Marylebone Cricket Club, half-persuaded by Spalding's glib tongue that they had thought of the notion themselves, immediately agreed to sponsor a match, and other cricket clubs followed their lead. In 1874 two teams, organized and led by Spalding, made the trip. The players, recruited largely from the Red Stockings and the Philadelphia Athletics, included the best cricket players in America— George and Harry Wright and Philadelphia's Dick McBride, all of whom

had often played the British game for money. Sam Wright, no baseball player but an able cricketer and the younger brother of Harry and George, also came along. The trip was widely publicized, and the players were accorded a smashing send-off that included flowers, champagne, cheers, and even tears. They were greeted with enthusiasm, astonishment, and a bit of condescension in England, where the natives had been taught that all Americans wore goat beards, kept saying "tarnation," chewed tobacco and spat freely, whittled all the time, and damned the British in every breath.

Baseball did not excite the British audiences, who found it perplexing, dull, and not at all suited to the British nature. They were pleasantly surprised to observe that the Americans, sunburned and heavily muscled as they

Cap Anson's champion White Stockings owned two of the country's hardest throwing pitchers, Fred Goldsmith and Larry Corcoran. Silver Flint, in his shirt sleeves in the back row, was the only man who dared catch their speed. Mike Kelly, who became the greatest name in professional baseball, was playing shortstop and outfield in Chicago. He later became a catcher.

were, could speak intelligible, if rather peculiar, English, dressed neatly, comported themselves decently, and might almost have been taken for gentlemen. And Englishmen gasped with delight, not unmixed with horror, at the way the Americans played cricket—with utter disregard for form or personal safety. Indeed the only players who did not show up well in the cricket matches against the British clubs were the Wright brothers and McBride, who were learned in guarding the wicket and wielding the bat heartily only against the "wides." The other American lads hauled off on any ball that was "over the plate," belting it from here to there and making four runs at a time. The "wides" they simply let go by, as they had learned to do in baseball. The Americans, allowed seven extra players as a handicap, won all the cricket matches but one.

Spalding's success at promoting this tour may have encouraged him to bend himself more earnestly to the development of a scheme he had long nurtured for putting professional baseball on more solid footing at home. Spalding, whose middle name was Goodwill, was forever laboring to make his own future more secure by building business goodwill that would accrue to his personal advantage. He noted that baseballs varied wildly in rubber content; some amateurs still tried to play with a ball that was made mostly for bouncing, while even professional games were disrupted by balls too lively or too mushy. Spalding worked for the adoption of a standard ball that would be supplied by a single manufacturer working to assigned specifications. The interesting angle to this scheme was that Spalding was to receive a royalty on every baseball sold.

But the major weakness of professional baseball lay not in the equipment but in the behavior of its people. Drink, corruption, and "revolving" were driving the kranks to other pastimes. Few fans enjoyed paying 50 cents to watch a befuddled outfielder weave about under a fly ball and fall to the ground before he could catch it. And most kranks preferred to believe that the players were all making an honest effort to bring their own side in first. As for "revolving"—moving from one club to another in search of a better payday—it usually meant that the best-heeled clubs soon owned all the good players. A poorer club might lose almost every game in a season's campaigning. It also sent angry club managers roaring into law courts, seeking recourse when a player, after pocketing a salary advance, showed up with a fatter contract on some other nine. Half a dozen of baseball's most sought-after stars in the Seventies were guilty of walking out on meager contracts to sign with wealthier, or more generous, clubs, and the subsequent litigation had further tarnished baseball's already begrimed image.

The old Amateur Association once had adopted a rule requiring that a player on any nine must have been a member of the club for thirty days before he could take the field in the club's uniform. But this rule had no more effect than the rule against paying ballplayers, and when the association went professional it was forgotten. The

Chris Von der Ahe, St. Louis grocer and saloon keeper, who financed the original St. Louis Browns. He built a statue to himself in the baseball park.

Philadelphia Athletics once even bought a ballplayer a new suit of clothes and paid his debts only to see him cavorting within a week in a Chicago uniform.

The scheme Spalding had been hatching was designed to tighten and strengthen league structure and to put enough power in the hands of the governing body to eradicate the basic evils. But it was also a plan to bar from membership in the league, association, or whatever, any underfinanced or poorly manned clubs such as had attached themselves so often to the Professional Association, to the dismay of kranks and club owners alike, who came to see sharp competition, not hopelessly one-sided clobbering matches.

The man who receives credit for dreaming up the formula that became the permanent foundation for Organized Baseball was William A. Hulbert, a director of the Chicago club, who with the help of a Chicago writer named Lewis Meacham, first presented a list of proposals for reforming the game. The proposals, appearing in the Chicago *Tribune* over Meacham's byline, constituted almost the complete plan for a new organization that became the National League of Professional Baseball Clubs. There is room for suspicion, however, that Al Spalding was more than an interested reader of these proposals, for he had been thinking (and talking) along the same lines for years. And Spalding had a genius for persuading other men (as he had persuaded the fine fellows at the Marylebone Cricket Club) that the idea he was selling them had sprouted in their own brains.

Spalding almost instantly became a prime mover in the scheme. Although he pushed the scheme earnestly and shrewdly until he saw it take life, Hulbert did not really share Spalding's faith. Indeed, he predicted that the new organization would probably last only five years. (In 1976, it will have lasted a hundred.)

Fathered then by a sportswriter, a businessman, or a ballplayer—or all three—the National League of Professional Baseball Clubs was born in 1876. It is ironic that the first step in its creation was accomplished by flagrantly violating one of the rules its creators vowed they would strengthen. For Hulbert, with Spalding's help, grabbed the whip hand in the association by stealing away four players already under contract to the Boston Red Stockings:

Spalding himself, outfielder-catcher Cal McVey, strong man Deacon White, and crafty Ross Barnes, the fair-foul expert. This was the very guts of the Boston club—the best pitcher in the league and three of its finest hitters.

The news of the transfer of these worthies from Boston to Chicago was supposed to be kept secret from the world—particularly from the Boston kranks—until the 1875 season was over. But a Chicago writer, gleefully sharing the secret, just could not keep from bragging about it. And when the shocking news reached Boston, the kranks were enraged. Small boys who had been wont to trail Spalding and his mates from the Commonwealth Hotel all the way to the ballpark, seeking an excuse to touch them or share a few words, now ran screaming at their heels: "Deserters! We'll dirty up your damn white stockings for you! Go to hell!"

Whatever pain these verbal assaults gave to Spalding, McVey, Barnes, and White, it was assuaged by thoughts of the extra dollars they were assured of in Chicago. There was some uneasiness at the prospect of being expelled from the association. But Hulbert comforted the four deserters with the assurance that the association needed them more than they needed the association. And this, as it turned out, was indeed the truth.

The association, with its strongest franchise gutted, looked shaky indeed, and club owners who had lived on faint hopes of better days ahead now lay awake in fear that the worst was at hand. It took but a few minutes' tough and persuasive talk by Hulbert (who had also made off with Adrian Anson, the Philadelphia Athletics' finest batsman) to convince the owners of the Athletics, the Mutuals, the Hartford Dark Blues, and the Red Stockings that their future lay with him and his new league, for which he had already recruited the teams in St. Louis, Cincinnati, and Louisville.

The clubs that made up the new league, first organized in Louisville and completed with the capitulation of the Eastern clubs, were no doubt the best in the country. The fly-by-nights and falterers, such as the clubs in Fort Wayne, Cleveland, Rockford, and Brooklyn, were allowed to stumble away into bankruptcy. The Chicago White Stockings, first organized in a vain effort to do the Red Stockings down, (they did beat them twice, but only after the Brooklyn Atlantics had done it first), was the strongest in the league in 1876 because they had stolen the best players. But Hulbert urged the other clubs to let bygones be bygones and appeased the Eastern owners by allowing Morgan Bulkeley, boss of the Hartford Dark Blues, to become president of the new National League of Professional Baseball Clubs. Bulkeley, who was about as qualified to run the league as he was to play third base for the Dark Blues, lasted but one season, then went back to Connecticut politics, his natural métier; Hulbert, the proper president, then came out from behind the throne and took the seat himself.

The St. Louis club that helped form the new league was then named the Browns. It was an outgrowth of the Unions, one of two clubs in St. Louis which had been defeated by the Brooklyn Atlantics when the Atlantics had made their own national tour in 1868, a year before the Cincinnati Red Stockings made theirs. The new league would allow only one club in any city, and that city had to own at least 75,000 inhabitants, so the Browns became the official representative of St. Louis. They fielded a strong team, too, almost beating out the unbeatable White Stockings for the first pennant (costing "not less than $100"). But the Browns were unable to draw customers enough to meet their payroll. (In 1877 the club lost $8,000, more than any other club in the league.) It may have been that their style of play had become a bit old hat, for they carried a catcher, Little Miller, who still believed the best spot to catch pitches was 20 or more feet behind the plate. In 1877 they had lost their star pitcher, George Washington Bradley, to Chicago. George was the first man to pitch a no-hit game in the National League; he did it against the Dark Blues on July 15, 1876.

Dickey Pearce, that crafty little fellow from the Brooklyn Atlantics, was at shortstop for the Browns of 1876, and Lipman Pike, the first Jew to play professional baseball, covered center field. In left field there was Edgar Cuthbert, famed as a demon slider. Pike was one of the mightiest hitters of his day, a man who swung the full length of his bat and delighted to send base hits rattling off the distant board fences. (Meanwhile Ross Barnes of Boston was piling up an average of more than .400 by poking fair-foul hits past enemy first and third basemen.)

The St. Louis owners hoped to pull out of the hole in 1878 by signing the greatest stars of the Louisville club: Charles Snyder, the club's captain, who played shortstop; William Craver and Al Nichols, infielders; Jim Devlin, the great pitcher; and left fielder George Hall. This gang seemed to make the

Browns the best in the league. But John Lucas, boss of the Browns, had neglected to check the references of his new employees. Craver, Devlin, Nichols, and Hall had all been dropped from the Louisville roster and barred forever from the league because they had been found guilty of taking money from gamblers to fix games—in the good old Professional Association tradition. The four may have imagined that, like Wansley and Duffy and Devyr of a few years before, they would all be promptly forgiven because of their value as merchandise. But the new league, which was more tightly organized and under the one-man control of Hulbert, would countenance no such charade. This gang were out for good, and St. Louis was forbidden to put them on the field. It was strongly suggested that Lucas knew the men were crooked and had signed them regardless. In a fit of anger at this charge, Lucas quit the league at once, and there were no Browns to go with the Reds, Whites, and Blues until a new team in a new league appeared a few years later.

Meanwhile, the White Stockings remained strong. But they did not remain unbeatable, for Jim White went back to Boston and Al Spalding retired from the pitching point, giving the job, except for two games, to George Washington Bradley, the league's only no-hit pitcher. (Actually, in that first season, using the new "dead" ball, Joe Borden of the Boston Reds pitched a no-hitter against Cincinnati, but the two bases on balls he gave up were counted as hits.) White returned to Boston because he found the living easier and the pay better there. Spalding quit pitching for two reasons: He had

noticed (he said) that he was "beginning to slip," although he was only twenty-six; and pitchers had begun to throw curves, a skill he had never mastered. Spalding's specialty always had been a deceptive change of pace. In his best days the curve was still just a stunt, hardly ever used against batters. (Candy Cummings, the supposed "inventor" of the curve, used to toss a curve to the first baseman to make the kranks yell once in a while. But it was a pitch that would as likely sail away from the catcher as the batter, so he

Young Charles Comiskey of Chicago led the Browns on the field. He started as a catcher, played in the outfield, and then took over at first base, where he first demonstrated the value of playing well off the bag.

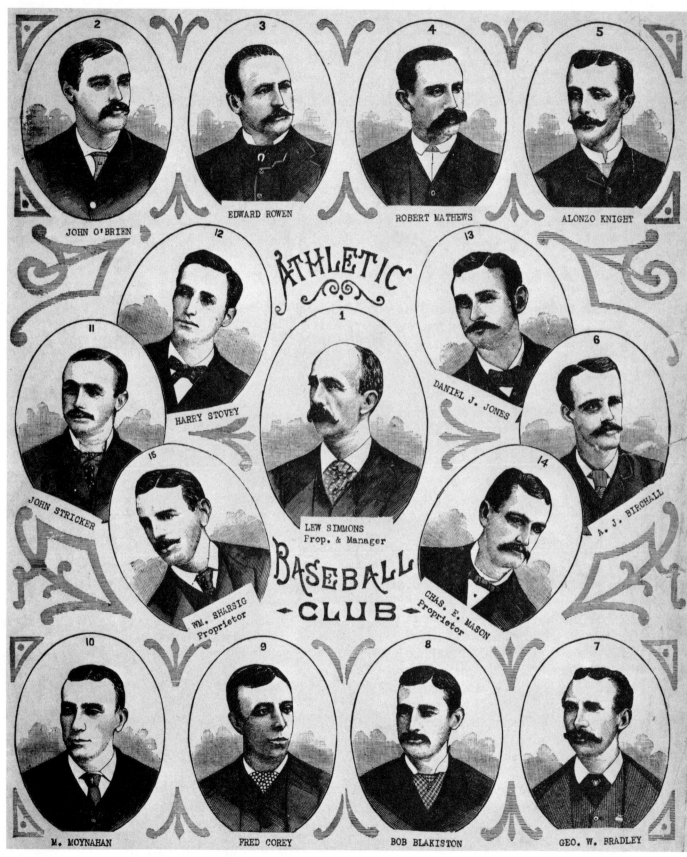

The Philadelphia Athletics of 1883, champions of the American Association (then a major league), featured George Washington Bradley, who pitched the first no-hit game in the Association; Bobby Mathews, one of the first curve-ball pitchers, and Harry Stovey (born Harold Stow), who stole 97 bases for Boston in 1890.

seldom used it when pitching to the plate.) With the onset of overhand throwing, however, pitchers began to make the ball break both in and out, and youngsters all over the land began to give more thought to learning how to throw a curve than how to swing a bat.

In Boston a new young pitcher named Tommy Bond, an Irish-born lad who had played for the Hartford Dark Blues the year before, was throwing curves at enemy batters and sending them reeling back to the bench. Whereupon the Red Stockings once more grew mighty and took that hundred-dollar pennant (it was called a "streamer") in 1877 and 1878. It was not until 1880, when the White Stockings had Mike Kelly in right field and Cap Anson in charge, that the White Stockings once more surged to the top.

The league meanwhile staggered from season to season as if Hulbert's prediction of a five-year life had not been an exaggeration. One club after another was expelled for failure to complete its schedule, and every season there were clubs that could not come up to scratch. Ultimately the league, which had jealously excluded all small-time clubs at the start, took to "appointing" members right and left, just to have someone for the big teams to play with. At one time or another Syracuse, Troy, Providence, Worcester, Indianapolis, Milwaukee, and Buffalo owned National League franchises, while the Hartford Dark Blues, the Louisville Grays, and the Cincinnati Reds all crept quietly away, to join the Philadelphia Athletics and the Mutuals of Brooklyn in the ranks of the teams that had no players on them.

Even the "successful" clubs in Bos-

ton and Chicago were not making money. Yet people did continue to turn out to watch games in good numbers, provided they could see a sharp contest or get a chance to marvel at some wondrous tricks with the baseball.

Tommy Bond of Boston was called upon in 1878, while his club was playing in Cincinnati, to prove that a baseball curved. Two 10-foot fences were set up, in a line, with a 20-yard gap between them and a post set in the gap. Tommy, a right-hander, stood on the left of one fence and after two attempts managed to pitch a ball that traveled to the right of the post and yet finished to the left of the far fence. There were wild huzzahs at the performance, and reporters dashed off to the telegraph to spread news of the experiment to an awestruck world. But a few squint-eyed characters averred that it was the wind that blew the ball back that way. So Tommy called on a left-handed pitcher named Mitchell to try the stunt from the right-hand side of the fence, and Mitchell did the trick backward, in defiance of the wind. Even so there were a few who saw it who went away unbelieving.

Bond, incidentally, was one of the first great pitchers who threw overhand. Spalding and his contemporaries continued to *pitch* the ball (that is, toss it underhand, but with considerable speed), even after the rules permitted a throw. When Spalding faded, the White Stockings brought in Larry Corcoran, a stumpy fellow who also threw the ball overhand and with such ferocity that he pitched his club to two championships.

Spalding was still part owner of the White Stockings, but the man who made them great was field captain

Adrian Anson, who had jumped from the Athletics when the new league was formed. Anson, destined to stay in big league baseball longer than any man then alive, first played for his father in Marshalltown, Iowa, on a team made up entirely of Ansons. He made Spalding's acquaintance while still a boy on his father's ball club, and he always recalled the great man (who led a barnstorming team to Marshalltown) as a tricky fellow who would try to overawe his enemies—then back down quickly if the enemy showed fight. Anson played hard for Spalding all the same, giving every ounce of his strength in the service of the club but never allowing Spalding to interfere with the doings on the field. Once when Anson was bellowing at an umpire, as he often did, Spalding hopped out of his front box to join the row. Whereupon, big Anse turned on Spalding and told *him* to butt right out of the affair. Spalding did as he was told.

More than any other captain (i.e., manager) of his time, Anson insisted that his players stay in condition. There were no candidates for the Keeley cure on the White Stockings while Anson was there, nor were any of the players permitted to carry oversized paunches on the playing field. They ran and worked until the sweat ran down in rivulets, and any man who showed up overweight was given more running to do. But Anson was as severe on himself as he was on his charges. He never granted riding room for a spare ounce on his frame, ate only bread and milk for supper before a game (when other players were, according to the diet standards of the day, swilling ale and tucking in beefsteaks), and kept a celibate bed from early spring to late fall.

Anson was a mighty batsman, and he made spectators yell by his skill at hauling down high throws at first base. (He played third base when he joined the club.) He was also an indefatigable "coacher"—shouter and heckler—who often brought in almost as many fans to hear him yell as to watch the White Stockings play. For Anson was not content with laying the rough side of his tongue on the uniformed enemy. He was just as likely to turn to the grandstand and aim an "oration" at the kranks, detailing the shortcomings of their hometown, the stupidities of their ball club, and their own personal delinquencies. After he had delighted young and old with such a catalog, delivered in a voice designed to carry over distant rooftops, Anson would turn back to the playing field, beat his hard hands together like two cricket bats, and roar: "Come on, fellows! Play the game!" And if any of them failed to heed him or played somewhat less than their best, Anson would comment on *their* idiocies as loudly and luridly as he had recited those of the clowns on the other side.

Anson was one of those who prompted the rulemakers to mark out lines within which a coacher was allowed to range, for Cap, as almost everyone called him, was wont to wander the whole baseline, from third base to home plate, ridiculing the third baseman one minute and bellowing into the left ear of the catcher the next.

Anson's most spectacular player while running the White Stockings, was Mike Kelly, the New Jersey lad who as an adolescent had been a battery mate of Edward "The Only" Nolan. In Chicago Mike, who had sometimes found it hard to temper his enthusiasm for good food and drink, grew lean and hard under Anson's tough regime. While Kelly was sometimes spoken of as "the big fellow," he was not a large man by present standards. Under Anson, Kelly's playing weight was 170 pounds which, for a six-footer in that era, was almost skeletal. But at that weight Kelly could run like a hungry hound, and with Anson to keep Kel's merry mind centered on hitting, he repeatedly drove the ball into the far reaches of the old ballpark.

In Chicago Kelly was most noted for his hook slide—a startling innovation then, when most sliders just dropped to the seat of the pants and rode into the base or dived for it headfirst and tagged it with one hand. (A decade earlier, base runners had been advised to run around the baseman and reach one hand down to tag it from behind.) The hook slide, designed to offer only the runner's toe to the baseman while the body went sliding off to one side, often brought Kelly safe into second when any other man would have been out. Soon Kelly's innovation became known as "the Chicago slide," and it was earnestly practiced by sandlotters all around the city. It provided a special satisfaction to spectators, who roared with glee as the enemy second baseman reached the ball out to tag a body that was not there. Nowadays when infielders are taught to let sliders tag themselves out by sliding into the ball, an old-fashioned hook slide is no matter for alarm. But in Kelly's day he traveled the circuit for many months before infielders learned how to put him out. And then, often as not, Kelly would come up with a new version by sliding right past the baseman and reaching one hand out to touch the bag on the way by.

Kelly strained other rules, too—not always with success but usually creating enough bewilderment to set the rulemakers to working at ways to stop him. Many of Kelly's stunts were designed simply to take advantage of the fact that at any game there was only one umpire, who simply could not watch two base runners at the same time. When Kelly saw a chance to make the move with the umpire watching the other man, he was not at all averse to taking a shortcut home from second base, without getting close enough to third to spit on it. But Kelly had other tricks to baffle, irritate, and outdo the enemy. He made good use of the new bird-cage catcher's mask by setting it on the plate as a runner came in from third. This often slowed the runner down, sometimes causing him to dodge the plate on the way in and occasionally ensnaring his feet so that he was sent somersaulting toward the grandstand.

For some reason, none of Kelly's tricks, some of which were mere extemporaneous bits of fakery, ever made him any real enemies. He was always the ballplayer's friend. When the Players' Brotherhood went on strike, Kelly, as the most famous ballplayer in the land, was offered a juicy bribe to scab on the strike. He turned the check down, even though his pockets at the time—as almost always—were empty.

Kelly, with his luxuriant moustache, sparkling eyes, full head of wavy dark-brown hair, and the letters on his uniform standing out a full half inch from his shirtfront, may not have been the biggest man on the diamond (that would often be Anson), but he was the one every krank strained to see. And Kelly always played as if he knew the

Schoolboy baseball players in 1887 were still playing the game barehanded. As the left fielder makes his "graceful catch," the infielders are mere spectators, with no one running out on the grass to take a relay and no one backing up the catcher in the event of a throw to the plate.

whole park was watching him. In St. Louis where the denizens of the Kerry Patch, the Irish ghetto, all habitually sat together in one section of the outfield stands, Kelly would frequently swap good-natured insults with the crowd behind him. (When not catching, Mike usually played right field.) He might invite them all to join him in a few choruses of "The Battle of the Boyne Water," an Orangemen's ballad that was designed to raise all the hairs along a decent Irish Catholic's spine. Or he might ask directions to the headquarters of the American Protestant Association—the notorious "A.P.A."—a name that was anathema to all the local Irish.

Anson's regular catcher during the White Stockings' championship years was Silver Flint. After Jim "Deacon" White went back to Boston, Frank Flint, called "Silver" because he was a towhead, came in from Indianapolis to do all—or almost all—the catching. Flint had been known as "The Only" Flint in Indianapolis, because he was the only man tough enough and bold enough to stand up to the hammering speed of young Edward "The Only" Nolan, the only man to pitch 30 shutouts in a season. In Chicago Flint was the catcher for two men who threw overhand, in the new style, and threw hard—little Larry Corcoran and big Fred Goldsmith. Yet Flint took his place behind the plate nearly every game, despite split fingers and cracked thumbs. He had a strong arm himself and could fire trolley-wire throws to any base.

Silver was no hitter, however. Indeed, he hit more like a pitcher than a catcher. But in his day, it was not easy to find a man who would catch up close against the cannonading of strong overhand pitchers, and who would snare foul tips right off the bat and still retain enough strength and agility to hop out from behind the plate and gun down a base runner trying to make second base on his own. So Silver Flint played on and on for Anson, helping to win championships in 1880, 1881, 1882, 1885, and 1886. During most of that time, ball clubs carried very few substitutes. Many clubs would have no more than ten or twelve on the roster, and if someone took sick, there might be a rush call to some team outside the league. (In 1878, the Cleveland Forest City Club had only *nine* players under contract.) Of course the schedules were not nearly so demanding as they are today. But in 1876 when Indianapolis played 114 games, The Only Nolan pitched nearly every one, and The Only Flint caught them all.

That was the year of course when Spalding came to Chicago to bring baseball glory back there. The championship was won (with a record of 52 won and 14 lost), but the team drew no great crowds and showed no golden profit. They played their home games in a field so run-down, with a rickety board fence and a splintery grandstand, that a Little League club today might disown it. After Jim White, finding no pot of gold awaiting him, had returned to Boston, Cal McVey took over the catching until Silver Flint was recruited. And before Silver Flint finished his stay in Chicago, Spalding had built a new baseball park with curtained boxes and push buttons to ring for service and had spent $1,800 "just for paint."

In Flint's first championship year, 1880, the club played 84 games, and Flint caught 63 of them. (Only Abner Dalrymple, the left fielder, played them all.)

Anson, meanwhile, had moved to first base from third, and on third he placed one of the strongest hitters and mightiest throwers in the game, Ed Williamson, a sturdy, solid fellow who could run like an antelope. Williamson hit as long a ball as any man in the organized game, and he threw farther than anybody had since the days of Jack Hatfield. In 1872 Hatfield had set the long-distance throwing record at the Union Grounds in Brooklyn with a heave of 400 feet 7½ inches. In 1888 in a contest held in Cincinnati, under the sponsorship of the *Cincinnati Enquirer*, Williamson had a try at Hatfield's mark. He threw the ball 399 feet 11 inches, and that was far closer to the mark than anyone else of that day could manage. Williamson already had set a hitting mark that would stand for thirty-five years. In 1884 he made 27 home runs, a mark that remained until Babe Ruth bettered it in 1919 at Fenway Park in Boston. As a player Williamson drew yells as much for his low, straight throws across the diamond —no more than knee-high they seemed—as for the fearsome long hitting and his speed on the bases. And he helped to win the nickname of "Chicago's Stone Wall" for Anson's infield.

Another corner of the stone wall was braced by the man who owned the biggest moustache in the game—second baseman Fred Pfeffer, a long-armed, long-legged young fellow who seemed able to reach in every direction to snag ground balls. He had to reach far, too, because Anson, like most other first basemen of that era, considered that the whole baseline between first and second "belonged" to the second baseman. Supple, slender, and swift, Fred seemed to relish covering the extra ground. He was much admired around the circuit for his gentlemanly ways, a contrast to the "manners" displayed by his cross-grained captain. But Fred was a man who liked to win ball games, and he was dangerous indeed at the plate when there were runs to be brought in. With the winning run on base, the bleacher bugs in Chicago, so many of whom were but a generation or less away from their Rhineland home, would call for "Unzer Fritz" to come deliver the killing blow.

In the outfield Anson's champions offered a young man who relied on prayer (he said) to help him collar fly balls. (Once he chased a fly ball into the stands and caught it while leaping over the seats, praying like sixty.) This was Billy Sunday, who left baseball to preach to multitudes in tents, urging them to hit the sawdust trail to redemption and leading them interminably in raucous choruses of "Brighten the Corner Where You Are." It was a pity indeed that fleet-footed Billy, who could outrun a small rabbit, did not employ his prayers at the plate, for he also hit rather like a pitcher or like a preacher. Still he made outs enough on seemingly sure hits to the outfield to help bring the White Sox in first.

The heavy hitting on the championship nine, however, came from Anson; from Abner Dalrymple, the left fielder; from Mike Kelly, the catcher; and George Gore, the center fielder. Of the 1885 winners, only Gore and Anson hit more than .300. But the others could deliver long blows when needed.

By this time there was a new star on the pitching mound for Anson, a slender lad named John Clarkson who, for a time, was accepted as the best pitcher in the game. Clarkson was a comparatively frail fellow, with an extraordinarily high forehead, such as would have seemed entirely meet on a reader of ancient rolls. But there was great control in his right arm, craft inside his skull, and blood in his eye. He was, however, sensitive beyond belief and could be thrown into a fit of depression by failure and particularly by faultfinding. Anson kept Clarkson winning by feeding him large doses of praise, for which John's appetite was almost unappeasable. And his exquisite fear of failure drove him to victory after victory. In 1885 he worked in 70 games and won 55 of them. Ultimately, Clarkson, like Kelly, was traded to the Boston Reds, which as a team soon became known as the Beaneaters. In 1889 in Boston Clarkson was craftier and stronger than ever. But the "sensitivity" that had alarmed his managers in earlier years turned at last into paranoia, and poor John died insane.

After cleaning out the National League faction in 1885, the White Stockings were challenged to match strengths with the new club in St. Louis, where baseball had been every other man's major preoccupation since just after the Civil War. The 1885 St. Louis club was named the Browns, but it was no kin to the original Browns, which had gotten mad and quit the National League in 1878. (Those old "Browns" passed their uniform-pattern on to the club in Indianapolis, where The Only Nolan was pitching. And because the Indianapolis nine could not attract paying crowds at home and had to play most of their games on the road, they were known as "The Homeless Browns.")

The new St. Louis Browns were born in the brain of Al Spink, a newspaperman who was to become cofounder of *Sporting News*. Canadian-born Spink, sports editor of the *Missouri Republican,* and his brother William, who was sports editor of the *St. Louis Globe-Democrat,* had tried to hold baseball together after the collapse of the 1878 club. They made a team out of Lip Pike, Dickey Pearce, Eddie Cuthbert, pitcher Joe Blong, and others on the old Browns roster and played games on Sunday before what Al Spink called an "array of empty benches" on the very field that was eventually to become Sportsman's Park. They even brought the Indianapolis Browns, with The Only Nolan and The Only Flint aboard, out to St. Louis to play a Sunday game in 1878. But, Spink reported, they did not take in money enough to pay trolley fares back to the hotel.

But the Spinks persisted, and at the least flicker of reawakening interest among the local kranks, they hastened to rebuild the park and erect a grandstand that did not offer broken legs and ankles to anyone who dared climb it. In 1880 they found a plump angel who, knowing next to nothing about baseball, was still ready to finance any outdoor recreation that promised to bring crowds of people into one place on Sunday, where he might sell them beer. He was Chris Von der Ahe, owner of a beer garden and grocery store close to the park. An openhanded, childishly vain man, Von der Ahe relished the image of himself as president of an organization as resoundingly respectable as "The Sportsman's Park and

Club Association." So he laid out the cash and the Spinks created the baseball team. The only one left to tell the tale of the original St. Louis Browns was Eddie Cuthbert, the daredevil sliding man, and he was placed in left field. He was also put in charge of recruiting baseball players throughout the land. When he had brought nine together who included himself, they all sat down on the outfield grass and agreed among themselves to play for a share of the gate receipts, as many another fine club of that day was doing. But when the first game was played against the St. Louis Reds on May 22, 1881, Cuthbert did not take part. His job was taken by John Magner, who became one of the Browns' mightiest hitters. The Reds won the game, 2 to 1. And there were no immediate opponents on hand for Von der Ahe's new Brownies to challenge.

Al Spink therefore wrote to another sportswriter, the famous Oliver Hazard Perry Caylor of the *Cincinnati Enquirer,* suggesting that he bring a team west to play in the newly freshened park. Caylor recruited a collection of ex-professionals, some of whom had served out their time in the National League, christened them the Reds, and took them to St. Louis. The players were to receive no pay, just day-coach fare, a stay at a second-rate hotel, and trolley fare to and from the park. If ever there were amateurs of the game of baseball, it must have been men such as these.

Among this gathering of devotees who came to St. Louis, where the new, independent "Browns" beat them, 15 to 8, was Dickey Pearce, inventor of the bunt, the trapped ball, and the fair-foul hit. This was 1881, and Dickey had

been playing baseball for pay since the 1850s, when he starred for the Atlantics of Brooklyn. (In the famous championship game in which the Atlantics gave the touring Red Stockings their first defeat, on June 14, 1870, Dickey had started the first double play in baseball. By deliberately dropping a pop fly and then picking it up to throw to second base, he put out the base runner—who was forced at second, from not having bothered to start down from first—as well as the batter, who had given up on himself and merely trotted toward first.) "What Dickey does not know about the fine points of playing baseball," one of his contemporaries wrote, "is not worth knowing." But by the time he came to St. Louis to play for his carfare, Dickey was seldom able to match his footwork with his headwork. He was then forty-five years old. Soon afterward he went to umpiring and earned no fame at the job.

Spink also brought in independent clubs from Chicago, called "prairie teams" because they played all their baseball in the wide empty lots then bordering the city. These clubs also played only for expenses. The rest of the receipts were divided between players and management. (The home

The All-American and Chicago teams that made the first world tour, organized by A. G. Spalding (center, in dark street clothes), brought a black mascot with them. Cap Anson sits to the left of Spalding. Next to him sits Fred (Unzer Fritz) Pfeffer and beside him, next to the mascot, is Ed Williamson, whose record of 27 home runs in a season stood until Babe Ruth broke it in 1919. Right behind Anson stands pitcher Lady Baldwin. Behind Spalding is John K. Tener, who became Governor of Pennsylvania. Ned Hanlon, who led the rowdy Baltimore Orioles in the 1890s, sits at Spalding's feet.

players got 60 percent among them, and the management paid all the expenses out of the remaining 40 percent.) With players coming to play for fun, and neither money nor marbles in the offing, it was naturally difficult to hold a team together or even deliver nine men in time to suit up for a game. A man who did not get a chance to play as much as he thought he should have might not show at all for the next trip. Or a chance to pick up a few dollars in some other uniform could lure away the regular battery.

At least once a prairie club came to St. Louis without a pitcher or a catcher, and the Spink boys had to hustle about town to dig up some strong boys to fill up the ranks of the enemy. When the Chicago Eckfords arrived one Sunday with two empty uniforms, Al Spink picked up a couple of youngsters he found pitching and catching in a vacant lot in North St. Louis and brought them in to become the Eckford battery for the day. The boys performed so well that day that the kranks voted the Eckfords the best club that had ever come from Chicago. The pitcher, Henry Overbeck, soon won minor league fame and the catcher, Kid Baldwin, later played for Kansas City in the Union Association and starred for seven years in the American Association for Cincinnati and Philadelphia. He was sixteen years old when he worked as a "ringer" for the Eckfords.

But the best club that Spink brought in from the open spaces was the traveling Rabbits of Dubuque, which once had had a league to play in but had beaten all the other clubs so badly that the league had collapsed around them. The Rabbits were managed by Ted Sullivan, one of baseball's original entrepreneurs (he discovered Old Hoss Rad-bourne), a pitcher who had become a manager. Born in County Clare, Ted had played baseball since school days with a big Chicago-born Irishman named Charles Comiskey, and he now had Charles on his club (at $50 a month) as center fielder, third baseman, first baseman, and occasional pitcher. (In the off-season, Comiskey worked for Sullivan's news agency, handling candy and magazines.)

The Browns beat the Rabbits 9 to 1, drew a fine crowd, and sold buckets of beer. And Al Spink was so impressed by the play of the Rabbit center fielder, who had gotten a two-base hit, that he wrote young Comiskey a letter that winter inviting him to join the Browns.

"Put your price as low as possible," Spink wrote. Comiskey had just married a young lady from Dubuque so he made bold enough to ask for $90 a month, almost double what he was earning. Spink promptly sent him a contract.

There followed a period of prosperity for the Browns and for Von der Ahe, with kranks crowding the stands and calling again and again to the aproned beer vendors to come bring another stein. For Comiskey, acting as field captain of his new team, showed St. Louis a type of baseball that thrilled the kranks to their teeth.

Harold Seymour, in his scholarly book on baseball history, says it is not true that Comiskey was the first first baseman to play off the bag, that this sort of play was already commonplace by 1882. But this is not how Spink recalled it, nor how men who played with Comiskey in the Eighties told about it. Arlie Latham, who played third base for the Comiskey Browns,

used to tell before his death of the excitement Commy stirred when he moved deep behind the bag to take pop flies or cut off short line drives. And George McGinnis, "change" pitcher for the Browns, insisted in later years that Comiskey, who had been moved to first base after missing an easy fly in center, "was the first man to field that position as it should be covered. He played a deep first base."

Certainly the men who had played that position in the National League in the Seventies, while a few of them may have been given to moving far afield after ground balls, were not in the habit of dropping way back on the grass, where they might not even be able to get back to first base before the runner. Charlie Gould, famed first baseman of the Boston club, hardly stirred from his position. Lumbering fellows such as Dan Brouthers of Buffalo, Cap Anson of Chicago, Roger Connor of Troy, Ed Mills of the Mutuals, and Dave Orr of New York, who weighed 250 pounds, did not consider racing back after fly balls as part of their job. Gould would not even move up the line to reach for a grounder. Neither players nor managers ever suggested that the pitcher move over to cover first base when the baseman was busy elsewhere.

But Commy had his pitchers racing for the bag whenever a ball was hit that Commy had a chance for. He also started the whole infield moving about, in a manner first employed by Dickey Pearce and George Wright when the game was young—shifting right or left, close in or out on the grass, depending on the habits of the hitter or on the tactical situation. He urged all his infielders to involve themselves in every play, backing up throws, covering open bases, and moving out to take relays. This constant movement on the field and the frequent rapid firing of the ball around from base to base kept kranks yelling, drew new hundreds to the game, and kept the beer vendors trotting back to Von der Ahe's saloon for new bouquets of steins.

Von der Ahe rejoiced in the clatter of the hundreds of nickels across his bar, Sunday after Sunday. (No stuffy Sabbatarians in St. Louis, where the Irish and the Dutch would not have allowed a New England Puritan even to raise his black umbrella.) But he rejoiced even more in the fame his ball club brought him. Not that he ever understood what his lads were doing on the field. Once, when a long blow to right field won him a ball game, he insisted to Comiskey that his players should "hit all balls to right field." He also was given to bragging that his bases were farther away from each other than they were in other ballparks, as his outfield was the widest.

Chris dressed himself, as his fame spread afar, in a manner that the newly rich of the Golden Age sometimes thought befitting their station: top hat, dazzling waistcoat, billowing cravat, a diamond stickpin the size of a ball bearing, and two-tone button shoes. But he took care also that his ball club traveled in style. Instead of the secondhand omnibus drawn by two tired plugs that most ball clubs of that day used to carry the team from hotel to ballpark or ballpark to railroad station, Von der Ahe (he pronounced it "Aw") put his hearties in open carriages pulled by prancing nags sporting blankets with the name "Browns" imprinted in large white letters. Chris built a row of apartment houses and named them after the

players. (He built saloons in the corner buildings.) When the club traveled to New York to play Jim Mutrie's Giants, Chris engaged a special train to tote not only the team but the loyal fans and the sportswriters, with Von der Ahe underwriting all the tabs, even the hotel bills for everyone. (One stowaway on the trip was a young newspaperman named Augustus Thomas, who later became one of America's most famous playwrights.)

Streaming along the sides of the Pullmans on that famous trip across half the continent were banners identifying the occupants as "St. Louis Browns, Four-Time Pennant Winners!" For by this time (1888) the Browns had joined in the formation of a new major league, the American Association, and had come in first four times. (Another St. Louis baseball club, the Maroons, made up mostly of players from an outlaw club, the St. Louis "Onions" or Union Association team, represented St. Louis in the National League in 1885 and 1886.) In 1885 with Comiskey and Ted Sullivan on their side, the newborn Browns, after winning the championship of the American Association, challenged Cap Anson's White Stockings, winners of the National League pennant, to a series that would decide the Championship of the World. The series was played all over the place, on the theory that baseball fans everywhere would like to watch the champions battle. There was a game in Pittsburgh and one in Cincinnati, as well as games in Chicago and St. Louis. The second game ended in a row, with Comiskey removing his club from the field in the sixth inning because the "home" umpire (the game was played in Chicago) refused to reverse what

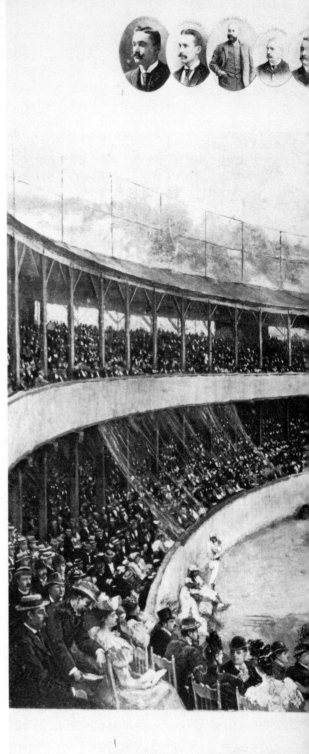

By 1894 when the Boston Beaneaters met the New York Giants at the Polo Grounds, crowds at baseball games had begun to be counted in the tens of thousands. But one umpire still called all the plays.

Commy considered an especially raw decision. The series was resumed, with plenty of rancor on both sides, but the championship was never decided. (Spalding's own *Baseball Guide* eventually reported the outcome as a tie.) And the prize money—$1,000 posted by the *Mirror of American Sports*—was divided equally between the clubs.

The next year, when the same two clubs again won the pennants in their leagues, Von der Ahe did not hesitate to approach Spalding for another series, despite the hard words they had had for each other. (Spalding had called Comiskey a "quitter" and had publicly vowed he would have no further truck with the American Association and least of all with Von der Ahe.) Spalding, with the gate receipts in view, was inclined to let bygones be bygones. But Cap Anson still nursed his grudge. He allowed that he would play the Browns only on a winner-take-all basis, perhaps feeling sure that the impecunious Browns would never dare run such a risk. But Von der Ahe and Comiskey accepted the idea avidly, never doubting that they could win.

And they did win, thanks to a wild slide by Curt Welch, who carried home the winning run in the deciding game by sliding in under a "pitchout" that had been designed to trap him off third. This became known as the $15,000 slide, for that was the sum of the gate receipts that were supposed to accrue entirely to the winner. Mike Kelly, the

Chicago catcher who had called for the pitchout, tossed his glove and mask high in the air and sent a few ripe curses after them. The St. Louis kranks tossed up hats and beer steins. And Chris Von der Ahe bellowed his delight until his throat grew sore. Winner take all! That was the way he liked to play.

In later years Arlie Latham privately confessed that many of the Chicago and St. Louis players had "stood in" with each other, agreeing beforehand to split their shares 50-50 no matter who won. But some Chicago boys had bet on themselves and wound up broke. Von der Ahe, one of the old-fashioned breed of dead-game sports, quickly peeled a few bucks off his own roll to see them all home. He also blew a good share of the take on a champagne party for everyone. (Chris had offered to bet Spalding $10,000 on the side, but righteous Al had spurned the offer.)

Poor Al Spalding was so thoroughly browned off by the unexpected victory of the Browns and the evaporation of the gate receipts that he immediately challenged Von der Ahe to a springtime series of six games—also for the "championship." Spalding told everyone who would listen that the defeat by the Browns could be laid entirely to the carousing of the players, led by Mike Kelly, who apparently conducted the whole team on an unscheduled tour of St. Louis' hot spots. Anson's prize pitcher, Jim McCormick, who had won twenty-nine games that season, got himself so thoroughly soused before one game that he was barely able to get the other side out. He gave up thirteen hits and six earned runs. When his turn came up next he could not even find his way to the pitcher's point, and Anson had to use short-stop Ed Williamson and outfielder Jimmy Ryan to get the ball up to the batter. The St. Louis batters dealt unmercifully with both.

In preparation for the springtime series Spalding sent his gang to Hot Springs, Arkansas, where the wealthy drunks of that era were wont to retreat to get the excess alcohol boiled out of their brains. Anson rode herd on the team and saw to it that they rose early, worked hard, drank only water and milk, and went early and alone to bed. The St. Louis Browns, meanwhile, put off their conditioning until the season was at hand. Their star pitcher, Bob Caruthers, to emphasize his determination to hold out until his salary was raised, went all the way to Paris and would not come back until Von der Ahe came to terms with him. When Bob did come back, flaunting his Parisian airs, it was just before the springtime series with the White Sox, and Bob was in no shape to pitch. Most of the pitching burden then fell to Dave Foutz, Von der Ahe's bad boy, whom he had summoned back to St. Louis during the winter and whose board he had paid so as to keep an eye on him. Dave had a sore arm and could not stem the White Stockings. Chicago beat St. Louis four games to two and claimed the championship. But no one paid the claim any mind. It was the only time a World Series had been held in the spring. And the White Stockings did not even win the flag that year.

The Browns did win, however, and in the fall they faced the National League winners, the Detroits—the only club in the league without a nickname. The Detroits were mighty in battle, for they had bought the current Big Four of organized baseball from the defunct Buffalo club: first baseman Dan Brouthers, who had long topped the league in extra-base hits and had actually driven out 14 home runs in a single season in Buffalo; second baseman Hardy Richardson, a heavy hitter who had held the league's fourth-highest batting average in 1885; shortstop Jack Rowe, a left-handed batter who had posted a .310 average in his next to last year at Buffalo; and third baseman-catcher Jim "Deacon" White, one of the original Big Four who had been lured from Boston to Chicago. The Deacon, now close to forty years old, was not going behind the bat too often (he played first, second, third, and outfield at Buffalo and occasionally caught a game there), but he was still meeting the ball with authority. His final batting average at Buffalo had been .292. The price for this whole gang was $8,000.

In Detroit Hardy Richardson went to left field, for second base was already covered by Sure-Shot Fred Dunlap, who was labeled the "King" at that position in the Eighties. (Other "Kings" were Mike Kelly, to whom the title clung the longest; shortstop Jack Glasscock; and Roger Connor, New York's outsized first baseman and one of the original "giants" who earned the New York team its nickname.) As long as men lived who had seen him play, Dunlap was named the greatest second baseman who ever held the position, not only because of his fielding but also because he had the best and most accurate arm in the game; despite his moderate size, he was a powerful slugger. Some of the game's followers insisted he was the greatest baseball player who ever lived. Dunlap never wore a glove—no matter that most of his contemporaries did—and he

could throw hard, fast, and accurately with either hand. Indeed, said some spectators, he never *threw* at all but just *slung* the ball with such power that it seemed to whistle as it traveled in from the grass.

The Detroits also owned Ned Hanlon, who was on his way to becoming the game's craftiest tactician and leader of the original Baltimore Orioles. Ned was one of the few Detroits who was not a great hitter. He held his job through his leadership (he was captain of the nine) and his ability to scamper all over the outfield to get underneath fly balls. He was especially good at "going back" for drives hit over his head. The catcher for Detroit was a big gentle fellow named Charlie Bennett, who was destined to end his career under a railroad car, when he slipped on a station platform at Wellsville, Kansas, where he had stepped off to talk to a friend. The moving wheels mangled Charlie's legs so that his left foot had to be amputated and his right leg removed at the knee. But this was in 1894, when Charlie was on the Boston roster. In 1887 he was still spry and strong and one of the best-known names in baseball.

Ned Hanlon won many a game with his crafty schemes and devices. Along with Anson and a few others he is sometimes credited with "inventing" the hit-and-run play. Whether he did or not, the deer-footed little Connecticut Yankee (5 feet 9 inches, 170 pounds) made frequent use of the play to confound his slower-thinking enemies. And in 1887, at least, he out-thought Cap Anson often enough to beat him and the Philadelphia club to the flag.

The owner of the Detroit club was a wholesale druggist named Stearns, who was so proud of his club's triumph that he could hardly contain himself. He was a sort of milder version of Chris Von der Ahe, always looking for new ways to make a score. Once the National League pennant had been secured, Stearns wrote to Chris, challenging him to a series for the championship. But this was to be a series the likes of which the nation had never before beheld. Stearns suggested fifteen games instead of six, so there would be no doubt about which team was superior. He suggested a purse be made up so that each member of the winning club could be rewarded with a prize of one hundred dollars. And he also suggested a really daring innovation: the use of *two* umpires at each game, one behind the plate and one "near second base" to call the plays at the bases. His plan also included the playing of the series in fifteen different cities, so the whole civilized world—what part knew its elbow from third base—might be enlightened and uplifted by the spectacle.

Chris quickly agreed to the fifteen games, but he wanted to play at least two in the hometowns and two in Philadelphia. As it turned out, games were played in New York, Brooklyn, Baltimore, Pittsburgh, and Washington, as well as in Philadelphia, Detroit, and St. Louis.

The first two games were played in St. Louis, with the Browns taking the first and the Detroits the second. The third game, the first World Series game ever played in Detroit, was won by Detroit in 13 innings. The clubs then moved to Pittsburgh, where Lady Baldwin of Detroit, the gentlemanly left-hander, mowed down all of Comiskey's hearties one after another, to win

by a score of 8 to 0. By the time the clubs got to Washington, Detroit had won seven games.

A doubleheader was scheduled, with a morning game in Washington and an afternoon game in Baltimore. St. Louis, with its hitters back in the groove again, beat Detroit in the morning 11 to 4. But in the afternoon, Lady Baldwin returned to dazzle the Browns again, and Detroit won the game that should have decided the championship. But they had played only eleven games and they had agreed to play fifteen. So back they went to Detroit, in the special train that the two openhanded owners (Stearns was just as free with a dollar as Chris Von der Ahe) had hired to carry, in style, players, newsmen, and loyal rooters around the baseball circuit.

In Detroit the major business was an old-fashioned carriage parade, such as had greeted the touring Nationals and Red Stockings some twenty years earlier whenever they reached a strange city. After that came a banquet that would have suited the court of Henry VIII, with several kinds of roasts and drink enough to add luster to the beaming countenance of Chris Von der Ahe. It was a marvel that, staggering away from this noontime spread, the overstuffed athletes were able to make it to the ballpark. But they all gathered there, with 4,000 happy Detroiters to watch them, and played nine innings of some sort of baseball. The Detroits, having already won the championship, also won this side portion, 6 to 3, with Lady Baldwin once more serving up the fast balls. In the fourth inning action was halted while a man wheeled a laden wheelbarrow across the outfield and straight to home plate. On board this

The Boston Beaneaters (formerly the Reds) of 1892 featured Mike "King" Kelly who is the biggest thing in the picture, with the blackest letters on his shirt. At extreme right in second row, wearing the sweater, is pitcher John Clarkson, who, like Kelly, was bought from Chicago.

craft were 520 silver dollars, a donation to Charlie Bennett from his Detroit admirers. Charlie, grinning with delight, grabbed the handles of the wheelbarrow and pushed it all around the bases while the crowd yelled approval.

The clubs went on to St. Louis and played out the string before dwindling crowds. When it was over Detroit had won eleven games and St. Louis four. But Chris Von der Ahe had never had more fun in his life and vowed to keep on winning pennants, to travel about the country again in a special train, and even, perhaps, to push his own wheelbarrow full of solid cash about the streets of St. Louis.

The Detroits did not win another

championship, for they spent the winter and most of next season sampling the hospitality of the many free spenders who wanted to continue to celebrate their triumphs. Before the next year was out, Detroit had dropped out of the National League, never to return. When big league baseball did come back there, it came with a new league behind it.

Chris Von der Ahe, however, his incredible nose aglow and his dark eyes a-light, was looking for new ways to brighten his own image. (He already had commissioned a statue of himself to be erected in the park.) He had made note of the fact that his ancient rival, Al Spalding, had turned Mike Kelly,

Chicago's golden boy, into solid gold by selling him for $10,000 to Boston. This struck Chris as a more exciting way to turn an honest dollar than even selling baseball tickets or five-cent steins of beer. And when Spalding let John Clarkson go to Boston for another $10,000, Chris would no longer be stayed. He had catchers and pitchers as good as anybody's, he told himself, and why couldn't he market them for high prices?

Without even discussing the matter with field captain Charles Comiskey, Chris sold pitchers Bob Caruthers and Dave Foutz, the very guts of his club, plus Doc Bushong, his first-string catcher, to Brooklyn for $10,000. His top outfielder, Curt Welch, who had made the $15,000 slide that won the 1886 Series, was sold to Philadelphia, along with shortstop Bill Gleason, for $5,000. This left Comiskey with only Silver King and Nat Hudson, of his original pitching staff, and Nat had won only four games in 1887. (Silver King, however, had won thirty-two, and he was a good deal easier to keep sober than Dave Foutz. Moreover, he was four years younger than Bob Caruthers, now called "Parisian Bob" because of his transatlantic holdout.) For a catcher Comiskey had Honest Jack Boyle, who had batted .240 in 1887. For a shortstop, he had nobody at all. When he heard the glad news of the sudden inflation of his boss's bankroll, Comiskey blew his stack. And kranks all over St. Louis and from every town near enough to send customers to the ballpark echoed his outrage, until it seemed that poor old Chris Von der Ahe must needs hasten out to some prairie cyclone cellar. But Chris soothed Comiskey, perhaps with a few kindly strokes on

Commy's own bankroll, and Commy set out scouring the local sandlots to find new bodies to fill his ranks.

In that era St. Louis was aswarm with footloose young men who knew of no better way to improve a summer afternoon than to play ball until dark, and Commy had no real trouble finding recruits. To help out Silver King and Nat Hudson, he hired a twenty-year-old Chicago Irishman named Jim Devlin away from the Philadelphia Nationals, and secured from Louisville in mid-season another twenty-year-old named Icebox Chamberlain, a squat right-hander who won eleven games. Then at shortstop he used a local sore-armed sandlotter, Ed Herr, until he was able to deal with Louisville for another veteran, Bill White, who could throw the ball better. Behind the plate, Commy placed Big Jocko Milligan, a mighty slugger from Philadelphia. And for his outfield he signed young Tommy McCarthy, who had played a few big league games in Boston and Philadelphia; McCarthy could run so fast and so far to pull down fly balls that the kranks soon named him their own—and to hell with Curt Welch. This new gang immediately began to win ball games, whereupon the local indignation was choked off before it had built more than a pint of steam. And Chris Von der Ahe was able to walk among his kind again, with men shaking their heads in wonder at his genius.

The trouble was that Chris, too, began to believe in his genius. He won the pennant again in 1888, took his gang to New York, and was beaten there by the mighty Metropolitans, whom the sportswriters had named the Gotham Giants (some *did* call them the

Mets). But his misdeeds of the previous winter lived on to make him miserable. The clubs that bought his heroes built winning teams around them and knocked the Browns out of first place in 1889. Then the Brotherhood Strike, which prompted Charles Comiskey to walk out on his $8,000-a-year job and line up on the side of "the boys"—the ballplayers—drove more than one club into bankruptcy and forever disrupted the close relationship Von der Ahe had enjoyed with Comiskey.

Commy came back to St. Louis after the strike. But fans had been alienated, players scattered, and the whole American Association had begun to totter. Eventually the two leagues joined, and Von der Ahe's Browns held a National League franchise. But Comiskey quit the club to become manager of the Cincinnati Reds, Chris moved his club to a park across the street from a race-track, and the whole show began to come unglued. In a twelve-club league, the Browns finished eleventh in 1892. Chris had some good players, notably the great "Pretzel Battery" of Ted Breitenstein and Heinie Peitz, who were loved by the St. Louis Germans. But he could not decide on a manager and kept shifting from one to another, starting with a part-time undertaker, Joe Quinn, who also played second base, settling for a while on the club prankster, Arlie Latham, then turning to a sportswriter named Diddlebock, and winding up with a two-fisted drinker named Tommy Dowd, who was laughingly called "Buttermilk Tommy." Tommy lasted until well into the 1896 season, when the Browns also finished next to last.

That year Von der Ahe set out to lure greater crowds to the park by giving them something besides the ball club to cheer for (and laugh at). He hired a Silver Cornet Band, made up of young ladies in striped skirts, built a chute-the-chutes in center field, staged boxing matches, ran horse races at night on the track across the street, and put on a Wild West show. But nothing availed him, not even the cash the local street car company put up to help finance these attractions. His club still finished eleventh. He had to sell Ted Breitenstein, his pretzel pitcher, to Cincinnati to pay some of his bills; he moved his living quarters to the ballpark; and he finally decided to operate without any field manager at all.

In the final year of the Browns Chris gave over the job of president to his assistant, Stewart Muckenfuss, hired Tim Hurst, famed boxing referee and umpire, to steer the club, and let Tim bring in a pack of new players. Tim brought in a few good ones and one or two who were slightly spavined, including the league's only left-handed catcher, John Clements. But a fire that burned down the grandstand (while 4,000 people sat in it yelling "Play ball!") and consumed most of that day's gate receipts, applied the death blow to Von der Ahe's ball club. Lawsuits bankrupted him and his club was sold to satisfy his creditors. Poor Chris ended his days operating a second-rate saloon on a side street, with his diamonds in hock and his gaudy clothes gone threadbare, and all the trophies of his baseball triumphs melted down in the fire.

The Year
of the Spider

THE 1890s are supposed to mark the beginnings of "aggressive" baseball, that is the winning of games through bumping, tripping, spiking, and taking mean advantage of the opposition, combined with organized bulldozing of the umpire. According to legend the inventors, or at least the heartiest practitioners, of this type of baseball were the old Baltimore Orioles, led by John McGraw and egged on by the crafty team manager, Ned Hanlon. But the Orioles were not the toughest team in the big league at all. The roughest, rowdiest, and most uncompromisingly "physical" of all twelve clubs in the overgrown National League was the Cleveland Spiders, led by Oliver Wendell "Pat" Tebeau, who had studied baseball and elementary mayhem in the Goose Hill section of St. Louis, where no man in a top hat dared walk more than a block without a gun in his hand.

The Spiders became "spiders" out of derision, at first. In the American Association (where they established two records by striking out seventeen times in one game and getting nineteen bases on balls in another) they were the Forest Cities, a collection of skinny, long-limbed, and bony-jointed young ex-semipros, who looked as though they could not lick their weight in week-old pussycats. Club treasurer George

W. Howe named them "spiders," when he first saw them all collected in one place with their knees and elbows sticking this way and that. This became the official name after the local sportswriters adopted it.

On the field the Spiders breathed fire. It was enough to make a batter pray he would not hit for extra bases, the way the Cleveland infield would undertake to render his route from first to third unsafe at any speed. If a man got past first base alive and unmarked—and that was by no means a certainty with big Jake Virtue there to make indentations in any runner's body—the hapless soul next faced, lurking near the shoals of second base, both Cupid Childs and. tough Ed McKean. Cupid Childs, who was bent on living down the name of Clarence Algernon awarded him by his mother, was not called Cupid because he was lovable. And Ed McKean was known as Big Ed, because he seemed twice as big as life when a man had to slide into him. If a runner was bound past this pair, he could be sure of earning a bruise from an out-thrust knee or elbow, if indeed he did not find a wayward foot in his path and perform a somersault into the dirt. If he had to slide into either one of them, the tag he received from the ball would open his lip or leave stitch marks in his hide.

At third Pat Tebeau himself lay in wait, and Pat could send a man careening clear to the grandstand by nipping the nap of the runner's shirt at just the right point in his flight. Or he might let a runner have a sudden hip to veer him off course and send him staggering.

Before this gang had been gathered, there had been other hearties, just as eager for action, peopling the Cleveland infield: Jay Faatz at first, who was not fat at all, but lean and wiry; and Cub Stricker, whose square name was Streaker, but who had started to spell it the way it was pronounced. Stricker especially was eternally ready for either fight or frolic, and he helped precipitate one of the most fearful rows the team engaged in—an uproar that sent a terrified umpire into hiding and brought out the city police.

The disagreement began when umpire Jack Powers first called Cleveland outfielder Jimmy McAleer ("most graceful in the game") safe and then out at second base, changing his decision when the New York catcher, Buck Ewing, came roaring out from behind the plate and bore down on Powers with indelicate phrases fouling the air ahead of him. But when Powers called McAleer out, the very heavens were rent with invective. Tebeau, Stricker, and Ed McKean joined Jimmy McAleer in flinging red-hot opprobrium, along with kicked-up gravel and other foreign matter, in the umpire's direction. Powers was shoved this way and that, until he seemed about to go sprawling. When his screams for help brought no immediate answer, he turned and sprinted for the clubhouse, with fear lending him a fleetness of foot not even the ballplayers could match. Happily Powers got in the door soon enough to throw the bolt. He crouched there trembling, while the Spiders threatened to splinter the barricade with their pounding fists, feet, and shoulders.

There being but 400 spectators at the game, and many of them reluctant to enroll for a lynching, the police soon had the crowd in hand, urged Powers to unbolt the door, and guaranteed his safety. Out came the umpire, tousled and sweating; the police, marching on

According to Connie Mack, this Baltimore Oriole club had "no gentlemen" aboard. Least gentlemanly of all was little John McGraw from Truxton, New York, the third baseman. Five of this team — McGraw, Wilbert Robinson, Joe Kelley, Willie Keeler, and Hughey Jennings — made the Hall of Fame.

either side, escorted him back to the playing field, while the local fans howled imprecations. The game proceeded with uniformed policemen lining both baselines. As the sides changed the cops would huddle around the umpire to keep him from all harm. He finished his job that day without suffering further physical indignities.

In later years the Spiders, with new and more fearsome faces in the infield, and Jesse "Crab" Burkett lending his dour presence to the outfield, engaged in a small riot at Louisville, where once again they questioned an umpire's judgment by shoving him back and forth among them. This time the Louisville club and fans took up for the umpire, and the Spiders suddenly found themselves outnumbered—but never outfought. This episode ended with the entire Cleveland club in the Louisville

jail, where they sweated out the night. In the morning Pat Tebeau, Ed McKean, Jesse Burkett, and Jimmy McAleer had to pay fines in court, while Tebeau was fined $200 by the league. Spider's owner Frank Robison, however, urged Pat to forget the fine, and he refused to honor the league order that Tebeau be suspended until the fine was paid. Instead Robison bought up some law and won an injunction to keep the league from interfering with Tebeau's career. The league did not further contest the matter.

Where the Baltimore Orioles did outdo the Spiders was not in toughness but, according to both biased and unbiased contemporary commentators, in dirty work, underhanded schemes, livery-stable language, and deceit. When the two clubs met in 1895 to battle for the Temple Cup, there was more excitement off the field than on it. The Spiders beat the Orioles four times out of five to take home the cup. But they very nearly did not get home alive.

After Cleveland had won three games at home, they moved to Baltimore to play the fourth and were greeted by a mob of Oriole fans earnestly seeking the Spiders' annihilation. When the Clevelanders left their hotel to take the horse-drawn omnibus to the park, they were met with a sudden shower of aged vegetables and spoiled eggs—mixed with more bruising objects —delivered by a hundred or more wild-eyed Baltimoreans. And even after they had lost the game 5 to 0, the Spiders were granted no surcease. Cupid Childs, before he could follow the example of his mates and lie flat on the wagon's floor, took a small rock on the side of his head. And the men who got off the bus at the hotel picked several dozen bits of rock and metal off the floor where they had been sprawled.

When the series was over and the Spiders owned the cup, Connie Mack, then steering the Pittsburgh club, voiced the sentiments of many of the league's more civilized citizens when he publicly exulted that "*gentlemen* had won the Temple Cup." McGraw and his cohorts were no gentlemen, and never pretended to be. They and their fans sat up nights devising vain tricks of every flavor to do their opponents out of baseball games. They hid baseballs in the deep outfield grass, to use when the right ball had rolled too far; they slipped "pounded" balls into the game to replace any that went out of play when the enemy was at bat; and they banked the baselines to favor their style of crafty bunting. They also used mirrors to flash lights in the eyes of

alien infielders, while for umpires, opposing players, or fans alike, they used language so foul that (one contemporary observer insisted) it drove some umpires to nervous collapse and prompted them to seek other means of livelihood. Said gentle George Wright, who had played baseball when lace-trimmed ladies were wont to wave handkerchiefs to cheer a pretty hit, "It is impossible for a respectable woman to go to a ball game in the National League without running the risk of hearing language which is disgraceful."

But McGraw and the Orioles were not to be shamed into slicing the ripe edges off their vocabulary. If the Spiders were tough, then the Orioles were nasty. And a good many fans rejoiced in the uproar. Even in Philadelphia, where brotherly love might have been expected to rear its head on occasion, the Boston club, led by tough first baseman Tommy Tucker, once was assaulted on the diamond and chased up the street by angry fans who flung tomatoes and rocks.

Before the century ended the Spiders were made tighter and tougher by the addition of one or two more who were adept at using shoulder, hip, knee, and spike to discourage opponents from advancing along the baselines. Pat Tebeau moved to first base, where he initiated base runners into the league by dealing each a solid shoulder in the face or ribs. Second base was still under the guns of Ed McKean and Cupid Childs. At third stood Roderick "Bobby" Wallace, a mild-mannered Scot who ran like a roe, and who soon became adept at using his spikes on a sliding base runner or flicking a man into orbit by suddenly grabbing his shirt as he tried to round the bag. Behind the plate was a monster named Jack O'Connor, called "Rowdy Jack" for the same reason that Jesse Burkett was called "The Crab"—because he was one. But at least their language, compared to the Orioles' *lingua franca* was halfway pure. And they had not yet learned to imitate McGraw's trick of cutting an umpire's toes into hamburger by constantly treading on them with sharpened spikes. Before Rowdy Jack came aboard, the Cleveland plate had been guarded by a tough veteran named Zimmer, called "Chief"—not because he was any part Indian but simply in recognition of the fact that he had once played for a club in New York State known as the Poughkeepsie Indians. Zimmer had never made a sliding runner exactly welcome at the plate. But he was a Sunday school operator alongside Jack O'Connor.

Rowdy Jack, like Tebeau, was a native of St. Louis, born in Goose Hill, where tough ball players could be found on every vacant lot. He had played his first baseball on the prairies that bordered the growing city, where Silver Flint had learned the catching trade before him. Jack O'Connor and Pat Tebeau became the stars of the Shamrocks of North St. Louis, a semipro club that carried around a conviction that the world did not hold a ball club that could beat them. Incidentally, Jack is supposed to have invented the trick of pretending, when he was coaching at first, to be the enemy first baseman, calling for a throw from a fielder and letting it sail by him to the grandstand, while two runs crossed the plate. Such a stunt has long been against the rules.

It is doubtful if even O'Connor was any more durable than Chief Zimmer, for the rugged old Chief early set a record by catching every game on the schedule (other clubs used to have a "pet" catcher to go with each pitcher). This was in the day when the "patent safety" glove was at last available to catchers, along with the "patent safety" mask and "patent safety" chest protector. But Zimmer caught with nothing but a thin, fingerless glove and never winced when the Mighty Cy Young fired his Gatling gun pitches.

Cy Young was the true star of the Spiders. An overgrown farm boy from nearby Peoli, Cy was one of the fastest pitchers who ever lived. Indeed, to the day of his death, when he was almost ninety, he never agreed that any of them—not Walter Johnson nor Amos Rusie—was any faster than he.

When Cy first sought admittance to organized baseball, he was scorned by a few—notably Cap Anson—as just another big farm boy. More than three quarters of the nation's strong boys in that day lived on farms or in rural communities, so there was no shortage of husky hayshakers who could throw a baseball hard enough to crack a board in a barn. But there was none quite so powerful as Cy, as poor Cap Anson very soon discovered. After stumbling around third base for his county ball club, Young turned to pitching when he was twenty-three and suddenly became the talk of the state. Anson actually made a special trip to see him—and turned him down.

Cy was pitching then for the Canton club at $40 a month. The boss of the Cleveland club did not share Anse's view. He paid $250 for the young man's contract and set him to work (at $75 a month) doing odd jobs around

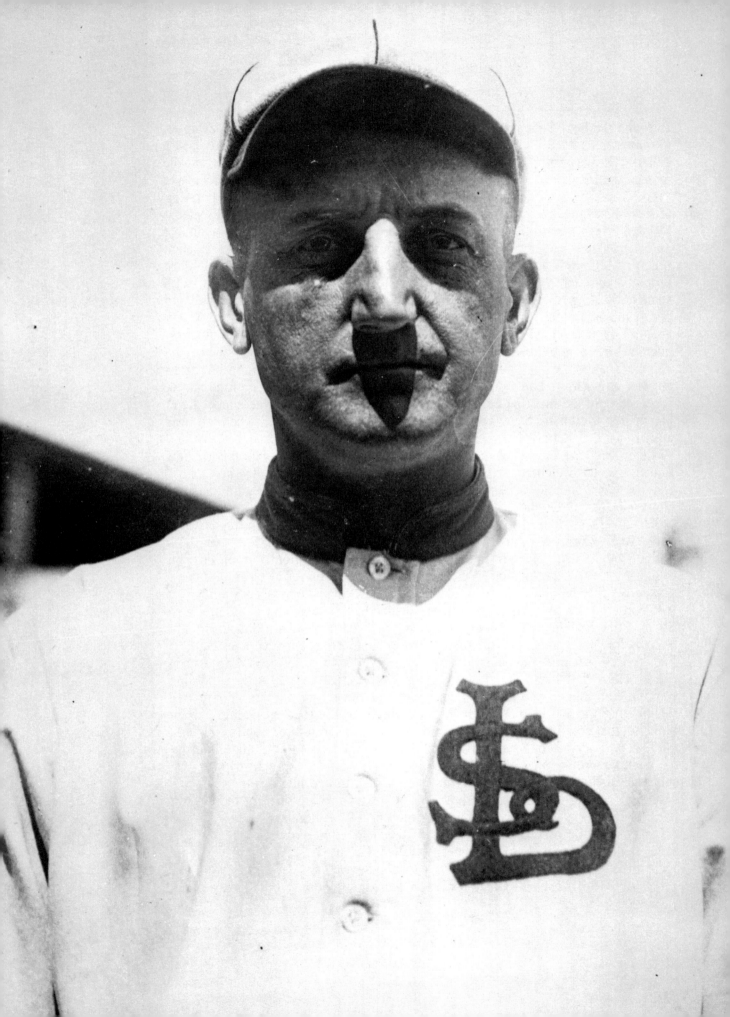

the park while the Spiders were on the road. In midseason Young pitched his first big game against Cap Anson's Chicagos. He gave the big town boys just three singles, struck out the side in one inning—including Cap himself —and won the game 3 to 1. Everybody in Cleveland was delighted, except Cy. He complained because he did not seem able to fire the ball full speed. For the first time in Cy's career, a catcher (who was Chief Zimmer) had stopped every pitch without trouble. His teammates explained to Cy that he had been working with the best catcher in baseball and that he was firing the ball as fiercely as ever. Having already pitched thirty-six games for Canton, big Cy pitched seventeen more for Cleveland and won 10 of them.

From that time forth Cy, whose real first name was Denton (farmers were all called "Cy" or "Rube" in baseball) pitched every time they'd let him and never seemed to tire. Fifty games a season were no chore for Cy. Eventually, he posted more victories than any man before or since—511. "More games," he told an inquirer, "than you'll ever see."

Unlike Anson, Cy was not a health nut. He ate heartily and included in his training diet generous quantities of red whiskey, which he drank unpolluted from shot glasses. And he pitched big league baseball from 1890 to 1911. Nine times he pitched forty or more complete games in a season. Five times he won more than thirty games in a season. In 1897 when he was thirty years old, Cy pitched his first no-hit game. In 1904 at the age of thirty-seven, he threw a perfect game against the Philadelphia Athletics. In 1908 when he was forty-

one, he pitched another. In 1911, forty-four years old and traded back to Boston from Cleveland for the second time, Cy suffered a spell of illness, found that he could no longer field his position as nimbly as need be, and decided to go back to his Ohio farm and chop wood. He lived to be eighty-eight, still chewing tobacco, still nipping good whiskey, and still convinced he had thrown a baseball harder than any other man who ever tried it.

There were other strong boys throwing the baseball when Cy was at his best, and most of them blossomed when the pitching distance was finally lengthened (in 1893) to 60 feet 6 inches. (When Cy came to the leagues, the plate was only fifty feet away.) One of the fastest—and one who was never afforded a real opportunity to demonstrate his skill—was Amos Rusie, the redheaded Indian Thunderbolt, who never would have admitted that Cy Young could match his own fastball.

For his day Rusie was a true Giant, in stature as well as in team membership. He was 6 feet 1 inch and weighed 200 pounds, taller and heavier than some of the men who had given the New York team its lasting nickname in the decade before he joined the club. In the eight seasons he pitched for New York, Rusie never won fewer than twenty games. Even so, he pitched far fewer games than he might have, had his boss not been so stingy and his own temperament so rebellious. In the season after they finally made the pitching distance long enough for Rusie's startling curve to find room to break, he won 36 games and struck out 195 batters.

When Rusie was brought in from

One of the original Cleveland Spiders was spidery Roderick (Bobby) Wallace, shown here in the uniform of the St. Louis Cardinals. He also played for and managed the St. Louis Browns in the American League, and kept on playing big league ball until he was forty-four. When he was sixty-three he managed the Cincinnati Reds. A pitcher, third baseman, second baseman, and shortstop, Bobby was often rated the best defensive player in the majors. He was also one of the best paid.

Indianapolis during the Brotherhood Strike to join, along with several of his teammates, a club that was to replace the striking Giants, his club was known as Mutrie's Mules, because they were altogether a spring-halt, a slow-moving and—except for Rusie—ill-starred lot who found themselves in the big league only because all the real big leaguers were playing in the park next door that belonged to the Brotherhood.

Mutrie was manager Jim Mutrie, baseball genius from Massachusetts, known as Truthful Jeems, a man who vowed always to play "honest ball" and evolved for his club the strange battlecry "We are the People!" He often was seen tooling around the avenues of the big city on his high-wheeled bike. Mutrie, who had played shortstop in New Bedford, Massachusetts, and captained the nine there, was hailed as a square shooter by New York fans and sports reporters. He was trusted with a night key to every newspaper office in the city, the ultimate honor in the profession. But not all his genius nor all his square shooting could turn the Mules into a baseball club. His mighty young pitcher from Indiana won 29 games for him, but he lost 34. At the end of the following season, in which young Amos won 33 games, including a doubleheader from the Brooklyns, Mutrie was out of a job. And soon after that, John B. Day, the boss of the club and Mutrie's long-time associate, walked out too, and young Amos was never again really at home with his bosses.

Rusie's idea of a fair shake was to be allowed to pitch every game in the schedule. When he played for Mutrie, Jim would promise the young redhead: "Win this game, and I may let you pitch again tomorrow." And Amos would pour his fireball in unceasingly until he had battered the enemy into the ground. He wanted no greater reward than to walk to the mound to start the next game.

But under the new management, Rusie grew wiser and more restive. Dividing his meager salary by the number of games he worked in, he discovered that he was being paid less than $6 an inning. His pleas for a higher rate were disdained by his new employer, Andrew Freedman, a Tammany stalwart who owned a bristling moustache, a bristling temper, an abrasive manner, a hot and piercing glance, a luxuriant head of curly hair, and a tight fist. Freedman bought the Giants to make money with them and knew of few better ways to make profit certain than by cutting down on the money wasted on wages.

Under Freedman, Rusie took care not to work quite so many games as before. But he still carried most of the load and won more than twenty games every season. Finally (abetted, Freedman insisted, by some rival such as a club owner who opposed him or wanted to beat him to the pennant) Rusie stayed away from the park altogether. If he thought his one-man strike would bring Freedman to his knees, Rusie had misjudged the temper of his boss. Freedman, who in his promotion of "syndicate baseball" had broken the league owners into two factions, was far more concerned with having matters his own way than with winning baseball games. So the mighty Indiana Thunderbolt, supposed to have been the fastest pitcher who ever threw a curve, stayed out of baseball three whole seasons —the season of 1896 and the seasons of

1899 and 1900. He had been earning $3,000 but had received somewhat less because of fines for his recalcitrant attitude — that is, his unwillingness to work in sixty or more games a year.

In 1896 big Amos asked for $5,000. Freedman offered him $2,400 and said he could take that or not play ball at all. So Rusie did not play at all. He kept his name in the papers, however, by issuing a forty-page pamphlet containing all his correspondence with Freedman. And Freedman's office muttered suspicions that the enemy club owners were financing Rusie's holdout to help get Freedman out of baseball. What did happen is that the Giants, who had beaten Baltimore for the Temple Cup but two years before, finished a feeble sixth in the standings. The next year, while a number of National League hitters were beginning to talk about making up a "Rusie Fund" to keep the mighty pitcher in comfort while he played ball only in the backyard of his Indiana home, Nick Young, the fretful president of the league, called all the owners together to try to pressure Freedman into composing the quarrel. Freedman dug in his heels; eventually the other owners kicked into a fund to pay Rusie $5,000 to sign a contract with the Giants.

Amos won 28 of the 38 games he worked in 1897. Neither he nor Freedman would talk about the quarrel or the settlement. But Freedman refused to issue courtesy passes to members of the Cincinnati team "as long as the team is in the hands it is." This needle was aimed at Cincinnati owner John T. Brush, once owner of the When Clothing Company in Indianapolis, original sponsor of Amos Rusie and suspected by Freedman of being the man who suggested Rusie's published broadside and financed his holdout.

In 1898 Rusie won "only" 20 games, held out once more, and never came back to the Giants. When he returned to the game, he was forty years old and had nothing left of his blistering speed. He had also divorced his wife and wandered footloose, with no coterie of club owners begging him to accept an honorarium for coming back to the game. On his eventual return, he pitched in three games, lost one, and never won any more.

Another strong-armed pitcher of the 1890s was Boston's Kid Nichols, whose fame, despite his winning thirty games or more in seven seasons, for a long time was in even deeper eclipse than Rusie's. Now the Kid is in the Hall of Fame, where he should have been when they opened the doors. Kid Nichols pitched fifteen seasons in the National League and, in all that time, had but two losing years—his eleventh (1900) and his last (1906).

Charles Nichols first applied for a job in big league baseball in 1886, when he was sixteen years old and had not got his full growth—which was to be 5 feet 10 inches. No one on the Kansas City club would take him seriously. But young Charles, in his gentlemanly way, kept asking first one team manager, then another. In 1887 when Charles was seventeen, the Kansas City manager finally gave in, took him to Lincoln, Nebraska, with the team, and let him pitch. Young Nichols won that game and the next four. Because he still looked more like twelve than seventeen, he was "Kid" to everyone from that time forth. (Later when his fame was wide, one or two writers tried calling him "The Only" Nichols, but the nickname would not stick.)

Nichols was perhaps the hardest working pitcher who ever made the big leagues. He would pitch, play the outfield, or take a spell at first base—or short or second, for that matter. He fielded his own position alertly, sprinted to back up the catcher or third baseman on throws from the outfield, and was quick to cover first on a ground ball to his left. He also hit the ball authoritatively, in one season actually topping all batters in the league for three months. He once hit two home runs and two doubles in a game, and all in one week, he won three of his own games with three base hits.

Three games in one week was no chore for Kid Nichols. He once pitched and won three games on three successive calendar days in Kansas City, St. Louis, and Louisville. (The game in Kansas City was actually against the St. Louis club, which had taken its "home" game there to coincide with a Knights of Pythias convention.) This was in the days when fouls did not count as strikes, and the pitching distance was still only fifty feet. When the pitching distance was lengthened, Nichols, like Rusie, grew more effective, until he and big Amos were considered the best in the business.

Before making the big leagues Nichols had pitched in Kansas City, Memphis, and Omaha, after refusing to take a salary cut to play for St. Joseph. At Omaha, when he was nineteen, he attained his full size and strength. There, he pitched 48 complete games and won 36 of them, striking out 357 batters with a scary fast ball that had the bush league hitters backing away.

As the "Omaha Wonder," he came to Boston to play for Manager Frank Selee's Beaneaters, where he was to remain for twelve seasons. In his first ten years in Boston, he won no less than twenty games each year. In eight years, he won more than twenty-eight and in seven, he won thirty or better.

In 1890 Nichols met his famous rival, Amos Rusie, head to head in a game that was for a decade afterward reckoned the finest baseball game ever staged in the National League. The game was played in the old Polo Grounds next door to the more famous Polo Grounds. (That site, known as Manhattan Field, then housed the New York club of the Players' League.) Nichols was two years older than Amos Rusie at the time, but they were almost equal in speed and strength. The game went thirteen innings. Rusie allowed three hits and struck out either eleven or twelve (authorities differ). Nichols gave up four hits and struck out ten. As seems only proper Rusie won the game on a home run by Silent Mike Tiernan, Giant center fielder.

Because of the frantic competition with the Brotherhood, which had taken away nearly all the original Giants, there were but 500 spectators on hand to watch this brilliant effort and tell their grandchildren about it. Nichols pitched in 47 more games that year, finished 46 of them and won 29. Rusie pitched in 66 more games and completed 55. He also won 29. But Kid Nichols also put in some spells in the outfield and sometimes collected tickets at the gate. (Once, later in his career, he took in 30,000 tickets at the new Polo Grounds. Visiting club owners who wanted an honest count often had

Cy Young, an Ohio farmer who always said he was the fastest pitcher in the game's history, pitched more games (906) than any other person in organized baseball. Working for Cleveland and for Boston (in both leagues in both cities) as well as for St. Louis, he won a record total of 511 games in 23 seasons.

The New York Nationals of 1894 had but three left of Mutrie's original Giants: John Montgomery Ward, sitting in the center with his arms folded and the mask at his feet; Mike Tiernan, to the right of Ward; and Roger Conner, standing directly behind Ward. The real star was Amos Rusie, the Indiana Thunderbolt, redheaded fireball pitcher whose holdouts almost disrupted the National League. He is second from the right in the back row.

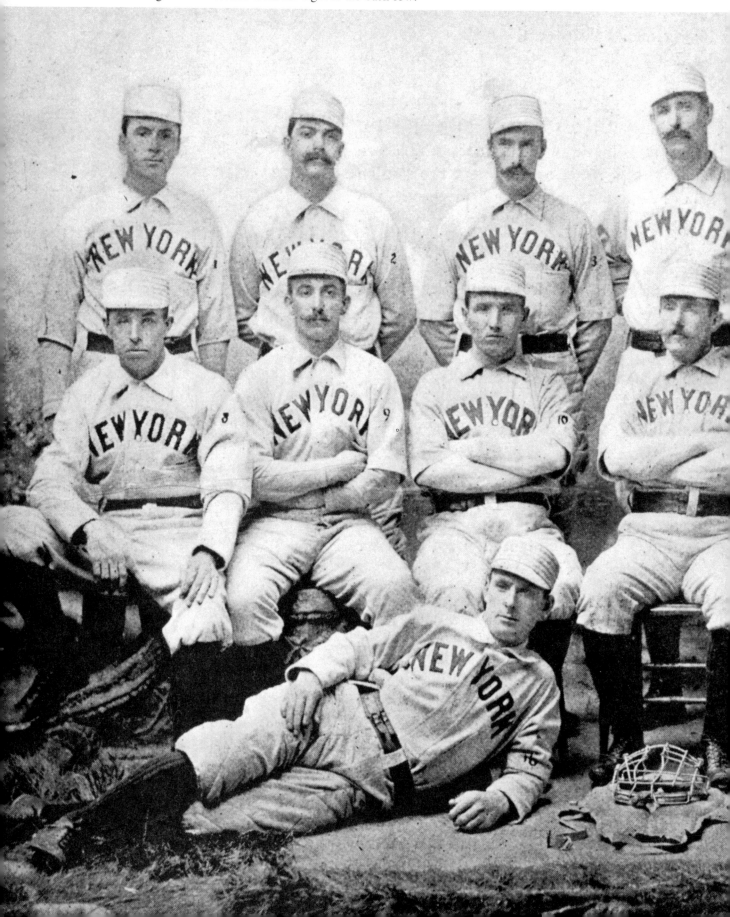

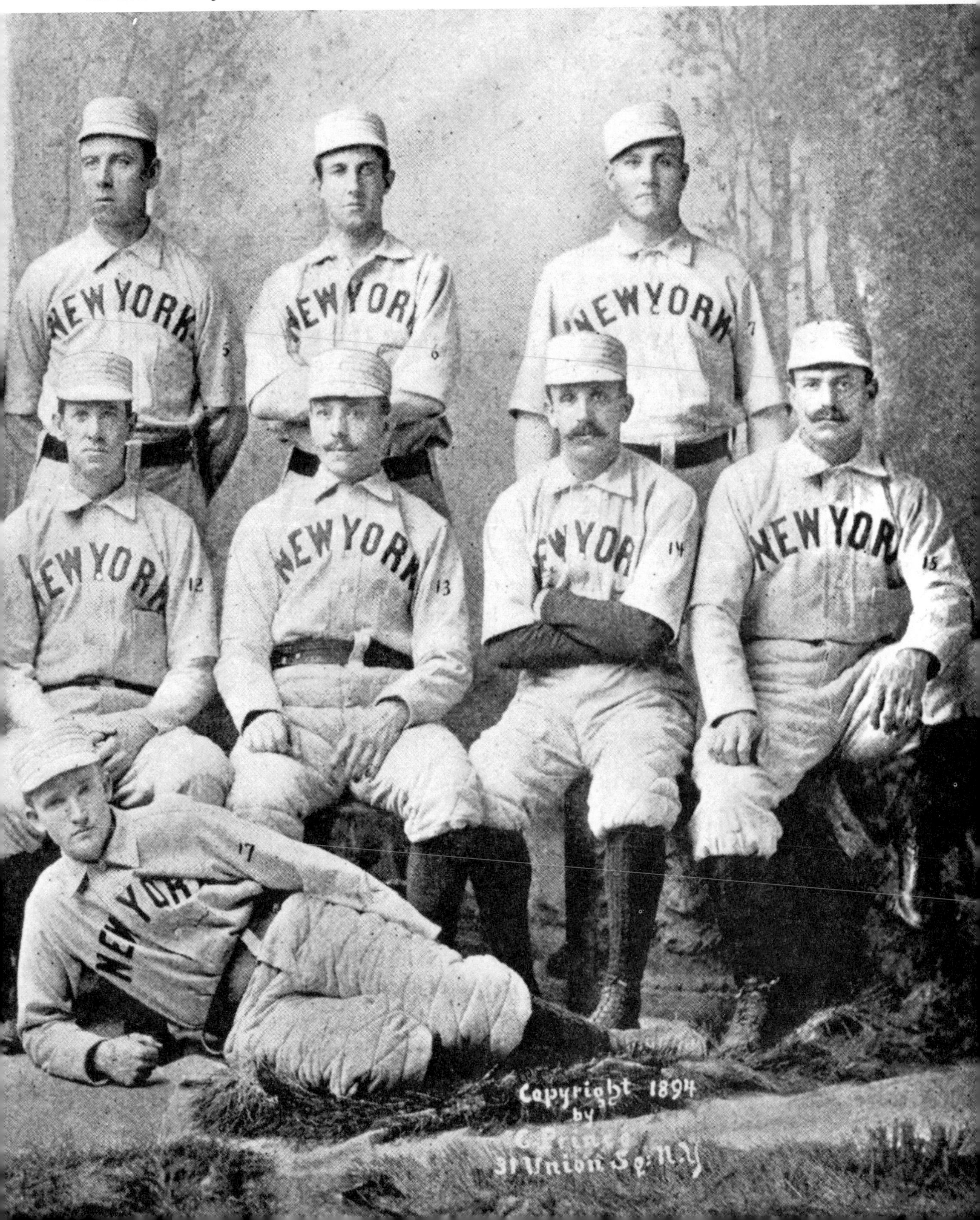

Copyright 1894
by
C. Price
31 Union Sq. N.Y.

to set their idle hand to guarding the turnstiles—or do the job themselves.)

There were doughty batsmen, too, who labored through the Nineties—Ed Delahanty, who once broke a baseball right in two, knocked over a shortstop (Bull Dahlen) with a daisy-cutter, and hit four home runs in one game (and who met his end in a midnight tumble off a railroad trestle into the Niagara River above the Falls); Willie Keeler of Baltimore, last of the left-handed third basemen (he was converted into an outfielder) who practiced placing the ball with a choked-up bat to land it in spots just vacated by moving infielders or outfielders; Hugh Duffy, one of Boston's Heavenly Twins, who still owns the highest batting average (.438) ever posted since the pitching distance was increased; Big Bill Lange, who quit baseball at the very height of his skill, and who was recalled long afterward by sportswriter Ring Lardner, when he taunted his contemporaries: "While you were sucking rubber nipples, I saw Bill Lange belt out his triples. . . ."

But the cheeriest, most beloved, and most eccentric of all was a Kentucky hero of the 1880s who lasted into the century's final decade: Lewis Rogers (Pete) Browning, Louisville's "Old Gladiator." Pete was the one man in baseball who truly loved to hit, who loved nothing more, and who thought of few things else. Whether you could call Pete Browning a ballplayer is debatable. He was no good on the bases, because he was afraid to slide. He was a menace in the outfield, because he shied away from fences —even from deep puddles. He had a horror of being hit. At the plate he became adept at squirming, dodging, and flinging himself out of the way of close pitches, so that he was almost never plinked by a thrown ball. But he could hit! And how he loved to talk about it!

Grinning, shiny-faced, gregarious, and invariably well-met, Old Pete was so often the subject of his own conversation that he took to referring to himself in the third person. "Old Gladdy is going to line them out this year," he would assure any listener. "Old Pete's lamps are full of base hits."

Pete was deaf in one ear. (It may have been the chronic abscess that made him so leary of running into fences, basemen, or baseballs.) And because he was partly deaf, he thought all the world was, too, so he conducted all his discussions at the very top of his lungs, whether they were with the bleacher bugs at his back in the outfield, the sportswriters in the locker room, or his cronies in the barroom where Pete took his fill of "German tea." Pete was the very image of good nature, always ready to placate those who might find fault with him and exchange compliments with those who praised him. Once he even apologized to his manager for hitting a home run when he had been asked to bunt. When he made ready to address the ball, some admirer in the distant stands howled to him: "Put it in the canawl, Pete!" And Pete instantly obliged. When he reached the bench he held out both hands to stay the wrath of his boss. "That goddam bug in the bleachers got me rattled!" he explained.

But when Pete failed to hit, he had no taste for human companionship and would flee to some private hidey-hole and remain there until he had recovered from his shame. Back at the ballfield again, he would assure his bleacher

In 1900 at the Polo Grounds, New York, carriage drivers attended their horses in center field during a game.

Cy Young, strong-arm pitcher for the Boston Puritans (not yet called the Red Sox), sets out to intimidate an umpire in the World Series of 1903. Boston vs. Pittsburgh.

Crowds at the first World Series (Boston, A.L. vs. Pittsburgh, N.L., October 3, 1903) were nearly unmanageable. They even lined up around the baselines until they were pushed behind ropes in the outfield. Many climbed over the fences. Huntington Avenue grounds, Boston.

When the new season opened in the Boston American League park, there were always celebrities on hand. Here Byron Bancroft Johnson (left), founder and first president of the league, sits with Lt. Governor Curtis Guild of Massachusetts, General Charles H. Taylor, owner of the Boston club, and the General's wayward son, John I. Taylor, who eventually took over as club president.

Lou Criger, catcher for the Boston Puritans, reclines on the bench beside straw-hatted Hugh Duffy of the Boston Beaneaters. Duffy posted the highest batting average in modern baseball: .440 in 1894.

fans, "The old lamps are full of sunshine! The old dogs are feeling great!"

Pete's prime concern was the condition of his "old lamps." A fastidious man who never appeared in public without clean linen and brightly polished shoes, he would never use soap and water on his eyes but he would keep them tightly closed all the time he was washing. Then, with his hide all duly hosed down, he would trot out into the forenoon daylight and look directly into the sun for seconds at a time. That was his way of driving all impurities from his precious lamps and filling them plumb full of hits.

Pete treasured his bats, too, owning about a hundred of them. He caressed them, honed them, oiled them, and rubbed them down as if they were made of flesh and bone.

Pete Browning started in the big leagues as an infielder with Louisville in the American Association and did not move to the National League until after the Brotherhood Strike. During the strike year (1890) Pete played with Cleveland, moved to Pittsburgh when the Players' League folded, put in half a season with Cincinnati, and then came back home again to Louisville. By 1894 when he played with Brooklyn and St. Louis, Old Pete was finished as a hitter, and there was no other skill he could hold his job on. Pete haunted the Louisville ballpark nonetheless, urging every

At the first World Series (Boston vs. Pittsburgh, 1903) hundreds of fans got in without paying.

visiting manager to appraise the brightness of the old lamps and to count the base hits residing there. By this time Pete had forsworn German tea and kept himself eternally in trim. But his old lamps, despite his assurances, had finally failed him, and the base hits had faded out of sight.

Pete had led the National League twice in batting during the 1880s when pitchers stood only fifty feet away. And he had led the Players' League with an average of .373. In 1885 he hit nine home runs, a healthy number in those days of the dead and sweat-darkened ball. In his final year in the National League, with St. Louis, Pete made a desperate effort to cling to his foothold in the game by playing every position in the field except catcher. He had pitched once for Louisville in 1884, allowing two hits while putting one man out, for an earned run average of 54.00. His effort with St. Louis did not make the record books.

Pete remained a favorite of the Louisville fans, however, throughout his short life. In his final years he became almost totally deaf. But his good cheer never deserted him, and only once did he lose his aplomb. That was when his admirers held a dinner and gave him a fat gold watch with his name on it. Pete accepted the watch with a bursting heart. But when the diners all shouted "Speech! Speech!", Pete could only gulp. Finally, after turning the watch over several times in his hands, he managed to blurt: "Where the hell is the chain?" Then, his shining face on fire, he sat down amid howls of happy laughter.

When the century ended, the professional game still suffered from the disaster of the Brotherhood Strike. Players' salaries had a ceiling of $2,400 (often ruptured for a few stars by means of bonuses and under-the-table payments). Batters were still getting adjusted to the longer pitching distances. And men like Billy Hamilton, Bill Lange, and Harry Stovey had learned to steal bases by the score —because so few pitchers at the new distance were bothering to hold the runners tight. And, with the ball traveling an extra ten feet, there was that extra time to make the base. But the day of the rowdy, the slugger of umpires, the defier of league authority, and the double-dealer had just about trod out its measure.

Of Giants and
Elephants and Tigers and
Burglars and Pirates
and Little Bears

THE new century brought a new major league to baseball, and, to the benighted umpire, freedom from fear. The umpires in the old National League had been a sorry lot, largely because no man with any gristle in his back could long put up with the threats, insults, and physical violence an umpire had to endure from fans and players, as well as the disdain with which club owners dealt with him.

It was actually the club owners who had the most to do with rendering the lone umpire's life not worth living. In the time when Nicholas Young, that poor, weak-stomached, weak-lunged, and weak-kneed imitation executive acted as president of the League, the haughty club owners took pains to bar from their parks any umpire whose work had displeased them.

Andrew Freedman in New York and John T. Brush in Cincinnati would simply insist that this or that man, be he Honest John Kelly or doubtful Jack Kerins, could not officiate at any game their clubs were involved in. And Nick Young would hastily shift the men around, marking one sick and putting one on the inactive list until it came his turn to go somewhere he might be more welcome. And should a manager or owner take sudden offense at an umpire assigned to his club, he might chase the man out and assign a ballplayer to decide the outs and call the balls and strikes.

Doings of this sort of course made

for "home" decisions of the most flagrant sort, spoiled many a ball game,
outraged some spectators, and drove
most of the decent umpires back to
working tramcars for a living. But
Byron Bancroft Johnson, the sportswriter who had fathered the Western
League and dreamed of turning it into
a new major league to be called the
American League, promised himself
that—if he did nothing else—he would
put iron in the authority of his umpires.
He did, too, and in doing so drove John
McGraw right out of the new league,
where John had seen a fortune waiting,
and back to the old league, where John
found a fortune after all. To McGraw,
an umpire was a natural enemy, an
incompetent in whose heart lived only
a dark desire to cheat McGraw and his
minions out of their due. One of the
politest names McGraw had for any of
this lot was the one he unfailingly
applied to Bob Emslie: Blind Bob. He
once barred umpire Johnston from the
Polo Grounds; when the league ordered
him back, Johnston, his knees knocking,
picked up a bucket to use as a place
to sit down and get his breath, but
McGraw took away the bucket.

That, however, was at a time when
Ban Johnson's firm edict that the voice
of the umpire was the voice of the
league had finally been adopted by the
National League, too. And McGraw no
longer could assign a substitute second
baseman to make the decisions for him.
Ban's league, after changing its name
to American, had to fight for its life
when it invaded the East. And even
after it had won a firm foothold, John
T. Brush, the owner of the Giants, and
John McGraw, their playing manager,
refused to accept its members as equal.
For a time, indeed, they almost man-

aged (with the help of Tammany Hall)
to keep the American League out of
New York altogether. It was made clear
to Johnson and his associates that any
vacant lot they undertook to build a
park on would quickly be sliced up into
streets by the city fathers.

Nevertheless, Johnson did find a spot
at the upper end of the island,
where the Columbia-Presbyterian Medical Center now stands, and got a high
board fence around it before Tammany
could say him nay. The New York
American League club, having tiptoed
into the second story of Manhattan in
this manner promptly became known as
the Porchclimbers—even the Burglars
—although they tried to call themselves
the Highlanders. Their manager and
field leader was a former Chicago
pitcher, Clark Griffith, who eventually
became known as the Old Fox. But he
was a young fox, as managers go, when
he came to New York, and he found
the forage thin indeed.

Having pitched for Boston and St.
Louis in the American Association and
for Chicago for the old league and the
new, Clark Griffith had thrown a lot of
baseballs by the time he accepted the
leadership of the New York Americans.
He was then forty-three years old, but
he pitched for his new club and even
won fourteen games his first year
(1903). Two years earlier while managing for the new Chicago Americans,
Griffith had led the league in winning
percentage. But in New York his arm
gradually wore out as his foxiness
increased. He won six games in 1904,
seven the next year, two the next, and
then never won another, although he
kept going to the mound in Cincinnati
and in Washington until he was fifty-
five. (He worked one inning of one

The 1906 New York Highlanders — also called the Porchclimbers — had a bush league look about them. The unmatching caps and particularly the silly miniature straw on the guy wearing a sweater would have driven Colonel Ruppert or George Weiss up the outfield wall. Yet these were the direct forebears of the proud Yankees. Sixth from right is Wee Willie Keeler.

game when he was fifty-five, giving up one hit and no runs.)

When the Highlanders played their first game in the new park, half quarried out of rocky and precipitous ground, there was still a deep hole in right field that the construction men had not had time to fill. Wee Willie Keeler, a former Baltimore Oriole, was the right fielder in the opening game, and he very nearly plunged into the hole in pursuit of a fly. Luckily, he was able to stop himself at the edge. The fans lived dangerously, too. Responding to the bush league atmosphere of the affair, they crowded behind the catcher and close along the baselines on both sides of the diamond as if they

were at a schoolboy game. Happily, no one was even injured by a batted ball.

In one early game, halted by rain, the inexperienced owners innocently invited all the fans present to come back the next day. There had been no rain checks on the tickets, so there was no telling who was really entitled to come in free. As a result, several thousand extra fans showed up for the free game, managing to break the boards in the fence in their eagerness to get inside. The two club owners (a pair of ex-bartenders named Frank Farrell and Bill Devery) were at first dismayed and then delighted to see that some few thousand New Yorkers really cared whether the

Highlanders won or lost. After that, however, they remembered to attach rain checks to the tickets.

Happily, Clark Griffith was not the mainstay of the New York pitching staff. The strong boy in the box was a fellow from North Adams, Massachusetts; stocky, tough, truculent, and strong as a moose, this fellow had won 28 games for the Pittsburgh Pirates in 1902. His name was John Dwight Chesbro. He was called "Algernon" and "Happy Jack" by his mates for the same reason that Clarence Algernon Childs, in the previous century, was called "Cupid"—because he was so much the opposite of what the names suggested. Happy Jack was not a big man, but he was built solidly and could pitch, it seemed, forever. In his second year with New York, he won 41 games out of 55, only to lose the pennant to the Boston Puritans (not yet named the Red Sox) on a wild pitch.

In later years Happy Jack's followers undertook to "clear his name" by insisting the pitch was a passed ball. But observers and teammates agreed that the pitch went high over the catcher's head, allowing the winning run to score. Whether the pitch was a spitball or not, history has not recorded. But spitters were Jack's specialty, and the ball did take off so far that even Lou Criger, one of the slowest-footed men in all the league, was able to score without sliding.

Clark Griffith had more to contend with than tough pitchers and wild pitches, however. His two bosses, Farrell and Devery, had been raised on the sidewalks, not to say in the gutters, of New York. Farrell at this time owned a gambling house, after a spell as a bartender, all-round tough guy and fight

promoter. Bill Devery, a policeman who had retired rich, owned a lot of political power—almost enough to offset that of Tammany's Boss Richard Croker. Neither one owned an awful lot of sense about baseball, but both thought they did, and both were given to telling Griffith how to run the club—not only what players to trade for but when to bunt, what pitchers to use, and how to select his line-up.

Foxy Clark fought a losing battle with the two of them, until the club itself began to reflect the inner dissension and the fans reacted by staying home—or going to see the Giants, where John McGraw brooked no back talk from players, owners, or even league officials. After five years Griffith quit, and the Bowery Boys chose as the new manager a tough-talking, angry young man who had been playing shortstop and driving the enemy to distraction with his fiery chatter. His name was Norman Elberfeld, but he was known everywhere as the Tabasco Kid because of the temper of his tongue. After taking charge he selected as his choicest target the New York first baseman, Hal Chase, whose name had not yet become a dirty word, but who annoyed many people by his free and easy ways with money, time, dress (he may have been the first hippie), and manner toward his betters. Hal played the horses freely (as did the club owners) and often wandered about the clubhouse to pick up bets. He didn't always wear a tie and sometimes wore shoes that looked like bedroom slippers. When the club was idle, as it always was on Sunday, Hal would hasten off to some one-horse hamlet and pitch for a semipro club, to pick up an extra few dollars. He even played baseball during the winter in

California under the name of Schulz. And those were not habits calculated to endear him to even the most even-tempered of managers.

But Hal Chase was the star of the club and the one man New York fans were willing to scale Washington Heights to watch. In 1908 he was unquestionably the finest-fielding first baseman alive, far better even than Fred Tenney, the Beaneater first baseman who had given his name to the tiny, pudding-bag glove he favored. (For decades afterward, boys who wanted to play first base asked for a ''Tenney'' for Christmas.) Tenney, who started as a left-handed catcher at Brown University, liked to get into every play and would dash clear across the diamond if need be to make a putout. Once he ran straight across when Cap Anson was at third, faking throws all the way until Cap did not know whether to dash for home or slide back to the bag. Cap made up his mind too late, and Tenney put him out.

Hal Chase had reflexes like a snake. Once he grabbed a hot line drive right off the bat of Nap Lajoie, when Chase had dashed in anticipating a bunt, and Nap had undertaken to ram the ball right down Hal's throat. Hal grabbed the ball in flight and calmly made a double play out of it. He could move right or left, run back for fly balls, and sprint in to kill sacrifices better than anyone before or since.

But none of the miracles Chase worked on the diamond could appease Kid Elberfeld. Chase, however, solved the matter by simply walking out and returning to California, where he could always make a dollar playing ball, and, it was freely said, make more than a dollar by throwing a game to the enemy

now and then, while betting against his own club.

Hal Chase's first loyalty was always to himself. But he was a charming man all the same, generous, quick-witted, well-met, a good-looking, light-hearted redhead who never had any real home but his hat and could perform almost any athletic feat the human mind could devise. He also dearly loved strong drink. He was, like most men whose youth had been misspent, a brilliant performer at pool and billiards. Hal was also a clever boxer and wrestler, a master horseman, and a dead shot with a rifle. He wandered the whole country over, shooting, riding, playing ball, betting on horses and ball games, taking a dollar whenever it was offered and, like as not, giving it away to the next guy who needed it. He was an excellent mimic and teller of jokes, enjoyed being the center of the stage, respected no one, feared no one, and never saw any reason for not doing just as he damn pleased. He died alone and practically forgotten, except by those who named him a disgrace to the game. A loner to the very end, Hal died of a disease hardly anyone had heard of—beriberi, a vitamin-deficiency ailment resulting from his childish self-indulgence and utter neglect of his body.

But during his best days in New York, Hal Chase was known and cheered for the great plays he made. No first baseman before him had ever charged the plate when a bunt was expected, and no man since his day has ever done it to such good effect. For Hal once actually turned a squeeze play into an unassisted double play by grabbing the bunt before it hit the ground and then lunging out to tag the runner

Keeler at bat for the New York Highlanders in a game against the Boston Puritans about 1906. Catching is Lou Criger, who turned down a $12,000 bribe to throw the first World Series. Umpire is the famed Silk O'Loughlin.

Action in the 1913 World Series. George Wiltse of the New York Giants is trapped on the baseline, pursued by Lapp, catcher of the Philadelphia Athletics, while Home Run Baker covers the bag at third and pitcher Eddie Plank moves in to back up Lapp. Giants won 3 to 0. Fans on apartment roofs outside Shibe Park could see the game for nothing.

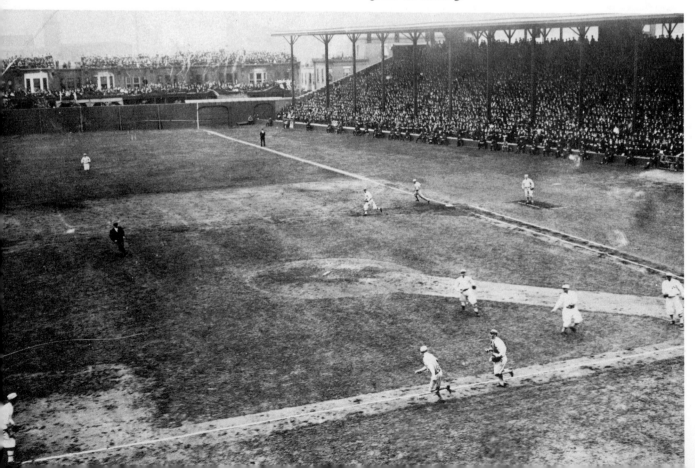

who was trying to score. It was almost commonplace for Hal to scoop up a bunt, tag out the batter, and then fling the ball to second or to third to get a putout there. Bunting was far more common in Hal's day, and so he had many opportunities to come charging to the plate. Batters with a runner on second and none out would often bunt instead of trying to hit to right, as they do today. And Hal Chase would often not only ruin the sacrifice by getting the ball to the base ahead of the runner, but would get the man going to first base, too, and so make the whole maneuver but vanity and vexation of spirit.

Hal was charged with an unusual number of errors—more than any other first baseman in the league—for four different seasons. At the end of his career he also led the National League in errors for one season. But most of his errors were the result of his daring and incredible efforts to lay his hands on ground balls or wild throws no other baseman would have tried for. And some were the result of a teammate's failure to anticipate one of his cannonshot throws in time. Hal made 22 putouts at first base one day. Only one man (Tom Jones of St. Louis) equaled that mark. One day in a doubleheader against St. Louis, Hal handled 38 chances, another major league mark for first basemen. But Hal was a solid batsman, too, who could place a bunt as well as any other player of his age. Clark Griffith said he never knew Prince Hal to miss laying down a good bunt on a squeeze play, no matter what enemy pitchers might do to thwart him. And his skill at hitting behind the runner on the hit-and-run play was equaled by very few.

While no one ever proved that Hal Chase had bet against his own club or had thrown games for money (he was cleared of charges in the only hearing he received), most men in baseball became convinced he was a crook and eventually no one would have him.

He came back to New York after Kid Elberfeld left, and he became manager for a while, without success. He lost his first base job when he was caught giving impromptu and unflattering imitations of new manager Frank Chance. Chase subsequently wandered from club to club, jumping in 1912 to the Federal League. Christy Mathewson, managing Cincinnati in 1918, did not want him on his club because Hal was not, Christy insisted, always trying to win. In 1919 Hal went to McGraw's Giants, and McGraw, who would put up with no hint of crooked work, let Hal go before the season was out. McGraw, seeing Chase in a hotel a season or two later, threatened to fine any of his players found consorting with the merry fellow, who stood tieless, hatless, and besandaled in the lobby to greet his old teammates.

After that, it was outlaw ball for Hal, with frequent appearances at racetracks and rodeos. His name was mentioned as one of those who had a hand in the great fix of the 1919 World Series, but by then he was out of baseball's reach. Still, the powers that order the professional game have decreed that Hal, despite his standing as the greatest who ever played the position, will never be remembered in the Hall of Fame.

Other than Hal Chase, the two greatest ballplayers of the young century were John (Honus) Wagner of Pittsburgh in the National League and Tyrus Cobb of Detroit in the American League. Both were great batsmen and

great base runners. Cobb was a fine outfielder, even though his throwing arm
did not measure up to others of his day.
Wagner was the finest fielding shortstop
of the first half-century. Men in bar-
rooms, in cigar stores, on street cor-
ners, at the ballpark, even in banking
offices and in rectories often would
argue heatedly that one or the other was
the greatest ballplayer of all time. John
McGraw said it was Wagner. Connie
Mack said it was Ty Cobb. And John
McGraw and Connie Mack were themselves the greatest managers of the day,
the most natural rivals, and opposite to
each other in temperament, methods,
word choice, and appearance.

John McGraw, by the time he had
become boss man of the New York
Giants, had turned from a spindly, big-
eared, fresh-faced kid to a stocky,
cocky, square-jawed, pugnacious man
of the world, who appeared in a neat
uniform on the field and dressed completely *à la mode* when out of the
ballpark. He was gentle, generous,
thoughtful, and kind off the field most
of the time. On the field he could be
loud, profane, vulgar, and quarrelsome.
Men who played for him would dream
at night of beating him over the head.
Some rival club owners almost frothed
at the mouth at the sight of him. Edito-
rial writers throughout the country
warned that "McGrawism" would ruin
the game. And gentle ladies removed
their sons out of earshot when McGraw
undertook to outline an umpire's failings to his face.

Connie Mack was gaunt, gentle, soft-
spoken, and nearly always cool. He appeared on the bench in carefully pressed
street clothes, with a stiff collar, neck-
tie, and stickpin. His hat was always
hard—either a derby or a straw sailor.

He never raised his voice to umpires
and relayed his instructions to his
fielders by waving a scorecard. He
addressed his players politely by their
given names and spoke of them in for-
mal terms. Chief Bender was always
Albert, and Rube Waddell was Eddie.
And Ty Cobb was Mr. Cobb. Where
McGraw was devoted to the idea that
bullying the umpire and needling the
opposition might give his team an edge,
Connie Mack espoused the notion
that a soft answer might turn away
wrath—and might bend the umpire's
next decision in the right direction.
Connie almost never used rough language; when hair-trigger George Stallings, manager of the Boston Braves,
offered him a punch in the nose during
the 1914 World Series, Connie was
merely bewildered. But McGraw was
notoriously openhanded, an invariable
soft touch for a down-and-out ballplayer. ("I got a lot out of the
game," he would explain. "They put
a lot in. Why shouldn't they get a
share?") On the other hand, Connie
Mack was more devoted to a dollar, it
seemed, than he was to victory. He
underpaid his players, annoyed them
with petty thrifts, and begrudged every
extra penny.

Cobb and Wagner, too, were almost
opposite in temperament. Cobb was
competitive to the point of viciousness;
he could not allow any man to come
in ahead of him in *anything*. (He once
nearly choked the breath out of a roommate who dared precede him into the
bathtub.) He was as quarrelsome as
McGraw and twice as vituperative. He
kept his spikes razor sharp to make sure
infielders made no effort to obstruct him
on the baselines. He would loudly challenge the enemy to try to throw him

World Series time at the Polo Grounds (about 1911) always saw the trees on Coogan's Bluff a-blossom with fans.

out. And when he *really* lost his temper, he could play like a demon. (Connie Mack always warned his players particularly the catcher, "Never get Mr. Cobb angry.") He engaged in fisticuffs (a sport in which he had no great skill) with teammates, with opponents, with umpire Billy Evans, and once with a fan who had been heckling him from the grandstand in New York. (This latter assault caused his immediate suspension by Ban Johnson, who witnessed the fray, and the suspension prompted a one-day strike by the entire Detroit team.)

Where Cobb seemed to live for baseball—or at least for victory —Honus Wagner treasured his leisure time, which he spent with his beloved hunting dogs. Honus hardly ever fought with anyone; he had good friends on every club. Yet Wagner was every bit as fierce a competitor as Cobb. He ran the bases hard and slid fiercely into second base to break up double plays. He stood his own ground on the bases against the most fearsome slider and would have tagged out a locomotive had he been required to do so. Honus could run faster than Cobb but was not quite so adept as Cobb at getting a jump on a pitcher. In the Cobb-Wagner era pitchers at last began to learn that the runners were stealing on *them* rather than on the catcher, and they studied out ways to keep runners close. Cobb, meanwhile, spent hours studying out ways to detect the move that meant a pitcher was about to throw to the plate.

Wagner also had a better arm than Cobb. He had enormous hands that seemed to swallow the baseball. He got his throws off explosively, often hurling a large helping of gravel along with the ball. He had started out as a pitcher, for he could throw with fearsome speed. But, alas, he could find few catchers who dared try to hold him. And he would miss the strike zone by an arm's length again and again. ("I used to strike out half the side and walk the other half," he explained.) At bat, Cobb and Wagner were nearly equal. They faced different pitchers and batted in different parks, so there is no saying for sure.

Cobb registered higher batting averages than Wagner. He twice hit more than .400, while Wagner never reached that figure. Cobb made more hits of every kind than Wagner did and stole many more bases. But Cobb's manager once set out to trade him for a lesser player—just because Cobb was fighting so much with his teammates. The Pittsburgh brass would no more have traded off Wagner than they would have given the ballpark to McGraw. (John McGraw and Barney Dreyfuss, Pittsburgh owner, were bitter enemies, and they had been since the day McGraw had screamed "Hey, Barney" at Dreyfuss, offering to lay him a bet on the game then in progress between their respective teams.)

Cobb and Wagner actually met head to head only once: in the World Series of 1909. Neither player contributed anything really memorable to the gaiety of the occasion, except that Ty Cobb stole home in the third inning of the final game. The Series, played in Pittsburgh's brand new Forbes Field and Detroit's ancient Bennett Park, where cobblestones still sometimes showed through the thin coating of loam, was the richest one to that date, with more than 20,000 customers gathering for the games in Pittsburgh. At this time Ty Cobb was still a comparative rookie (age twenty-two) while Honus Wagner, at thirty-five, was supposed to be slowing down. But Honus remained tough. Cobb, on first base at one point in the Series, shouted down to Wagner: "I'm coming on the next pitch, kraut head!" Come he did, and the throw beat him to the base. Wagner took the ball and held his ground as Cobb, with his filed spikes flashing, rocketed in. Grimly, Honus put the tag on Cobb and made him out. "He split my lip for me!" Cobb growled afterward in grudging admiration.

Wagner led his club in hitting in that Series, with a .333 average. He stole six bases. Cobb stole only two bases and batted .231.

McGraw and Mack met head to head three times in the first part of the century, as they led their clubs into the World Series in 1905, 1911, and 1913. The 1905 Series was, for fans who admired strong pitching and tight scores, the most thrilling of the lot. Crowds climbed on fences and rooftops and trees—as in Boston, the 1903 Series had sent fans up telegraph poles—to satisfy themselves that they had at least caught sight of the doings. For baseball's greatest pitchers were having at each other in this Series, and the two craftiest managers were seeking out the gambit that would do the enemy in.

McGraw had learned his craft at the knee of Ned Hanlon, in Baltimore, when Hanlon had come out from Pittsburgh to lead the Orioles to fame. Connie Mack, whose full name of McGillicuddy had seldom been used even by his neighbors in East Brookfield, Massachusetts, had put in some seasons at Pittsburgh, too, and one under the leadership of Hanlon. So the two geniuses had sharpened their wits for a time, at least, against the same stone. Both men were practitioners of ''inside'' baseball—the scheming out of ways to move a runner base by base until you have him all the way around. Both set greatest store on good pitching and catching—Mack having served all his active baseball years behind the plate.

Between them, McGraw and Mack had most of the great pitchers of the day. Connie owned Chief Bender, the twenty-two-year-old Indian who was just beginning to attain his finest form; Edward (Rube) Waddell, the eccentric left-hander whose name was known in every cigar store in the nation, from his having led the American League in winning percentage, after winning more than 20 games for Philadelphia the three preceding seasons (and who once had run off from the team to find some happier clime where he could go fishing more often); Eddie Plank, the college-bred lefty who had won 26 games that season; and Andy Coakley, who had just completed his only good season in the majors, with 20 wins and 6 defeats.

McGraw owned Christy Mathewson, top pitcher in the National League, with 32 wins that season and 34 the year before; Iron Man McGinnity, leading pitcher in the league in 1904 with 33 wins and only 8 defeats; and Red Ames, a twenty-two-game winner in 1905.

As it turned out, Mack could not use Rube Waddell, and McGraw did not need Red Ames. The big Rube, in welcoming Andy Coakley aboard the train that carried the Athletics to New York after they had won the pennant in Boston—Coakley boarded in Providence—had undertaken to smash Andy's brand new straw skimmer. (It was traditional then that straw hats were to be demolished on Labor Day, and often fans would pitch their skimmers onto the diamond after a ball game, marking the end of the summer.) In the wrestling match that followed Rube's effort to put his fist through Andy's hat, Rube was thrown against his seat and badly bruised his left shoulder, so that he could not use his mighty arm. But when the Series began and Rube was not listed to start, some fans muttered that Mack's Bad Boy had sold out to the gamblers.

It probably would not have mattered if Rube *had* pitched, for every pitcher in the Series, on both sides, pitched well enough to win. All the games were shutouts. And in the only high-scoring game, which the Giants won, 9 to 0, Andy Coakley allowed but one earned run. (There were five errors in this game, three by Lave Cross, the Athletics' third baseman. The Giants also stole five bases.) Christy Mathewson, the Bucknell football star who had helped the Pittsburgh pros beat Connie Mack's *football* Athletics three years earlier, won three games in this Series, in which he allowed no runs for 27 innings, struck out 18, gave up 1 walk, and granted but 14 hits. In that era in New York, the word for ''Old Reliable'' was ''Big Six''—the name of the most renowned volunteer fire company in New York during the previous century. Mathewson was named the Giants' Big Six and never did know where the name came from. (''Big six-footer?'' he wondered.)

The two New York winners, Mathewson and Joe McGinnity, each displayed a pet pitch that was designed to unseat the reason of eager batters. Mathewson's was his fadeaway, a pitch he had learned from a worn-out minor leaguer and which he perfected through patient practice. It was a reverse curve, like a screwball that, being thrown with almost no pressure from the thumb, had a tendency to drop off suddenly as it curved away from the hitter, with some of the effect of a knuckleball. McGinnity, the tireless Joe who liked to win doubleheaders, threw his ''Old Sal'' underhand. It spun right up out of the ground at the batter, as big as a playground ball, inviting the man to bust it in two with his bat. But nine times out of ten, if the man hit it at all, he sent it blooping up into the air where an infielder could catch it. McGinnity was the loser (and Bender the winner) in the only game the Giants dropped. But still, Joe gave up only five hits, and all the Philadelphia runs were scored on errors (by first baseman Dan McGann and third baseman Art Devlin.) The third Giant pitcher, Red Ames, worked only one inning—the ninth of the game McGinnity lost. He gave up one hit.

Throughout this era little boys worshiped the pitchers more than the hitters. Besides the monumental figures in New York and Philadelphia, there were men elsewhere who often left fans agape at the wonders they worked.

In Chicago there was Mordecai Peter Centennial ''Three-Fingered'' Brown (born, of course, in 1876), a disabled infielder who, after mangling one finger in a corn chopper, discovered that he threw a ''natural'' sinker—a wide curve that dropped suddenly on its way to the plate, like a sparrow dying on the wing. When Brown was helping the Cubs win championships, he had the aid of a big strong right-hander named Eddie Reulbach, who led the league in win percentage three seasons running (1906, 1907, and 1908). Eddie had no trick pitch nor was he the fielding demon that Brown was. (Having started as a third baseman, Brown would scramble around the infield like a spider.) But few were the men who could hammer the ball in as hard and as long as baby-faced Eddie. In his first year in the big leagues, after startling the natives in the Vermont bushes, Eddie pitched all the way through an eighteen-inning and a twenty-inning game.

Then there were others, relatively unsung now but known by nickname to almost every man and boy when the century was young: Orvie Overall, the California college boy; Wild Bill Donovan, whose reputation for wildness kept the enemy batters helpfully loose at the plate; and Jack Coombs of Philadelphia, who, like Amos Rusie, had mastered a pitch that broke straight down—not out and down like a common curve but dropping like a rock—the sort of pitch that had made old Toad Ramsey invincible.

Infielders, having learned at last to play in tight combination to accomplish two and three outs on the same batted ball, grew famous in groups. The famous Boston Beaneater combination of Tenney, Collins, Lowe, and Long had been broken up by the advent of the new league, and the most noted defensive gang—longest known to fame, that is, but probably not the most gifted—was the trio of bear Cubs in Chicago—Tinker, Evers, and Chance. The forgotten man in this group was third baseman Harry Steinfeldt, who hit .471 in the 1907 World Series. In the 1906 season he batted .327 and led the league in runs batted in. But Harry's name would not fit into a rhyme, so he remained a "Who he?" even after fourteen years in the majors.

Joe Tinker was not a great hitter, but he handled twenty-seven chances in the 1908 World Series without an error. Johnnie Evers was a crab, not just because he scuttled about the infield but from his quarrelsome ways on the diamond. (Off the diamond, he was gentle as a pussycat.) And Frank Chance, known as Husk, was tough. In the 1907 Series he had a finger broken by one of Bill Donovan's wild pitches, spit tobacco juice on the hurt, and kept right on playing. (Another devotee of eating tobacco was the hard-boiled catcher for the Red Sox, who became their manager—"Rough" Bill Carrigan. He did not use tobacco juice as an antiseptic but liked to spit it in the

A quartet of Miracle men: George Stallings with the pitchers who brought the Boston Braves to the 1914 World Championship. Left to right: Dick Rudolph, Manager Stallings, Lefty Tyler, and Bill James.

Marquard   Crandall   Ames   Schlei   Murray   Marty   Seymour   Wiltse   Doyle   Snodgrass
Richmond   Mng McGraw   O'Har

eye of any base runner rash enough to slide into him at the plate.)

Among the most widely famed hitters of that era was a man who never came close to matching Babe Ruth—John Franklin "Home Run" Baker. He earned his nickname not so much for leading the American League four times in home runs (9 in 1911; 10 in 1912; 12 in 1913; and 8 in 1914), but because he won the 1911 World Series for Connie Mack by hitting two home runs at the proper moments. And Frank was the anchor of the most famous infield combination of the day: Connie Mack's $100,000 infield of John McInnis (first it was Harry Davis), Eddie Collins, John Barry, and Baker. This line-up seemed nearly impregnable when it crouched behind one of Connie's strong-armed pitchers, and Eddie Collins is still considered, in some circles, to be the greatest second baseman to play in the majors.

The Boston Red Sox also had a combination that was reputed to be

the best ever built. It was not an infield combination, however, but the outfield trio of Duffy Lewis, Tris Speaker, and Harry Hopper. Of these, Tris Speaker was the best, both as a fielder and a hitter. His most noted skill was his ability to "go back" after fly balls and take them over his shoulder on the dead run. This talent enabled Tris to position himself close behind second base to field line drives and soft fly balls that ordinarily would have dropped in for base hits. He also became a fifth infielder and once, in the 1912 World Series, performed an unassisted double play at second base, catching a short fly by New York Giants' Art Fletcher and continuing on the dead run right across the base before the runner, Art Wilson, could get back. Tris, a tough Texan who had tried to be a pitcher, developed this capacity to "go back" through endless practice, with old Cy Young hitting fungoes to him and Tris taking off at the sound of the bat. He finally learned to judge by the crack the bat made on

Schaefer Devlin Latham

Robinson

The New York Giants of 1909 owned more than their share of clowns. Far right is Arlie Latham, who once, while playing third for the St. Louis Browns, flew headfirst over Cap Anson's head, avoiding a tag, and landed on his feet on first base. On one knee in the center of the picture is pitcher Bugs Raymond, who used to do a war dance around first base whenever he got a safe hit. Third from the right, holding a baseball under Chief Meyers' ear, is Prince Germany Schaefer, who liked to run out his home runs going backward around the bases. Wilbert Robinson, sitting at the far right, sometimes drew laughs without meaning to. The man with the big grin at the far left is no comedian but Rube Marquard, born Richard Marquis in Cleveland, Ohio, star pitcher who was known briefly as the Eleven-Thousand-Dollar Lemon.

meeting the ball just about how high and far the ball would travel.

Hooper and Lewis were, like Tris, unusually fast afoot. Both were good hitters, too, although not league leaders. Enemy batters used to complain that with this trio out on the grass, there was just no such thing as a fly ball's dropping safe or any hope of a "Texas League" bloop hit when Tristram of Texas stood guard. Duffy Lewis often played unusually deep, as Tris played shallow, and he made a specialty of climbing a small left-field incline, called "Duffy's Cliff," to pick certain doubles off the fence. As for Hooper, he made a number of spectacular catches in right field and threw men out from almost everywhere. His most memorable catch, however, was probably the "illegal" one he made while lying on his back atop a collection of friendly bleacherites. Harry, chasing a long ball off the bat of "Laughing" Larry Doyle of New York in the 1912 World Series, threw himself backward

over the low bleacher fence and gloved the ball while he lay there, entirely out of the playing field. The umpire allowed the out, and Larry Doyle lost his home run. Larry never did complain about it.

The Sox, incidentally, had one of the game's greatest pitchers working in that Series, too, but his career was cut so short that his accomplishments never have been properly memorialized in the record books. He was "Smoky" Joe Wood, who wound up his career as an outfielder with Cleveland.

Joe, owner of one of the fastest pitches of his day, won 34 games in 1912, using the new cork-centered ball that had replaced the dead ball—the pitcher's friend—of earlier days. Ten of Joe's victories were shutouts, and his earned run average was 1.91. (In 1910 his earned run mark was a meager 1.68.) Joe struck out 258 batters in 1912 and gave only 82 bases on balls.

In 1916 he held out for a paycheck to match his skills. In 1917 he was traded to Cleveland and came up with a sore arm, which forced him to turn outfielder. In 1918 he batted .296 and led the league in triples. Joe's lifetime earned run average of 2.03 would earn him a place among the top three or four in that department, had he only pitched about a dozen more games.

Boston's most celebrated ball club, however, the 1914 "Miracle" Braves, held no really famous stars, with the exception of their friendly and hard-working catcher, Hank Gowdy—and poor Hank is too often recalled for his famous stumble, when he lost a foul fly because he had dropped his mask right at his own feet and then stepped in it. The worker of the miracle that year was a high-strung and hot-tempered genius named George Stallings who, after managing in Detroit and Newark, had succeeded Kid Elberfeld as boss of the New York Americans.

George, however, was no more able to put up with playing suggestions from the front office than Griffith had been, and he walked right off the job with his neck on fire. In Boston he had full charge; through craft, conniving, sharp judgment, and sharp words, he took the 1914 Braves from the bottom of the league to the top between mid-July and the end of September. Then he beat Connie Mack's supposedly invincible Athletics in four straight games. This was the ultimate miracle, for Connie Mack had a roster that read like a future Hall of Fame. (Indeed, six of the 1914 A's, including Connie himself, earned spots in the Hall of Fame; the five others were Chief Bender, Eddie Collins, Frank Baker, Herb Pennock, and Eddie Plank. Only two of the Braves made it, Rabbit Maranville and Johnny Evers, and Rabbit made it less on his play than on his popularity with the sportswriters.)

George Stallings, however, using his own form of psychological warfare, managed to get the jump on the A's—already unsettled by desertions to

John McGraw, grown plump and prosperous as manager of the New York Giants, liked to startle people at banquets with his pet margay.

the Federal League—and kept them off balance. He pretended personal enmity toward Connie Mack (he even offered to punch the courtly gentleman in the nose) and ordered his players not to answer when the Philadelphia players extended even the mildest of greetings. When the two games in Philadelphia had been completed and both won by George, he announced there would be no return trip to Philadelphia so there was no need to leave any equipment there. And when the Braves just managed to grab the first game in Boston, making it three games to zero (thanks to two doubles and a home run by Hank Gowdy), Stallings canceled the train reservations and announced that the Series was as good as over. It was, too. But George never got into another World Series.

Most of the Western clubs, except Chicago, had little chance for the World Series. But in 1919 Cincinnati had its first and became involved in the scandal that was supposed to mark the end of baseball as the National Game. For this was the year that the Chicago White Sox—or most of the club's key members—conspired to dump the Series into the arms (or paws) of the underdog Cincinnati club, thus enriching a few gamblers, bankrupting a few more, and ending the careers of some of the league's finest players.

This was not the first time games had been given away. It was not the first time gamblers had attempted to fix the Series—which always carried heavy ''action'' in the hotel lobbies, cigar stores, and taverns of the nation. In the very first American League vs. National League series in Boston in 1903, gamblers offered Boston catcher Lou Criger $12,000 to allow a few extra runs to come in. Lou refused the offer but was badly shaken by the veiled threats accompanying it. He said nothing about it until years later.

Even some of baseball's most glorious names had been known in their active days to bet against their own clubs, to accept presents from other clubs for trimming a contender, to ease up on a friend at the plate, or to conspire to allow some favorite to get the extra hits needed to win a batting title. (Mickey Mantle, in recent days, accepted a fat pitch delivered by a friendly pitcher, who wanted to help Mickey crack the 500 mark for homers.)

But this fix was certainly the most flagrant. It was exposed in spite of the efforts of some baseball writers and some of the game's brass to stifle the first public reports, which were written by Chicago sportswriter Hugh Fullerton. And it scared hell out of most of the club owners, who could imagine an aroused public pulling their rickety ballparks down around their ears. It was almost half a century before the owners realized that there was really no need to be so damn *pure* as they first set out to be. While the scandal did not, as it has sometimes been said, bring about the creation of the quasi-public office of Commissioner of Baseball, it did frighten the owners into subjecting themselves, with a show of grace, to an authority that was at least partly in the interest of the fan and the ballplayer. (Nowadays that Commissioner's throne remains empty even when the current appointee is sitting in it.)

The Golden Age of baseball, therefore, beginning as it did right after World War I with the coming of age of Babe Ruth and his array of imitators, rose out of the ashes of the Black Sox holocaust. And it was the inspired slugging, for which the bad boy from Baltimore set the style, that taught the baseball fans that ''inside'' baseball held only a fraction of the thrill that came from seeing brand-new baseballs belted outside of the playing field.

There were, of course, still old-time place hitters working and making records even after Babe Ruth turned from pitching to the outfield and moved from Boston's cramped Fenway Park to New York, where they built a modern stadium to hold the crowds who doted on him. Ty Cobb still frightened pitchers and infielders in this day. And when men belittled him for not hitting home runs, he allowed that he could hit them any time he wanted, had that been his style. To prove it, he hit three balls over the fence in a single game, hit two more the next day, then went back to his choked-bat style.

There was also George Sisler, one of

Honus Wagner of Pittsburgh, the Ty Cobb of the National League, was not ashamed to choke his bat in order to put a hit into a vacant spot.

the sharpest-eyed men ever to stand up to a pitcher, who, in 1922 equaled Ty Cobb's season average of .420. Sisler, who played first base for the St. Louis Browns, started out, like Babe Ruth, as a pitcher. He never equaled Ruth's records at that job, but he pitched well enough to have made himself a major league career on the mound. The trou-

ble was that George just hit the ball too well to be kept out of the line-up. In September of 1915, his first year with the Browns, Sisler played both ends of a doubleheader at first base, pitched the first game of a doubleheader the next day, and played first base in the second game. At the end of the season George was playing regularly in the outfield.

In 1916 he became the Browns' regular first baseman. But George still stood ready to fill in whenever and wherever he was needed. Left-handed or not, he also played two games at third base.

When a sore foot limited George's agility at first base, he went back to the outfield. And he still managed to pitch three complete games, winning one and losing two but giving up an average of only one earned run per game. Throughout his fifteen active seasons, even after he became club manager, Sisler remained ready to go to the mound when need be. He worked as a pitcher in at least one game every season for seven years, until he was waived out of the league.

Unlike the other George, who became Babe to the world and Jidge to his teammates, Sisler was a college man. At the University of Michigan in the second decade of the century, his batting and pitching were so spectacular that he had bids from half a dozen teams in both leagues. But he came to St. Louis because his college coach, Wesley Branch Rickey, had gotten a job managing the Browns.

Sisler was always a model of spirit and deportment. He was the best-liked man on the diamond. He would go out and play when other men would have deemed themselves too crippled to perform. In 1922 when he hit .420, George badly damaged his right shoulder while trying to dig up a low throw at first base. The doctors who strapped him up warned him that he might end his career if he did not stay out of the line-up.

But the pennant was hanging on a September series with the New York Yankees, and George was damned if he was going to sit on the bench and watch the championship elude his mates. He came to bat forty times in the first eleven days of September and made twenty-one hits. In the series with the Yankees, when he was really swinging with only one arm, George had a chance to tie the American League record, then held by Ty Cobb, of hitting safely in forty consecutive games. On the sixteenth of September he made a hit to tie the record, and the next day he hit safely once more to set a mark that stood until Joe DiMaggio ran his string to 56 in 1941. (Joe also broke the National League record of 44 games in a row, held by Willie Keeler.)

Typical of George Sisler's spirit that sometimes won games already counted as lost was his performance one day when even his own club had decided the game was over and had begun gathering up the bats. George rolled a ball back to the pitcher, and almost everyone began looking for the exits. Not George. He dug as hard for first base as if he had banged a hot ground ball to short. In a once-in-10,000 freak accident, the ball stuck in the webbing of the pitcher's glove, and by the time the pitcher had pried it loose, Sisler had crossed first base and the Browns went on to win. For Sisler could fly on the baselines, faster than most of his contemporaries. He led his league in base-stealing four times. In 1927 after he had been marked all through because his batting average had dropped below .300, George batted .327 and came in first in the league in stolen bases with 27. He had been "all through" once before, when a severe sinus infection that involved the optic nerve had kept him out for the entire 1923 season. But in 1924 when he had been made manager of the Browns, he batted .306 and the next year hit .345.

When New York Highlander fans were invited to attend the next game free after a rainout, no one could tell who was entitled, and so the crowd almost pushed the players off the field. New York vs. Philadelphia, July 4, 1907.

In 1928 Sisler, once more labeled finished, was waived clean out of the league. He was with Washington then, apparently closing out his career at age thirty-five, and had batted only .245 in the first 20 games. So he went to the Boston Braves, batted .340 in 118 games, and wound up with a total combined average of .331. He played three seasons in Boston, never again dropping below .300 in batting. Then he got a job as a player-manager in the Texas League and kept on beating the ball until he was thirty-nine.

Like Hal Chase, Sisler was an accomplished athlete in almost every field. Had he not starred so tri-umphantly in baseball in college, he might have been one of Michigan's great ball carriers on the football field. He was a star punter and dropkicker and could run the 100-yard dash in near-record time. He also was a top performer in billiards, swimming, boxing, and ice skating. And even umpires agreed he was one of the nicest men alive.

There were not, for a fact, too many nice guys in major league baseball through the prewar days. When Ty Cobb joined the Detroit club in 1905 as an eighteen-year-old rookie with a high opinion of his own skill, he had to fight for a chance to take batting

Ty Cobb, of Detroit, the American League Honus Wagner, kept his hands well apart on his bat. He sharpened his spikes, chopped off his sleeves to make them fit, and sometimes played with holes in his stockings.

Hal Chase, star of the New York Highlanders and slickest fielding first baseman in history, was barred from the Hall of Fame because he bet on ball games and was suspected of throwing games for money.

practice. The veteran players not only shoved him away from the plate, but the pitcher would take aim at him, his mates would saw his favorite bat in two, trip him on the baselines, and even lock him out of his hotel room. A gentler soul would have given up without ever getting through spring training.

Every town, it seemed, had its pet roughneck—McGraw in New York, Carrigan in Boston; Cobb in Detroit. Besides Ty, Detroit had a catcher named "Butch" Schmidt who was so tough he used to pound nails into a plank with his fist. He also gave a sound beating to Ty Cobb, repeating the lesson when Cobb came back for more at a later date. The Chicago White Sox had hard-boiled Chick Gandil and Swede Risberg, who used to frighten their own teammates. According to another of the Black Sox, Joe Jackson, Risberg "threatened to bump me off," when he started to confess his part in the 1919 World Series fix.

In Brooklyn there was Bull Dahlen, the fearless shortstop, who had been playing ball since 1891 and had twice been on the Brooklyn roster. Bull, who had once been knocked flat when he was rash enough to get in front of a ball hit by mighty Ed Delahanty, is one of the few ballplayers since Ban Johnson entered the game who actually punched an umpire in the head. He finished an argument with umpire Cy Rigler one day by letting the man in blue have a fist in the face.

Pittsburgh had Fred Clarke, who seemed to dote on cutting down second basemen with his spikes. And managing the St. Louis Cardinals for a while was Roger Bresnahan, one of the greatest catchers the major leagues ever saw, a graduate of the McGraw school of

Mordecai Peter Centennial Brown was called "Three-Finger" Brown because he lost most of his right index finger in a corn chopper. Pitching for the Chicago Cubs from 1904 to 1912, Brown had eight winning seasons in a row, with six consecutive years in which he won twenty or more games. In 1908 he accepted 108 fielding chances on the pitcher's mound and never made an error.

oratory, and a man who talked so tough that his lady boss, Mrs. Schuyler Britton, could not stand him. He was "not the type," she told her attorney, that she wanted to have managing her club. Why, he didn't talk fit to eat!

There were also, in these prewar days, a goodly number of great performers who, for one reason or another, ultimately found themselves half-forgotten. Of course, the great batters—Napoleon Lajoie of Cleveland, "Wahoo" Sam Crawford, Harry Heilmann (whom Ty Cobb turned into a champion by changing his batting style), Elmer Flick (who looked as if he might match Cobb in hitting and base running), Cobb, Wagner, and Ed Delahanty—and the mighty pitchers —big Ed Walsh and Urban Faber, the spitball kings; Joe McGinnity; Rube Waddell; Chief Bender; Eddie Plank; Mathewson; Ted Lyons (one of the first of the knuckle ballers); and Walter Johnson—the matchless Big Train— have had their fame well cultivated.

But who talks nowadays of Noodles Hahn, who pitched six seasons for Cincinnati, starting 225 games and finishing 209 of them? But for an injury to his arm in 1905, Noodles might have matched any of the Hall of Famers. Playing with a club that seemed devoted to the second division, Noodles, during his too-brief career (he was twenty-six when he injured his arm), won 127 games and lost 91. In his eight active seasons he exceeded 20 wins four times.

And what minstrels sing of Big Bill Dineen, except as an umpire? Yet Bill, in the first World Series between the National and American leagues, won three games for Boston. A veteran of the defunct Washington Nationals and a refugee from the Boston Beaneaters of the National League, Big Bill won 21 games for the Boston Americans two years in a row (1902 and 1903), then won 23 in 1904. The next year, he pitched a no-hitter against the White Sox.

Of even lesser renown these days is the first "hero" of the 1903 World Series—Deacon Phillippe, the lean Pittsburgh right-hander from Rural Retreat, Virginia, who also won three games in this almost interminable Series, was awarded a diamond stickpin and a thousand handshakes—and then blew the game that would have meant the championship. The Deacon, who had pitched a no-hitter for Louisville in 1899, won twenty games or better his first five years in major league baseball and never had a losing season in his thirteen-year career in the league.

But the Cleveland fans probably would not have swapped any of these for their own "Big Six," Adrian (Addie) Joss, winner of a "perfect" game against the Chicago White Sox in 1908. Ailing through most of his career, Addie—a long-legged, slab-sided fellow—had to quit the game in 1910 after starting out with another no-hitter. In his off-time Addie worked as a sportswriter, specializing in articles on how to play the game, for he was known as one of the craftiest ballplayers of his day, who fielded his position like an infielder and hit well enough to go to bat in a pinch. He also played first and third base and put in a few innings in the outfield. His lifetime earned run average of 1.88, second best in the books, indicates that had not illness cut him down, he might have earned a niche in Cooperstown. He died two days past his thirty-first birthday—al-

"Savior" of baseball, after the Black Sox Scandal, which broke in 1920, was Kenesaw Mountain Landis, first Commissioner of Baseball. Striking a dramatic pose at the 1943 World Series, he almost knocks the hat off Colonel Larry MacPhaii.

most exactly a year after he had pitched his last no-hitter.

Perhaps most talked about of all in the early 1900s—except for the great men who earned the World Series headlines—was one of the game's foremost eccentrics: Arthur "Bugs" Raymond, a spitballer and part-time bartender who worked for St. Louis and New York in the National League, after having been "discovered" and then quickly undiscovered by Ed Barrow of Detroit. Outsized, red-faced, amazingly strong, and given to frequent cavorting about the diamond, Bugs gave fans a hundred stories to tell wherever he played—in Rockford, Illinois; Waterloo, Iowa; Jackson, Mississippi; in Detroit; Atlanta; and Savannah (where he first took to tending bat); and in Charleston; St. Louis; and New York. Besides his spitball he had a scary fastball that might have been as good as Rusie's or Johnson's or Cy Young's had Bugs not been quite so devoted to burning his brief candle at both ends.

But Bugs played ball for fun and rejoiced in his accomplishments. Like most pitchers he loved best to hit the ball, and managed this so seldom that whenever he did drive the ball into fair territory, he would do a sort of Indian war dance around the base after he had arrived safely. Once, indeed, he celebrated a foul ball—a long, long drive that would have been a home run if it had stayed inside the foul line. It went clean over the left-field fence in Boston, and Bugs watched it in wonder. It counted as one strike, and Bugs never swung at the next two pitches. He was busy waving his bat and shouting his delight as the pitcher wheeled over strikes two and three. Then, still rejoicing and his red face shining like the new sun, Bugs danced and pranced all the way to the bench.

Poor Bugs never won enough baseball games to earn fame equal to that won by his capers and his carousing. He set a record of sorts in 1908 when he lost 25 games while winning only 14. In his first year with the Giants (1909), he won 18 games and never came close to that mark again. More than once Bugs appeared on the ball field wearing an unhealed hangover, and one day he won a game without even a two-minute warm-up—he had arrived bleary-eyed one hour late, just in time to ask for the ball.

If Bugs won a game, as he sometimes did, he promptly celebrated his good luck by toasting everyone in his favorite barroom. If he lost one, he immediately set out to drown his sorrows in the same setting. When the team took a train from one town to the next on the schedule, old Bugs would invariably climb aboard, barely able to make the steps, but full of jollity. Bugs died when he was thirty.

In Brooklyn the greatest pitcher alive in the century's youngest days was not Mathewson, Walter Johnson, Chief Bender, or Rube Waddell but George Rucker, nicknamed Napoleon and called "Nap" by the Brooklyn fans. (All the game's leaders were either "King" or "Napoleon" in those distant days. The nickname stuck to only a few.) Nap was a gentleman from Georgia who never played for any big league team but Brooklyn. When the young left-hander was pitching bush league ball in Augusta, Georgia, Connie Mack owned title to him. But Connie already had the best pitchers in the league, so he let George go to Brooklyn, where he became the left-handed

Larry Lajoie, leading batter in the American League and Cleveland's best second baseman, greets Honus Wagner, Pittsburgh's shortstop and the National League's top batter.

workhorse. Uncomplaining and soft-spoken, willing and strong, George pitched game after game in which his mates would quietly disintegrate around him. Like most of the Brooklyns, George usually did his best work against the Giants, and had he ever belonged to a club of the Giants' class, he might have made marks that would still be standing. McGraw once offered $30,000 for his contract, but Rucker's boss, Charles Ebbets, would not even talk about a deal.

So George kept working in this lowly vineyard at a meager wage, taking the mound in forty games or so each season for seven seasons and only twice com-ing out with a better than .500 average.

In 1908 when he won 18 games and lost 20, Rucker pitched a no-hitter against Boston. It was not until 1916, his last year in the leagues, that he finally found himself on a champion-ship club. By then Nap had retired to the bullpen and won but two games the whole season. In the World Series he pitched only two innings and struck out three. The game had already been lost, and Nap had been suffering all year from bursitis. But Manager Wilbert Robinson, who wanted Nap to have at least one go at the Series, sent him in. Fans on both sides roared old Nap a welcome, which was also a farewell.

The Golden Years

MODERN baseball was supposed to have begun in 1911 when the official major league ball was given a cork center. But the game really grew beyond earlier imaginings just after World War I, when peace, gradually rising wages, and industrial growth plus the home run mania triggered by George Herman Ruth created new fans and new enthusiasms. In the 1920s crowds at all athletic events began to outnumber the populations of small cities. College football could no longer be contained in backlot gridirons with one set of wooden stands. Professional boxing promoters aimed at million-dollar gates. Sane men and women could even be persuaded to gather in festering numbers to watch some slightly retarded member of the race spend several days dangling from the top of a flagpole.

It may have been that the lower middle class and the working poor had all suddenly, from having their innocence eroded by the bitter realities of the war, arrived concurrently at the conclusion that nothing was better for a man than to eat, to drink, and to be merry. Certainly the "Work and Win" ethic grew faint and fretful as sophisticated men and women learned it was possible to strike it rich with one quick throw of the dice—on the stock market, in Florida real estate, or by staging spectacles of one sort and another. And baseball players found out that games could be won and paychecks fattened by one mighty swing of the bat.

No one else could have been better cast to lead and to epitomize the new hedonism than George Herman Ruth, a young delinquent who had become addicted to beer when he was eight years old, who grew strong in the belief that there was no need to mortgage the present to pay for tomorrow, and that a youth should enjoy what he wanted whenever he wanted it. Bright, headstrong, vulgar, aggressive, profane, crude, and simplehearted, Babe, no matter what solemn-sided experts may have said about Cobb and Wagner, was probably the best baseball player who ever lived. But he was far more than merely a great pitcher, a great batter, a great base runner, a great fielder, and a great strategist. He was a great personality, who glowed so with the joy and the love of life that he commanded every room he entered. Round-faced almost to the point of caricature, and so wide-nostriled that he probably could have winded a war-horse in a footrace, Ruth was handsome nonetheless. His hair was glossy, ink-black, and luxuriant. His eyes were dark and alive. His mouth was mobile, quick to smile, to writhe in sudden anger, or to pout in childish self-pity. His voice was deep, resonant, and truly musical. (He loved to sing.)

Before overindulgence had somewhat distorted his belly, young George was physically well-formed, more than 6 feet tall, with large strong hands, long arms, hard-muscled forearms, and solidly muscled legs. He had a mincing, pigeon-toed way of walking that he had imitated from the man he most admired when he was a boy. That was Brother Mathias—a huge man of muscle: 250 pounds and more than 6 feet tall—who had charge of discipline at St. Mary's Industrial School for Boys, run by the Xaverian Brothers in Baltimore. This school, to which young George was five times committed after it had proved difficult to keep him out of the barroom where his father worked and impossible for his mother to discipline him, was Babe Ruth's true home until the day he was signed to a baseball contract by the Baltimore Orioles. And it was at the school that Babe learned baseball —first, as a left-handed catcher, then as a pitcher, and always as the heaviest hitter in the school.

Grown-up and still largely delinquent in his behavior—as are so many poor boys who come into sudden riches —Babe Ruth became the most imposing figure of his age. It was he, not Judge Landis, who "saved" baseball from the fate the nervous magnates saw yawning before them after the Black Sox scandal of 1920. Babe lifted the game to new heights of excitement, and he kept it on the front pages of newspapers throughout the land. It is doubtful that the "public" would have turned away from baseball just because a World Series had been fixed. The depth of public tolerance for dirty work in sports has never been properly sounded. But Babe Ruth created a new public, not just out of the children who were helping the population figures increase by geometrical progression, but also from people of all ages, some of whom knew less than beans about baseball strategy and lived only from one long, screaming hit to the next. And then there were those who understood only that their own meager selves would somehow be glorified could they

Dazzy Vance, darling of the Brooklyn fans, liked to rear back and get his left foot far out front when he pitched.

but for an instant get close enough to a famous person to lay a finger on him, catch his attention for a breath, or actually carry away his signature or a snatch of his clothing.

Because of this, Babe Ruth's burgeoning figure overshadows the whole history of organized baseball during the supposed "Golden" Age of Sports. (Professional football, long the stepchild of games-for-pay, profited in like manner from the explosive exploitation on film and paper of the astonishing doings of Red Grange of Illinois.) Cobb, Speaker, Wagner, Sisler, and many of the great men of earlier seasons still trod the diamond in the days of Ruth. But they and many others, including the dozens who learned to imitate the Babe by driving the juiced-up baseball out of the park, were all dwarfed by the man who was earning many times more money than any ballplayer had ever been paid before. (When Babe, at the height of his career, was refused $50,000 a year by General Manager Ed Barrow of the Yankees, he was offered that amount by Yankee owner Jake Ruppert. But Babe insisted on $52,000, because he had "always wanted to make $1,000 a week.")

The New York roster held the names of a number of extraordinary performers who were happy enough to trail along in Ruth's shadow. Two, indeed, tagged along off the field and earned some minor recognition in baseball circles as members along with Ruth of the Yankees' "playboy trio." These were Waite C. Hoyt, son of a man who had won some small fame in the theater, and Joseph Dugan, one of a whole parcel of Dugans who had worked at one time or another for the New Haven Railroad.

Hoyt was no youthful delinquent nor graduate of an industrial school. He came from a comfortably fixed middle-class Brooklyn family and had been brought up strictly according to the standards of the day. He had been a high school pitching hero and would have gone on to college had not a chance to make money in baseball lured him away. He was still of schoolboy age when John McGraw signed him to a contract—or signed Waite's father, inasmuch as the boy was a minor. Waite first had made an effort to join the Brooklyn Dodgers, appearing at Ebbets Field one day, along with a few dozen other youths, for a "tryout." He was hardly noticed except by one puck-faced outfielder named Stengel (called "Dutch" or "Casey" by his mates.) Casey always recalled Hoyt as the big kid who had shown up in a "pair of bloomers his mother must have made."

McGraw had a sharp eye for youthful talent, however, and he took the boy on board despite his misfit uniform. He sent Waite down South for "seasoning" among a group of hard-boiled minor leaguers and faded National League stars and then shifted him to New England, where Hoyt's hide was further toughened by exposure to skinflint management and hard-drinking companions. Although Hoyt actually put in one training season in Texas with McGraw and stayed with the big team long enough to pitch an inning and strike out two big leaguers, McGraw finally had to let go of Waite's contract to make room for more seasoned players.

At the age of eighteen and a "veteran" of the National League, Hoyt was playing for the minor league club in Lynn, Massachusetts, when he was invited to come talk to the Boston Red Sox. Apple-cheeked and innocent of eye, Hoyt had a hard time convincing the man at the gate at Fenway Park that he was really a ballplayer. But once inside he convinced everyone. It was at Fenway Park that Hoyt first met Babe Ruth, whom he learned to call "Jidge." (Ruth called him "Kid," as he did almost everyone, and later called him "Stud" as he did all his intimates.)

Hoyt was among the stars sold to the Yankees by Red Sox owner Harry Frazee, following Babe Ruth southward by one year. Hoyt's record with the Red Sox was undistinguished (so was the club he worked for), but in New York he became a star, with 19 victories in each of his first two seasons. Hoyt by this time had grown hardened to the taunts that he received for daring to look so much like a child. A big, solidly built young man, he was no bait for the bullies and was able to hold his own in a row. He was also as ready as Ruth was to sample the excitements of the big city. While young Hoyt never hoped to match the Babe stride for stride in touring the town, he and Dugan often helped to turn the Babe's company into a crowd.

With his quick wit and sharp tongue, Dugan may have been the merriest of the three, but even he had to own himself overmatched against the jolly Jidge, who could tour the hot spots all night and hit home runs on the morrow. Dugan, who roomed with Hoyt on the road, would occasionally disappear on secret errands of his own that awakened his roommate's curiosity. One morning when Dugan had ducked out of the hotel lobby with no word about his destination, Hoyt took after him and shadowed him to a nearby church, where he found young Joe devoutly lighting a candle.

"In hopes I will get some help with my hitting," Dugan explained.

"Well, light one for me then," Hoyt urged him. "I'm pitching today."

The extra candle was lit. But that afternoon poor Waite was promptly blasted out of the box. Dugan shook his head in sympathy.

"Some bloody Protestant," he explained, "sneaked in and blew the candle out."

The Yankee line-up in the 1920s was a frightening one, which sometimes cowed their enemies into submission merely through displays of power in batting practice. There was no scheming, scrambling, pecking, and bunting—not even much base-stealing—for these hearties. When they got a man on base, the aim was to jolt him all the way around with a blow against the fence or over it.

Of course, the most renowned of the sluggers were Ruth, who set the style, and Lou Gehrig, who followed in his wake. Young Lou, an awkward fielder to start, and something of a social butcher as well, had a hard time winning his way into the hearts of his tight-knit and cold-eyed teammates. He was too much the boy scout in his talk and too much the rover boy in the way he brought gifts from his mama (including leaky bundles of pickled eels!) into the clubhouse. But Lou made it finally, by dint of his complete devotion to the job, his willingness to perform whatever job was handed him, and his refusal to let any physical ailment—major or minor—deter him from performance of his duties. Lou was no carouser, no stage personality (both Ruth and Hoyt had good singing voices and were suc-

Carl Mays of the Yankees used to bend close to the ground to hide his underhand pitch. He killed shortstop Ray Chapman of Cleveland with a fastball in 1920.

cesses on the stage), and no wit. But he did learn to field his position with dexterity, if not grace, and he brought joy to every teammate's heart with his murderous drives into the far outfield and into the nearby streets to bring runs home by the bundle.

Out-thundered by these mighty bats were a number of young wallopers of almost equal worth, who occasionally shared the headlines with Ruth and Gehrig or, at least in the springtime, threatened to run them a race. There was Jimmy Foxx, known to teammates and opponents as "The Beast," the strongest and best of all the right-handed batters. There was Mickey Cochrane, rated the equal of Roger Bresnahan as a catcher, who could run, and hit and inspire a pitcher or a whole ball club—and who eventually demonstrated that he could manage a championship club when he brought a pennant to Detroit in 1934.

Connie Mack, in Philadelphia, owned both Foxx and Cochrane to begin with, and he also owned some of the fastest and craftiest pitchers in the league, as he always seemed to. Not all of them lasted long enough in the leagues to qualify as Hall of Famers (Waite Hoyt, for instance, stayed "up" for 21 seasons).

Connie Mack also owned another mighty hitter destined for the Hall of Fame under the made-up name of Simmons, given to him by an impatient rewrite man who could not get his real name, Szymanski, straight over the telephone. Al, playing for Aberdeen of the Dakota League and Milwaukee of the American Association, at first did not impress his watchers with his batting ability. He had a habit of aiming one foot toward third base. This "foot

in the water bucket" stance, which was to become Al's trademark, was supposed to make it impossible for him to hit with any power or to hit an outside pitch at all. But Al was really keeping his front foot free, as good hitters often do, and he did not hesitate to step into the pitch when it came.

The Milwaukee club, perhaps despairing of curing him of this habit, had shipped him down to Shreveport, Louisiana, and it was there that Connie Mack spotted him. Connie had owned an earlier slugger from Milwaukee, a first baseman named Joe Hauser, who could hit a ball as far as Babe Ruth could and might have matched Babe's records had he not, in a freakish accident, split his kneecap so that it was never properly repaired. (Despite one weak knee, however, Joe became a minor league sensation and hit 65 home runs one season in Milwaukee.) Al Simmons remained sound of wind and limb, however, and held his own with all the great hitters of his day. He hit the ball far, and he hit it often, finishing one season with a mark of .392 (Harry Heilmann beat him out that year with .397).

Al felt he was in baseball heaven in Philadelphia. When he was an amateur ballplayer in Milwaukee, he had written to Connie Mack asking for a tryout. Connie never saw the letter. After Connie bought him for a small price, Al returned to complete the season at Milwaukee and batted .398 in the remaining 24 games. The Milwaukee bosses ruefully counted over to themselves what they might have sold him for if they had kept him there all season.

Stroking the baseball regularly into the near distance throughout those Golden Days was a happy young man

Waite Hoyt, at the age of thirty-two, after helping the Philadelphia Athletics win a pennant, came back to his hometown, Brooklyn, to pitch for the Dodgers. But before the season was out, he had returned to the New York Giants, the team that had first signed him, sixteen years before.

named Bottomley and called "Sunny Jim" after a mythical figure whose picture smiled up at the nation's young people from the label of a cereal box. Sunny Jim Bottomley was really sunny, a man who looked and acted as if he was having the time of his life playing baseball. He wore his baseball cap pulled around at a jaunty angle, so the bill was always askew. And he swung his bat lustily at every sort of pitch. Jim hit many a home run, with the new "Babe Ruth" baseball, and one day knocked in 12 runs in a single game against Brooklyn (September 26,

1924). He once tied for the league lead in home runs, once led the league in triples, and twice led in two-baggers. Beginning in 1924 he drove in more than 100 runs each season and ended his career with more runs batted in (1,422) than runs scored (1,177).

Once Jim hit a home run and had to explain that he didn't really mean it. The ball, driven with all Jim's strength into the far-off stands, had injured a spectator. A legal complaint against Jim set forth the accusation that he had swung at the ball deliberately and "with the intention of creating a situation

Rogers Hornsby stood as far away from the plate as he could get, in the rear, right-hand corner of the batter's box. He won seven league batting championships.

commonly known as a home run.'' No, Jim solemnly told the court, he was just trying for a hit. And anyway, there was ''never any malice in my home runs.''

There was never any malice in anything Jim did on the diamond. He helped raise Branch Rickey's St. Louis Cardinals to new heights in his best days and earned as devoted a following in St. Louis as Babe Ruth knew in New York. Jim developed his strength swinging a hammer in a blacksmith's shop in Illinois and earned his first few baseball dollars playing for the town team in Witt. He was a fierce com-

petitor all his life, the man who kept the St. Louis infield alive, and often the one who led the club home with his mighty bat. He played 13 seasons in St. Louis, 11 with the Cardinals, and 2 with the Browns. In between times, he played first base for the Cincinnati Reds.

Sharing the clubhouse in St. Louis through most of Sunny Jim's great years was another hard-hitting infielder, who could knock the ball as far as Jim could, hit it more often, and was destined to wind up his active career the same year Jim did (1937), although he had started seven years ahead of him.

Rogers Hornsby, who played at Jim's side in the infield, and even filled in for Jim at first base a few times, also ended his own playing career, after considerable wandering, right where Jim did—with the St. Louis Browns.

There was nothing sunny about Rogers Hornsby. He was a cold-eyed, calculating, intense man who found nothing funny in baseball—least of all in hitting. He seemed in some ways to be the reincarnation of Cap Anson, although he was inches shorter than Cap. But he was just as fanatic about physical condition, just as cross-grained, and could wallop a baseball with equal intensity. Like Cap, he was full of private prejudices and knew how to nurse a grudge. He was perhaps less likable than Cap, for he was inclined to go his own way and to seek his own ends without being concerned too much about the men he might have to bump aside.

Hornsby entered major league baseball in 1915 as a shortstop, and the following year he played every infield position for the St. Louis Cardinals. His third year in the majors, he led the National League in triples, and by 1920 he led in runs batted in and posted the highest average in the league: .370. He also hit more two-baggers than anybody else in his league.

Hornsby's market value at this point in his career was set at $350,000. That was what the Giants had offered for him, and it was more than the purchase price of Babe Ruth. To prove he was worth it, Hornsby then set out to lead the league in batting the next five seasons in a row, three times batting more than .400. In 1922 he hit 42 home runs,

tops in the National League. Hornsby became manager of the Cardinals in 1925, and he continued managing for most of the next eighteen years. (He succeeded Jim Bottomley as manager of the Browns in 1937.) When he was not managing or coaching somewhere, he went in for barnstorm exhibitions of hitting, touring the nation with a small bag full of his own private brand of baseballs that were guaranteed to fly off his bat twice as fast as the regulation ball.

Once an old friend, doing a little exhibition pitching when past his own prime, asked Rogers not to slam the ball back quite so hard, as the old-timer's eyesight did not permit him to get out of the way of a screaming line drive with as much agility as was sometimes needed. Hornsby made a sour face and promptly hammered a ball through the box that almost took his old friend's head off. Rogers never backed away or gave ground for any man. He made no bones about the fact that he liked to play the horses, as John McGraw and umpire Bill Klem did. And the mere fact that Baseball Commissioner Kenesaw Mountain Landis disapproved of this pastime never deterred Rogers, although the icy old man's opposition was said to have interfered with Rogers' advancement in baseball.

Anyone who ever met Hornsby remembered his eyes. From the time he was a skinny kid playing shortstop in Texas, they were cold and clear as pure ice. Whether the clarity of his eyes had anything to do with his ability to sight a baseball down a bat is a question. But most people believed that his unusual eyes made him a great hitter.

Another thing that made him a great hitter was his unusual stance. At the Cardinal training camp in 1916, Bob Connery, who had "discovered" Hornsby playing Class D baseball in the Western League, talked the young man into changing his batting stance—to stand in the farthest corner of the batter's box, as far from the plate and from the pitcher as a hitter was allowed to stand. No one in baseball ever stood quite so far from the plate as Hornsby did. And hardly anyone ever hit every type of pitch with the power and consistency of Rogers Hornsby. His distance from the plate, he said, gave him time to level off on any pitch that came into the strike zone.

Although Hornsby still holds the "modern" batting record of .424, set in 1924, he first attracted the attention of his discoverer not by his bat but by his agility in the field. As a hitter, in the minors, he was strictly a choke, poke, slap, and bunt man and would never have set any batting marks in the majors. All the same, he might well have held a job on his fielding for, after trying every job in the infield, he became the best second baseman in the business and grew particularly adept at making a quick throw to first, right across his chest, without any pause to shift his feet.

Eventually, Hornsby was traded to the New York Giants, immediately after he had led his club to a World Championship in 1926. His boss in St. Louis, Sam Breadon, had long before promised himself that he was going to get rid of cantankerous Rogers first chance that came along. For Hornsby had called him a tightwad to his face, in the final month of the season. And after the season was over, Hornsby had turned down a one-year contract and insisted on a long-term agreement at a fat raise, just as most managers who have won championships usually receive in reward. Breadon, who did indeed admire the smell and the feel of a dollar bill, said no. And before the argument had time to grow bitter, Breadon swapped Hornsby to John McGraw for second baseman Frankie Frisch and pitcher Jimmy Ring. That, cried the St. Louis fans and sportswriters in almost a single voice, was the lousiest deal ever visited on a suffering public. It would *have* to be rescinded. But Sam Breadon locked himself away, took his telephone off the hook, and rode out the storm. Championship or no, Rogers Hornsby could go snarl his epithets at someone else.

Hornsby's name, will be forever linked in baseball history to that of Grover Cleveland Alexander, who was, or could have been, according to many who watched him, the greatest pitcher who ever lived. But poor Grover, who was "Pete" to his friends, was practically a professional drinking man whose idea of a celebration was a night in which the drinking stopped only when he could no longer lift the glass without help. Pete's name has been glorified enough in the Hall of Fame and in the countless stories told of his supposed greatest moment when he held off the mighty New York Yankees on a misty October day in the 1926 World Series.

The haze of time, deeper even than the haze which made old Pete's fast ball doubly effective that day, has distorted the details of that moment, so that it is sometimes recalled that, suffering from a hangover, he struck out Tony Lazzeri in the last of the ninth, with the winning runs on base.

But it did not happen just that way.

Sunny Jim Bottomley, hard-hitting first baseman for the St. Louis Cardinals in 1926, always
wore his cap a little askew. He owns the record
for runs batted in in a single game — twelve.

It was the seventh inning of the deciding game of the Series when Jesse
Haines, the Cardinal pitcher, his finger
bleeding from pitching his knuckler,
walked Lou Gehrig to fill the bases with
two out. At that point, Hornsby, the
manager and second baseman, sent to
the bullpen for Old Pete. Pete had won
his game the day before and had been
expected, and entitled, to put in a night
of celebration. But when Hornsby
looked into Pete's eyes as he met him
in short left field, the eyes were clear
and steady.

Old Pete thereupon threw a strike to
Tony Lazzeri, tried to burn another one
past, and saw Tony rip into it to send
it on a whistling line over third base,
into the stands. It was foul by a foot
and counted as strike two. Old Pete
calmly cranked up again, ignoring the
runners, and sizzled a strike over the
outside corner. Lazzeri let fly at it with
all his strength, missing it completely.
But there were still two innings to go,
and Alexander did not run into any
further theatrics. In the ninth inning,
after Combs and Koenig had made out,
Pete walked Babe Ruth who was shot
down trying to steal second.

Pete was forty years old when he won
that game. He had been in the National
League, with Philadelphia, Chicago,
and St. Louis, since 1911, and had won
33 games ten seasons earlier. He had
4 more seasons of pitching ahead of him
before his mighty physique at last gave
way. He ended his days being shifted
about from boardinghouse to boarding-

house, living on the tiny pension baseball awarded him, lest it be accused of allowing one of its greatest heroes to die in want. (Eventually the payments had to be made directly to the boardinghouse keepers, lest poor Pete sop up the entire stipend before he got around to paying for his food.)

Unlike many another Golden Age hero, old Pete never wound up with the Boston Braves. Christy Mathewson did (he was named president when Judge Emil Fuchs bought the club in 1923). Joe Dugan did. Babe Ruth did. George Sisler did. And so did Rogers Hornsby. They were not all there together, but even if they had been, it is doubtful they could have lifted the sorry Boston club much higher in the standing.

The Braves were by no means the worst club in the league. That was usually the Phillies. But the Braves never seemed to accomplish what their roster promised in those days, when everything was getting bigger or growing higher, when everyone was becoming richer, and when summer days were made still longer by adding an hour of daylight on at the end.

The Braves, for all the money that was spent and all the great names that were recruited to inspire them, seemed to grow soggier by the season. They played in a ballpark too big for any six outfielders to cover. And their rival club, the Red Sox, were, if anything, sorrier still. Yet they staggered through the Golden Twenties without ever rising higher in the standing than fifth place.

Still, the Braves created continual excitement in the city and managed to set the style for lush quarters, lavish publicity, generous salaries, and open-handed treatment of the fans that gradually brightened the face of organized baseball everywhere. Judge Fuchs, who went bankrupt operating the Braves, was never meant to be a baseball man, for he possessed a genius for misjudging the potential of a ballplayer or a manager; he was also too soft a touch to run the team himself (he tried it once when, like Chris Von der Ahe, he grew impatient with incompetent managers).

The Braves did have a few glorious moments on the field. One, which preceded Judge Fuchs' arrival by about three years, was the longest game (in number of innings) ever played—a 26-inning tie (1 to 1) with the Brooklyn Dodgers, in which both pitchers, Joe Oeschger of the Braves and Leon Gadore of the Dodgers, pitched every inning. (They did not, as some legends have it, ruin their arms in the process, either. Both men did some fine pitching in later seasons.) And in the first year (1923) of the Fuchs regime, the Braves shortstop, Ernie Padgett, playing his first season in the majors, made an unassisted triple play against Philadelphia to help keep the Phils one notch below them in the standings. Bill Wambsganss of Cleveland had performed an unassisted triple play in the World Series against the Dodgers a few years earlier, but this was the first time any National Leaguer had contrived any such stunt since the league was brand new. (Paul Hines of Providence was credited with putting three men out all by himself in 1878.)

And one day in Brooklyn, where amazing things go unreported every week, the Braves, with some help from the Dodgers, turned a two-base hit into a double play. The ball was hit by Babe Herman, a much maligned outfielder who was sometimes accused of having been hit on the head by fly balls. ("Never!" Herman insisted. But he granted he might have taken one on the shoulder.) Actually, Herman thought he had hit a triple, and he would have made three bases on it except that he forgot there were runners ahead of him. "Dazzy" Vance, president of the Dodgers' 0-for-4 club, thought the third base coach had ordered *him* to stay at third. (Actually, the coach was telling Herman to hold up.) So Dazzy slid *back* to the bag as Herman slid into it. What Herman had overlooked was that, in charging blindly for that extra base, he had gone right by Chick Fewster, another Brooklyn base runner, leaving poor Chick with no base to slide into at all. Herman was automatically out on the play, and Chick was called out when he tried to find a hiding place in the outfield to keep from being tagged.

The Braves owned no Babe Hermans or Dazzy Vances to add notes of hilarity to the doings on the diamond. But they did list on their roster for a time a few of baseball's lesser "characters," whose fame often outreached their playing skill.

For a catcher, they had for a time an overgrown high school lad from Somerville, Massachusetts, named Francis Hogan, but nicknamed "Shanty" when his habit of devouring everything within reach that was not too tough to bite nor too thick to drink gradually turned him into a figure the size of a small outbuilding. (Some did say Shanty became Shanty because he was a shanty Irishman by derivation. But fans found his nickname especially apt when he blocked out part of the playing field with his bulk.)

Shanty was tough as well as large. He was hit right in the face by a pitch

from Chicago's Guy Bush one day, and he trotted down to first without even rubbing his near-broken jaw. Shanty was the man who prompted the rebuilding of Braves Field, it being the custom in those days for every club owner to try to arrange matters so his heavy hitters could put balls into the stands. To suit Shanty Hogan's hitting habits, Judge Fuchs built a whole new section of seats in left field to absorb long fly balls hit by Hogan and turn them into home runs. Unhappily, Hogan never made too much hay there, nor did Rogers Hornsby, an even mightier right-handed hitter, who liked to hit a ball where it was pitched. But right-handed batters belonging to the enemy found the new target inviting, indeed. One June three right-handed *pitchers* from Cincinnati—Pete Donohue, Ray Kolp, and Eppa Rixey—all drove home runs into the new seats on successive days. Whereupon Judge Fuchs ordered a canvas screen erected to close the target altogether.

The judge was always doing his best for his club and for the fans, even if his efforts were sometimes misguided. He brought baseball up to date by introducing radio broadcasting—a form of entertainment many an old-timer classed with larceny. (Charles Comiskey, at one time, had closed his park to Western Union telegraphers, insisting that they were stealing his baseball games and cutting down on attendance.) In the early days of radio, too, many a baseball magnate solemnly foresaw whole townships of empty seats if anyone dared sneak out the details of a ball game to men and women who did not pay their way in. The judge, however, was a born publicity man, and he knew that filling the

Al Simmons, who helped keep the Philadelphia ballpark jammed full during Baseball's Golden Age (the 1920s), was traded to the Chicago White Sox and opened their season with a home run before a skimpy crowd in St. Louis, April 13, 1933.

air with baseball news would just broadcast the baseball fever. Judge Fuchs also emptied his pockets to finance the successful campaign to bring Sunday baseball to Boston.

Another thoroughgoing original, whom the Braves brought aboard for a time was Art ("the Great") Shires, first baseman, heavyweight boxer, football star, and professional college student. Art attended more colleges than he could recall, playing football on "scholarship" and using a wholly different pseudonym at each school. At Wesley College Art was Art Shires. But at Marshall College he was Dana Prince. At Canisius he was Bill French. At Geneva he named himself after the great Boston infielder who first hit four home runs in a single nine-inning game—Robert Lowe. And once he dropped out of college altogether because he could not recall what name he had used when he had enrolled.

Lou Gehrig, fresh out of Columbia, was learning to be a first baseman in 1923. He already knew how to hit.

Bill Terry, manager of the New York Giants, was calling the strategy in 1936 and trying to perform it as well. Here he attempts a sacrifice bunt in the 1936 World Series against the Yankees, but the strategy failed as Dick Bartell was thrown out at second base by the Yankee pitcher, Bump Hadley.

Long before Art wound up with the Braves, he had named himself "The Great," had challenged half the world to mortal combat, and had actually got into a fistfight with his manager in Chicago. (He was also arrested in Chicago by a policeman, who charged that he had found a pair of brass knuckles in Shires' pocket.) Art made his first appearance in Boston in the prize ring at the Boston Garden, where he beat Braves' pitcher Al Spohrer, who also expressed pretensions as a boxer, into a state of semiconsciousness. Art's ambition, often uttered aloud, was to fight Hack Wilson, home run hero of the Chicago Cubs, who was seven inches shorter than Shires but came closer to matching him in weight than poor Al Spohrer did. Commissioner Landis, however, who was bound that baseball's skirts would never be sullied by prize-ring resin or racetrack dirt, refused to allow the match.

Art was really a better ballplayer than his detractors would grant. But Art undertook to live in the manner of a latter-day King Kelly, with clothing two hops ahead of the fashion, screaming shirts and ties, and a regal hotel suite. He strutted about the town informing his public of what great feats of strength and daring he was about to exhibit. Unhappily, Art smashed up his knee before he ever set any records in Boston, and when he recovered from the injury, he was quickly shuttled down through the minor leagues, never, or hardly ever, to be heard from again.

The Braves only true hero in this era was one they raised themselves, Wally Berger, a mighty home-run artist from California, where he had hit forty home runs for the Los Angeles club. Berger, like Hornsby, was a right-handed hitter.

But unlike Hornsby, he undertook to drive every pitch out to the horizon.

Braves Field was perhaps the least accommodating ballpark in the country for men who hit for distance, its outfield reaches resembling in depth the full expanses of the Boston Common. But Berger managed to send fair balls over fences just the same. He did not hit forty home runs for Boston. In his first year he hit thirty-eight to lead the National League.

Berger drove one homer over *both* fences in center field in the home park, which had been cut down by the erection of an inner fence after the management discovered that there was no glory to be gained or hay to be made simply through owning the biggest outfield in Christendom. That blow of Wally's traveled over 475 feet and landed on the railroad tracks outside the park. He had hit one almost as far the day before. He also, in that first year, struck out 69 times. (Hornsby never struck out more than 65 times a season in his whole career, and he often had more than twice as many walks as strikeouts. Berger, in his whole career, *never* had more walks than strikeouts.) But Berger won ball games for the Braves and provided Boston fans the first homegrown hero to cheer for since before World War I.

And Wally Berger repaid the Boston fans in most concrete fashion before his career was over, for it was his bat alone that won fourth place (and an extra few thousand dollars) for the Braves in the 1933 season. This was the highest mark the Braves had reached since the end of the war. And it all came about when Wally Berger should have been in bed. When the game that was to decide who was fourth and who was fifth began on

the first of October against the Phillies, the Braves were just half a game behind St. Louis. Wally Berger, carrying a fever, had come to the ballpark but was too sick to suit up, so he crouched in a box seat near the bench and nursed his sniffles.

Then, in the seventh inning—with the bases full, two out, the Braves one run behind, and Rabbit Maranville, close to his forty-second birthday, due to hit—Manager Bill McKechnie called for Berger. Wally had come to the dugout only moments earlier, after having decided to get into his playing garb after all. But he was still hot from fever and bleary of eye. Nonetheless, when McKechnie summoned him, he picked up his two bats and strode to the plate to hit for Maranville. He stood there until the count was two strikes and three balls. Then he drove the next pitch over the left-field fence. The Braves, and the scattered few customers, broke into a frenzy nearly as wild as the one that had greeted the pennant nineteen years before.

Meanwhile, a few blocks away, the Red Sox also had spent most of the Golden Years in the depths of their own league. What heroes the team had owned —Babe Ruth, Waite Hoyt, Joe Dugan, Carl Mays, Bullet Joe Bush, Iron Man Sam Jones, and Herb Pennock—had all been shipped down river to help pay off Harry Frazee's debt to Colonel Ruppert. Now they had to make do with men like Ike Boone, Ira Flagstead, Dudley Lee, and Jack Rothrock. Yet they did own mighty pitchers (a few of whom would thrive in later years in greener pastures), and once in every ten or twelve weeks, there might be events at Fenway Park that for an instant would awaken visions of the days of Carrigan, Jake Stahl, Tris Speaker, and Smoky Joe Wood.

Best of the Red Sox pitchers in this era were a husky, tireless lad named Ruffing from Granville, Illinois, who had lost a few toes in a mine explosion; a tough, strong-armed veteran (he was twenty-eight when he joined the Red Sox) named Ed Morris, out of Alabama; and a local semipro named Danny MacFayden, who never could pitch anywhere as well as he could pitch in Boston. Danny, like Shanty Hogan, had come from Somerville High School, where he had been a schoolboy sensation, and he might have had to put in several seasons in the minors had not the Sox been so pressed for someone who could throw as far as the plate for nine innings in a row.

Red Ruffing pitched more games than anyone on the staff and lost more games than anyone in the league. Yet anyone who watched him on the mound knew that the big, mild-mannered redhead could throw fast, crooked, straight, or slow and put the ball just about where he wanted it. It was often whispered, or even growled out loud, that Big Red was not really putting his heart into his work in Boston. Certainly, he did not take long to become a star, when he found his way at last to the Yankees, where all good little Boston boys were going. In Boston he lost 47 games out of the 77 that he worked in during his last two seasons. But when he got to New York, Red won most of his games every season but one for the next fifteen seasons. In his fourth season with the Yankees (1933), he led the league in strikeouts.

But hardly anyone was winning baseball games for the Red Sox, and Ruffing at least was ready to work dou-ble shift if need be. Danny MacFayden, slight, bespectacled, solemn, and looking exactly as he did when pitching for Somerville High and Hebron Academy, managed a winning season. So did big Ed Morris, who was stabbed to death at a testimonial "fish fry" in Florida before he had a chance to go to the Yankees, as Ruffing and MacFayden did. Morris actually won 19 games for the Red Sox one year. He would have brought a price of $100,000 if he had lived to be traded.

It may have been that the whole losing atmosphere in Boston infected the players, for others besides the pitchers turned into stars when they escaped from the zig zag confines of Fenway Park. Jack Rothrock, second baseman, right fielder, third baseman, catcher, and pitcher, as well as shortstop and first baseman, became a star for a season or two with the St. Louis Cardinals. And Billy Rogell, who earned boos in Boston when he tried out at shortstop, second base, and third, turned into a championship shortstop with the Detroit Tigers. Only Danny MacFayden failed to thrive on foreign soil, and he was a Boston boy to begin with. After leaving the Red Sox, he failed to pitch winning ball again until he came back to work for the Braves.

If gloom was deep in Boston through these merry seasons, however, joy was uninhibited in New York, where the Yankees won pennant after pennant, the Giants were often in the thick of the struggle, and the Dodgers were everlastingly embroiled in their undying feud with John McGraw. And joy was only partially confined in Philadelphia, where the futile Phillies offered a sorry contrast to the sparkling Athletics, who were usually trying to wrestle the pen-

This is what Babe Ruth looked like, pitching and playing outfield for the Boston Red Sox in 1919, when he first broke the home run record. He pitched in 17 games that year and played outfield in 113.

nant away from the Yankees and were drawing crowds that often overflowed into the grandstand aisles.

Brightest and best of the sons of McGraw in this era probably was the hard-hitting first baseman, Bill Terry, a confirmed Confederate from Tennessee, who had never taken any courses in how to snuggle up to sportswriters so that he missed out on some of the more fulsome publicity that was being awarded without let to much lesser men.

Bill Terry actually quit baseball long before he ever played in the major leagues. He had starred as a high school pitcher in Atlanta, had signed with the local club in the Southern League, put in a year in class D, and then was sold to the Shreveport club in the Texas League. Here, he pitched and played the outfield, breaking no fences and setting no records, even though he acquired an earned run average down near one and a half runs per nine-inning game. He got married during his first year in Shreveport, turned into a mediocre pitcher his second year, and promptly decided to quit baseball and find some line of work that held fatter paydays.

A fat payday was all Bill Terry looked for in baseball. After he had been out of the professional game for four years, living in Memphis where he showed himself occasionally on the sandlots on Sundays, and worked the rest of the week in the office of an oil company, he was approached by John McGraw, who had heard of Bill's Sunday exploits and wanted him to try out for the Giants. No longer a wet-eyed youth, but a family man who was more than ordinarily concerned with his security, Bill told McGraw that he would

try out for the Giants only if he was guaranteed a big league salary. McGraw, who admired a man who would stick his chin out in this manner, thought about Bill all the way home. When he got to New York, he wired Bill a firm offer of a substantial year's salary. So Bill went back to baseball.

With the understanding that he belonged to the Giants, Terry started out as a pitcher for Toledo, where he won ball games on the mound and beat out long hits as a pinch hitter. But McGraw was thinking of him as a hitter rather than a pitcher, so Bill, after a couple of months, became a first baseman. Next year, after he had boosted his batting average to .377, he was made manager of the Toledo club. Before the season was over in the big leagues, Bill Terry was back with the Giants, a first baseman for keeps and, for all anyone knows, perhaps already viewed by McGraw as his successor.

The Giants already had a first baseman when Bill Terry came aboard. He was George Lange Kelly, a long-legged fellow, nephew of Big Bill Lange, the man who had been, for a brief period, the fastest base runner and the hardest hitter in the game. George, called "High-Pockets," was a right-hander and so under a certain handicap at first. But George was agile and strong armed. He could play third or second just as deftly as he played first base. And had he not been so good with his glove, he could still have remained on the roster because of the hearty way he could lay into a pitch. George hit enough homers (23) to lead the league one year, and he also laid in a large supply of doubles, more than anybody except Rogers Hornsby. Thus he was not about to move out of his job to make room for any veteran-rookie, even one with as heavy a bat as Bill Terry's.

So Bill started out his major league career as a pinch hitter, and not such a fearsome one. Had McGraw been appraising him on his pinch-hitting alone, he'd have kept Bill forever on the bench or sent him home. Instead, when George Kelly fell victim to an infected tooth, McGraw put Bill on first. Whereupon Bill responded to his boss's confidence by getting nine hits in twenty times at bat, including three home runs. Bill did not replace George Kelly at first. But whenever a soft spot developed in the batting order, McGraw would shift big George to the outfield or to second base and let Bill take over at first.

Perhaps Bill Terry's greatest days were those of the first World Series he ever played in, when he helped the Giants hold off the Washington Senators for a while and actually turned the mighty Walter Johnson into a soft touch. Batting left-handed, Bill was no man to be intimidated by Johnson's frightening sidearm cross fire that had driven many a right-handed batter away from the plate pale and shaking. Bill, who doted on fast balls, busted the 1924 World Series open as he alternated at first base with George Kelly. Bill faced Walter Johnson ten times and counted up a home run, a triple, two singles, and three bases on balls. His overall average for the fourteen times he came to bat was .429, best for both teams. George Kelly batted .290 in nine times at bat. Perhaps if McGraw had let Terry play the base every game, he might have rescued that Series. But nobody really begrudged poor old Walter Johnson his championship, the only one he ever took.

Next season McGraw began alternating Kelly and Terry from game to game, letting Bill play first whenever there was a right-handed pitcher in the enemy line-up. Bill, from playing more or less regularly (he got into 133 games, sometimes as pinch hitter), boosted his batting average by 80 points. Bill did not become the regular first baseman, however, until George Kelly was traded to Cincinnati in 1927. From that point on, Bill Terry's average never sagged below .300, and his salary, as his boss Horace Stoneham once bitterly revealed, "increased 200 percent." Bill was still in the game for money, and he never failed to emphasize this fact when contracts were offered. He had a good business in Memphis, had lived before without baseball, and when he threatened to stay home if his salary was not raised, Stoneham and McGraw knew he meant it.

Bill was a big man, more than six feet tall, and well muscled. He batted left-handed and had the strength in his arms and shoulders to have been a mighty home run hitter. But like Rogers Hornsby, Bill liked to hit the ball where it was pitched, driving outside pitches to left and pulling inside pitches to the short right-field fence. He also drove many an extra-base blow far out toward the Polo Grounds clubhouse, for center fielders to chase after. In 1930 he attained his highest batting average: .401. But had he been hitting in the more florid 1950s, when power rather than average was what fattened paychecks, Bill probably would have concentrated on home runs and might have hit seventy in a season.

It was not that Bill did not like baseball or was not addicted to it. He did not play semipro ball in Memphis because he needed the few extra dollars. Nor did he haunt the training camps, after his retirement, in search of customers for fuel oil. He loved baseball and played it with fervor, both at bat and in the field, where he was one of the cleverest fielders of his day. But he was damned if he was going to play for less than he was worth, when he had leverage enough to get it.

Terry was a gracious enough fellow, but he was given to straight talk, which sometimes sounded too blunt to be polite. And once when he did attempt a wisecrack to the sportswriters, it lived

to haunt him. For it was Bill Terry who first uttered the tired joke: "Is Brooklyn still in the league?" He uttered this famous rhetorical question in January 1934, before a group of New York sportswriters who had gathered to hear Bill, who was then managing the Giants, make his pennant prediction. We should win this year, said Bill, but the Cubs, Pirates, and Cardinals may give us trouble. But what about Brooklyn? So Terry smiled and offered his offhand gibe that soon made a headline in every paper. There was even a banner flown in the Ebbets Field stands

Here is Babe Ruth in 1927, when he set the record of 60 home runs that stood for more than thirty years.

that season, reading "Yep. We're still in the league." And Brooklyn fans, who had a measureless capacity for bearing grudges, named Bill Terry enemy number one.

In previous years Brooklyn had had a first baseman who Flatbush fans declared was the equal of any Bill Terry, or any two Bill Terrys at first base. He was not really, but he often came close. His name was Jacques Fournier, and the greater part of his playing career had been spent in Chicago and St. Louis, with one brief spell in New York as first baseman for the Yankees. Even at that, big Jacques had put some six years of professional ball behind him before he got into the big leagues.

He had started playing sandlot ball as a catcher in Aberdeen, South Dakota. Before he was twenty, he signed with Portland in the Coast League, then without shifting cities moved to the Northwestern League that same year. When he was eighteen years old, he signed with Sacramento in the Pacific Coast League and became a first baseman. He started the 1911 season with Vancouver, in the Northwestern League again, and ended it in Moose Jaw of the Western Canada League, where he took top spot in the league in batting with an average of .377. He also led the league in doubles, triples, runs scored, and total hits. Jacques was then nineteen years old, and the big leagues finally took note of him. But Jacques, still short of his twentieth birthday, had a hard time hanging on in the majors.

Jacques started with the Chicago

In his final year with the Yankees (1932) Babe Ruth gave this picture to his new teammate, young Frank Crosetti.

White Sox and won headlines for his play in spring training. When he played for real, however, and the pitchers started throwing him curves, young Jacques looked like a sandlotter. He finished the season with Montreal of the International League. He came back to Chicago next season and hung on for four.

Then he was out again, with Los Angeles in the Coast League and it was in-again, out-again for Jacques for some time. The New York Yankees picked him off the Los Angeles roster when their first baseman went to war. He was yanked right back when the White Sox proved he belonged to them. Then he was taken up legitimately by the St. Louis Cardinals. And in a game with them, when he had been turned into a pinch hitter, Jacques was once in the game, on the bench, back in the game, then back on the bench, all within a few minutes.

The Cardinals were playing the Chicago Cubs when it began. First Fournier was sent to hit for shortstop John Lavan and received a base on balls. When Jacques reached first base, he was called back so Leslie Mann could run for him. Mann took his position a stride off the bag, and Jacques sat down. The first baseman took a sudden throw from the catcher and laid the ball on Mann, who was called out. But Mann had not even been officially announced! So the Cardinals charged out to argue the point. How could a man be out when he wasn't in? Jacques went along with the mob, and while everyone was centered on the umpire, Jacques idly took up a stance on first base. Then, with a show of irritation, he shouted that *he* was not out of the game, but right on the bag where he belonged.

The umpire, Charles Rigler, happy for a solution to the problem, retracted his first call, named Fournier safe at first and ordered the action to proceed. Mann then came in *officially,* and Fournier left the game again.

Throughout his career, Jacques was quick to devise things to do or say that would outdo an opponent or drive him into a frenzy. When he was in the minors, he once set an opposing base runner onto an umpire by telling the man that the umpire had called him out when he had really called him safe. When the man left the bag to yell at the umpire, Jacques tagged him, and he was *really* out. And in his final seasons with the Dodgers, Jacques was the leading bench jockey, a master at seeking out the word, phrase, or general topic best calculated to redden an enemy pitcher's neck and disturb his equilibrium.

But Jacques could also bang a baseball into fair territory with great regularity and eminent success. Once he had been shifted from St. Louis to the narrower and friendlier confines of Brooklyn's Ebbets Field, he lifted his batting average from .294 to .351. A right-hander who batted left, Fournier was supposed to be weak against left-handers and a sucker for a curve. He worked so hard at his weaknesses, however, that he became one of the few left-handed batters who could murder left-handed pitchers, even when they threw him curves.

On July 13, 1926, Jacques hit three consecutive home runs off left-hander Bill Sherdel of St. Louis. (In 1924, he led the National League in home runs with 27.) In Brooklyn he also became a truly miraculous grabber of high, low, wide, or mile-high throws, so that his fans were constantly celebrating his accomplishments. But when Jacques, for his quick thinking, quick tongue, aggressive play, and years of service was named field captain, the home fans turned on him, naming him the author of all the disasters the Dodgers fell heir to, which were manifold. But they were none of Jacques' doing, and even if they had been, there was no justification in reason or decency to submit the man to the screamed obscenities that began to overwhelm him. Perhaps he became the target because his position at first base set him closest to the loudest mouths in the park. Perhaps the taunts were prompted by Jacques' own penchant for yelling insults (but never obscenities) at the enemy. Whatever the cause, the result was an offer by Jacques to resign from the club and quit baseball for keeps. This threat, printed, of course, in all the newspapers, had the effect of winning back to Jacques (called Jake by everyone) the loud vocal support of the fans who loved him and of shaming some of the loudmouths into silence.

But Brooklyn, throughout this era, was the haven of the wildest breed of fan—as it probably had been since the day some fifty years earlier when a spectator had jumped on outfielder Cal McVey's back to make sure he did not field a fly ball. As a matter of fact, the doings in Brooklyn probably better epitomize this Golden Era, when the whole nation seemed partly mad, than the glorious deeds that were brightening ballparks in other more sanctified cities in the land.

The stupendous Yankee outfield of Ruth, Meusel, and Combs, with Lou Gehrig backing up Ruth's fearsome war-club with his own; the golden-armed pitching staff of Connie Mack, where grim "Lefty" Grove fired lightning, while George ("the Moose") Earnshaw and big Rube Walberg followed with curves that crackled and hissed, and old Howard Ehmke and grizzled John Picus Quinn aimed nothing balls at the plate; the snarling Chicago Cubs, who could outscream and outcurse the Brooklyn bleacher bugs, while Hornsby and Hack Wilson dared aspire even to the throne of Babe Ruth; the rollicking Pittsburgh Pirates, for whom the Waner brothers led all the rest in breaking the seams on baseballs and breaking training rules; the upsurging Washington Senators with Joe Judge entering his second decade as the club's first baseman, and with Walter Johnson's incredible side-arm speed finally beginning to earn its due; the Giants of John McGraw, who looked as if they might battle the Yankees every fall to see who would rule baseball and bragged of pitchers such as Art Nehf and Hugh McQuillan, who were as good as any ever trained up by Connie Mack, plus hitters such as Irish Meusel, Travis Jackson, Ross Youngs, and Frankie Frisch, who could hold their own with the Waner Brothers —all these unquestionably worked wonders that would one day pop the eyes of generations unborn. But the Dodgers, in their helter-skelter way, without hope, cohesion, and strategy, and practically without a manager, earned the unremitting attention of radio and press, the love of rich man, poor man, beggar man, and thief and kept their fans everlastingly between delirium and despair.

To match Lefty Grove, they had their own Dazzy Vance, who cut the sleeve of the underwear on his pitching arm

Walter Johnson, believed by many to have been the fastest pitcher who ever lived, was a gentle, kindhearted man who had great fear of hitting a batter. He threw only fastballs, with a sidearm motion. His tremendous hands almost swallowed the ball. He chopped off the sleeve on his pitching arm to get more freedom.

to befuddle the batter, who pretended he had never been named Clarence, and who organized an inner circle of hell raisers on the club with the one aim of drinking illicit beverages long past the curfew hour without being caught at it. To share headlines with Babe Ruth, they had Babe Herman, whose fame still echoes. And in a class all by himself, they had Rabbit Maranville, aging hero of the 1914 Braves, who still loved to frighten his teammates by climbing out on fifteen-story windowsills to walk about in the rain. And then there were the mad, mad fans.

The stands in Brooklyn were generally a madhouse anyway, with about as much organization as there was on the bench, which was hardly enough, as my uncle would say, for a man to bless himself with. For a quarter, one of the hard-bitten ushers in the place would permit a bleacher fan to help himself to a box seat—and then leave the benighted fellow to fight it out for possession of the seat with the legitimate ticket-holder. Still, there were fans who, through one stratagem or another, always managed to hold the same spot in the park, where they might scream their devotion to their chosen deity and hurl taunts and curses at John McGraw or any who wore his collar. Surely had a Giant outfielder, chasing a foul ball to the rail, fallen into the clutches of that lot, his body would have been picked to the bones before striking the deck. Baseball management in those days had not yet learned to sell soft drinks in paper containers or pour them out and keep the bottles. So umpires in Brooklyn frequently had to dodge flying bottles. Once, when Bob Emslie called Heinie Groh of the Giants •safe at second base on a force play, the fans

hurled so many empty bottles in Bob's direction that the game had to be stopped while the ground crew gathered them up. (In those days, bottles were all returnable.)

But the fans' greatest day arrived in September 1924, the year in which Dazzy Vance won 28 games and struck out 262 batters. (Vance led the league in strikeouts not only in 1924, but for the next four years.) On the seventh of September, a Sunday, the Giants played Brooklyn at Ebbets Field. The Giants were in first place and Brooklyn was in second, only half a game behind. Win this, and they'd move into first. Everybody in Brooklyn, for sure, must have decided to come see their heroes take the lead. Tickets were sold out hours before the game was to begin, and the management warned the police that there would be 50,000 at the gates. (The stands could hold, in a tight squeeze, just a few more than 40,000.) Before the gates had opened, there were certainly 100,000 fans on the streets around the park. Many of those who had been unable to buy tickets had brought winch-bars and tire-irons, instead. Brushing aside the woefully outnumbered police, scorning the screams of the terrified gatekeepers, and no whit daunted by the weight of the corrugated iron curtains that kept the entrances closed, the fans set out to pry their way into the park. The gates were wrenched off their hinges and dropped to the walk. While mobs raced through the openings, screaming like liberated fiends, others, too impatient to struggle through a narrow gate, swarmed up the concrete walls, clutching parapets and outcroppings and often losing their holds and bouncing on the sidewalk.

There were uncounted broken bones that day, besides the several dozen serious injuries that brought ambulances howling from every quarter of the borough, attracting new thousands to the scene who marveled, cheered, or joined the rush.

More than 7,000 nonticket-holders made it into the seats and defied all efforts of the proper ticket-holders to oust them. Thousands who held tickets arrived to find such a crush at the gates that they could not even get close enough to wave their tickets at the gatekeeper. The Commissioner of Baseball, his halo of white hair undoubtedly a little askew, finally got into the park to see the end of the seventh inning. But there were many who gave up the struggle and went home. There was no counting the total number of men and women who crammed their bodies into those confines that day. It was simply "the greatest crowd ever to watch a baseball game in Brooklyn," where nobody watches professional baseball in the flesh any more. The Giants won the game, 8 to 7. And the Brooklyn management blamed the police—not for the loss of the game but for the destruction of the gates and the incursion of freeloaders. The crowd had torn back the huge sliding doors that had been opened just wide enough to admit one ticket-holder at a time. They had broken turnstiles or simply jumped over them. And they had left the Cedar Place gates in ruins. The police said that the management had sold too many tickets. But all surely would have been forgiven had the Dodgers come in first. As it was, they never caught the Giants at all that year and did not come close again until Vance and his merry men had long been gone and McGraw was dead, as well as Wilbert Robinson, Brooklyn's blundering field boss of that Golden Age.

George Sisler, recruited off the University of Michigan campus by his coach, Wesley Branch Rickey, became the greatest first baseman in the American League with the St. Louis Browns. He hit .407 in 1920 and .420 in 1922.

Hard Times
and Soft Baseballs

THE Great Depression of the 1930s, which laid low so many banks and businesses and turned so many stockbrokers into working men, actually left major league baseball relatively undamaged. In smaller cities and in the minors, however, there were lean days, indeed. But in spots where great clots of the nonworking were gathered, baseball actually prospered. In Baltimore, for instance, where a young bachelor named George Weiss had taken over the minor league Orioles on the death of Jack Dunn, the club really burst into bloom. The park was repainted, spavined players were traded off for young and hungry ones, and a number of great hitters were developed —so that fans, who had been boycotting the place for several seasons, crowded into the park once more and filled the owners' pockets with profit.

Elsewhere, too, ballparks, which probably proved a comfortable and cheap haven for men who had drained their spirits by slapping the pavements all day in vain search of paying jobs, found their turnstiles comfortably aclick. Yet there were certainly echoes of discontent in the parks and evidence everywhere of hard times. The wild excesses of the 1920s had simmered down. No longer did petty politicians go streaking through crowded city streets at the tail of a screaming procession of siren-equipped motorcycles. No

153

more did crowds coalesce from no-where just to watch a man shuffling about in a circle, to stare up at the air for minutes on end without knowing what they looked for, or to follow a young man carrying a stuffed elk head through the streets. Executives who had been wont to stop into the office only to nod their throbbing heads at their employees, then hasten to a handy speakeasy to start once more to cele-brate the apparently eternal golden flow they and their cohorts bathed in, now appeared sober and scared as early as the office boy to discover what new di-sasters would be heralded in the morn-ing mail.

When President Hoover had ap-peared at Shibe Park in 1929 for the fifth game of the World Series between the Cubs and the Athletics, the fans had greeted him with a scattering of boos and shouts of "Beer! Beer! We want beer!" But the following year, beer was the least of it. When the President appeared for the opening game of the 1930 Series, again in Philadelphia, the cheers were thin and there was much glum silence. Profits had not been high for the winning Philadelphia club that year—but that was because the race had been decided early in September, so that the final month offered just a view of a pennant-winning ball club marking time. The World Series still filled the park and left thousands gathered at scoreboards everywhere. Salaries for the veteran champions were high by the standards of that day. (Al Simmons, the American League batting champion, was drawing $33,333 a year.) But for the players on the lower rungs, pay was thrifty ("Pepper" Martin, hero of the 1931 Series, drew $4,500 a season), so that there was still plenty of gravy left for the stockholders.

Some of the hoopla drained out of the game when the National League, although refusing to admit it had done so, deadened the baseball and thus cut down on the number of home runs. Somehow a return to the days when runs had to be schemed and scrambled for and when victory went to the players who fought their way from base to base seemed more in keeping with the times. And it surely was poetically appropriate that Pepper Martin, an ex-vagabond who rode to his first baseball jobs cling-ing to the brake rods of a freight car, should appear as the unquestioned hero of the Depression Series, which took place in 1931, when there were many hundreds of thousands of men through-out the land who had nothing to keep them from idling in front of an electric scoreboard to see how the Series came out. It was natural, too, that everywhere except in Philadelphia, the popular choice to win that Series was not the gilt-edged Athletics, but the scruffy St. Louis club in which no Golden Lads disported themselves and which was bent on avenging the previous year's loss to these same Athletics—pennant winners in the American League three times in a row.

Pepper Martin, the Cardinals' ex-hobo outfielder, who was destined to become the greatest name in baseball for a few weeks in that dark time, bore the prophetic middle name of Roosevelt. (His full name was Johnny Leonard Roosevelt Martin, but nobody ever called him that.) And for many a ragged and discouraged citizen in that era, Pepper bore witness that Happy Days were, if not quite here again, at least somewhere within view.

Pepper came into the Series carrying very little fame. He had hit an even .300 in the season, which was his first

In the 1934 World Series tough Mickey Cochrane of Detroit met tough Ducky Medwick of St. Louis at the plate. Ducky was out.

Mel Ott, boy-wonder outfielder of the New York Giants, used to carry his bat low and his front foot high as he stepped into a pitch, as if he couldn't wait for it to get to him.

full season with the club (he played in 39 games in 1928 and 6 in 1930). But he had become a regular mostly because he insisted on it. After a season of pinch-hitting and bench-warming, he had told the boss, Branch Rickey, in the spring that he wanted to play regularly or be traded to some club that would use him. Rickey knew Pepper well, had bought him for $300 from the Greenville, Texas, club, and would never forget his arrival at the training camp in Florida, dressed in worn hunting clothes, unshaved, hair full of cinders, and face soiled with train oil, after a night in a Georgia jail. He knew Martin meant what he said, and he awarded him the job in center field, trading off Taylor Douthit to make room for him.

In the World Series the stars were meant to be Lefty Grove, Al Simmons, Mickey Cochrane, George Earnshaw, and Rube Walberg—all of Philadelphia. And no one, except possibly Martin himself, expected the Cardinals rookie outfielder to outshine the mighty Mule Haas, Athletics center fielder, who had just completed the best year of his career with a batting average of .323. But Martin, in the first game, even though he was unable to beat Philadelphia all alone, did reach Lefty Grove for three hits. And he stole a base on Mickey Cochrane.

In game number two, Martin apparently decided he was going to have to win the thing singlehanded. While Wild Bill Hallahan was holding the Athletics to three singles, Martin plucked a single and a double and stole two bases. He scored both runs as St. Louis won 2 to 0. He was batting sixth in the order at this time and when game number three began, he was still far down the list. With Lefty Grove pitching again,

Martin hit a single and a double, while thirty-eight-year-old Burleigh Grimes staggered the Athletics with a two-hitter.

The fourth game was a work of art by George Earnshaw, a work that was marred only by the rude hand of that scoundrel Martin, who made two hits and stole a base. That was enough to convince Manager Street that maybe Martin was no flash in the pan. He moved the little dirty-faced center fielder (5 feet 8 inches and 170 pounds) up to fourth in the order for the fifth game, and Pepper responded by going promptly into orbit. In four times at bat, Martin made three hits—including a home run—and drove in four of the five runs scored by St. Louis. Philadelphia could make only one run off Wild Bill Hallahan.

Pepper could not accomplish anything at bat after those first five games. But he had made twelve hits already, and that was a new record. He wound up the Series with a batting average of .500 in seven games, five stolen bases, and five runs batted in. And to remind the fans everywhere who had really won the Series, Pepper made the final out in the final game—a breathtaking one-hand shoestring grab of a sinking liner hit by Max Bishop.

The Cardinals at that time had not yet turned into the Gas House Gang, the combination that really seemed to own baseball through most of the 1930s. That fellowship was created and its nickname awarded only after Leo Durocher had been brought in from Cincinnati to fill the hole left at shortstop, when young Charley Gelbert nearly blew his foot off in a hunting accident. (Leo had got his first "break" in professional baseball when a shortstop prospect with Hartford in the Eastern League broke his leg, and Leo was summoned out of a factory job to fill in for him.) Leo's fame as a hard-boiled, loud-mouthed, and quarrelsome manager has dimmed the fact that he was a fielder almost as fantastic as the great Hal Chase. While Leo never owned Hal's batting skill or displayed his consistency in the field, he did keep the despairing Cincinnati fans awake and even excited by his almost daily contribution of at least one impossible fielding play, either at second base or shortstop. In the fastball league (Miller Huggins was said to be the *only* man on the Yankees who could stand Leo), Leo had acquired the nickname of All-American Out, which clung to him throughout his playing career. But in St. Louis, he fit right in with the scrambling, bragging, dirty-faced, dirty-mouthed, quarreling, conniving, bullying, raucous, and joyful crew whom Leo himself first named a bunch of gas house players.

Gabby Hartnett of the Chicago Cubs gives Detroit slugger Hank Greenberg a demonstration of how a tough catcher blocks home plate. Detroit, October 3, 1935.

In the 1930s, Dizzy Dean was a thirty-game winner with the champion St. Louis Cardinals — full-grown, aggressive, and full of confidence.

Paul Dean, according to brother Dizzy, was the fastest pitcher in the league. He had a big, rearing-back motion just like Dizzy's.

Frankie Frisch in his days as the Fordham Flash, college-boy star with the New York Giants, poses beside a chewed-up base. He went on to be the gallant leader of the St. Louis Gas House Gang.

For along with Leo, the Cardinals carried "Dizzy" Dean, whose personality dominated baseball from the moment Babe Ruth began to fade; "Ducky" Medwick, slugging outfielder who was as ready to belt out an enemy with his fists as he was to lay into a fast ball with his bat; Pepper Martin, who always looked as if he had been sliding in cinders with his old pants on; Rip Collins, late of Rochester, a left-hander who batted on both sides of the plate; "Kayo" Bill Delancey, catcher at Columbus for Dizzy's kid brother, Paul Dean, and a man who would likely have made the Hall of Fame if tuberculosis had not ended his career after only two full seasons; "Showboat" Ernie Orsatti, who doubled as a stunt man in Hollywood in the off-season; and other seemingly ill-assorted but well-attuned characters. The gang itself was welded into one, however, by the personality, determination, and aggressiveness of Frankie Frisch, the happy Dutchman, who had been raised by McGraw into a fair facsimile of the tough old master. Frisch's first concern was to win, and this was the one charge he offered his rowdy followers. They could live as they liked, drink, sleep, stay awake, or go blind. But if they failed to win, they could resign themselves to going back to the cotton mill or the filling station. And nobody—*nobody* was going to keep the Cardinals from climbing to the top. So the good-time Charlies and the me-first monsters all joined hands to fight their way united into the big money.

Dizzy Dean foreswore some of his dizziness and made ready to pitch every other day if need be. Ducky Medwick, who held out for more money with the sullenness of a mistreated mule and the social charm of an unmated rhinoceros, still stood up to beanballs and verbal abuse and knocked the foe's best pitching into the seats. Brother Paul kept his mouth shut, agreed with everything Dizzy said, and was ready to pitch any time Old Diz wasn't up to it. Leo Durocher kept his lip unbuttoned but offered none of it either to his teammates or his boss, at least for this season of 1934. And Frankie Frisch cursed, reviled, exhorted, and rejoiced, lending all his breath, all his muscle, and all his ingenuity to the impossible job of beating Bill Terry's Giants to the flag. (Actually, he was chiefly concerned as the season grew late with beating the Cubs out for second place, for the Giants ran off with the race, or seemed to, and had their Series tickets all printed and their line-score sheets distributed for pasting in all the New York tavern windows, before anyone realized that the Dean brothers and their uncouth playmates were winning all the baseball games.)

It was late September before anyone outside of Frankie Frisch and his immediate circle gave the Cardinals a look-in at the pennant. But the Gas House Gang, a few of whom had tasted the sweets of the World Championship just three years earlier, began to dream dreams of luscious five-figure checks and long, long automobiles. Pepper Martin, who had been dumped back on to the bench two seasons before and had then come back to hit over .300 again, was pawing the earth in his best style, hungry for another whack at that World Series gold pile. Even Dazzy Vance, inherited from the Dodgers the season before and now but a red-nosed imitation of his once glorious self, threw in a winning game (his only one) and worked in 19 others. But the major mound work, especially in the final ten days when the gang suddenly realized they could actually catch the Giants, was provided by the Dean brothers.

In the final week either Paul or Dizzy pitched in five games out of six. The pennant was won in the last two days of the season, with Paul Dean (who had just thrown a no-hitter against the Dodgers) winning the next to last game, 6 to 1, and Dizzy taking the final game, 9 to 0. Actually, the pennant was won before that last game was over, when the Dodgers beat the Giants 8 to 5, even though Carl Hubbell himself had been rushed into the breach to stay the disaster. But Dizzy paid the scoreboard no mind and pretended not to hear the happy roar of the fans. He fixed his mind on one batter after another, gritted his teeth, and pitched his shutout.

The World Series was about as wild an affair as the game had seen, for it brought together some of the most aggressive—that is, quarrelsome—players in all of baseball. Almost the only famous roughneck of the day who did not make the scene was shortstop Dick Bartell of the Phillies, known as Rowdy Richard to the sportswriters, who then as now doted on alliteration. Dick, famed as the man who had cut down this man and that with his spikes, had probably thrown more punches than any active player. It is too bad he could not have been on the Detroit roster this season of 1934, for he would have had an opportunity to take on the whole Gas House Gang with his bare hands. But Dick did not reach Detroit until 1940, when he had begun to mellow a little. In his stead the Tigers offered their manager, Mickey Cochrane, a man who would shout defiance into the face of

an oncoming Sherman tank or would have snatched a baseball, if it happened to be in play, out of the mouth of a hungry tiger.

The city of Detroit, with the advent of this Series—their first in twenty-five years—had worked itself into a state of chauvinistic fervor that would have been wholly appropriate had they been girding up their best youth to go stand off the Visigoths. When tough Mickey Cochrane got himself a minor injury of some sort, he became, in a newspaper headline: "Our Stricken Leader." The Cardinals, who had less of the boy scout about them than any outfit in professional sports, did not fail to seize on this oozing bit of overcooked corn and squeeze the last drop of ridicule from it, until Cochrane was ready to bite his bat in two. Dizzy Dean particularly loved to run a needle under the flesh of the enemy. He walked into Detroit batting practice one day and tried for a few licks. Approaching the great Detroit home run hitter, Hank Greenberg, he asked to see what type of war club Hank was about to use against the Cardinals. Hank handed him the bat. Dizzy hefted it judiciously and gave it back. "Throw it away," he said. "I'm pitchin'."

Hank had no need to throw his bat away. He did hit .321 in the Series, and in the fourth game he hit two doubles and two singles to drive in three runs. But he also struck out nine times in the seven games, with Dizzy laughing raucously each time. The Tigers, who came into the Series the betting favorites, really suffered from the pitch of emotion the city had got them into. Game number one, which ancient Alvin Crowder had started in a managerial surprise move like Connie Mack's use of old Howard Ehmke in the 1929 Series, might have been won by Detroit, even though Dizzy Dean pitched against them. But the Tigers made five infield errors, with two by third baseman Marvin Owen. After the Cardinals won the game 8 to 3, Dizzy Dean apologized on the radio for not pitching a shutout.

St. Louis, too, was stirred to near-hysteria by the World Series. Owner Sam Breadon of the Cardinals got it into his head that somebody might try to kidnap Dizzy Dean and hold him for a million-dollar ransom. Either to save that million (which he knew he would *have* to pay) or to save the Series, Breadon hired armed guards to walk up and down outside Dizzy's hotel door all night long.

It is doubtful, however, if any six kidnappers could have made off with Dizzy. He was at the height of his strength, at the peak of his skills, and at the absolute pinnacle of his rather short career. He had won thirty games that year—the first pitcher to do so since Old Pete Alexander was in his prime some twenty years earlier. And he had made good on almost every brag, striking out batters when he offered to do so, and throwing "nothin' but fastballs" when he told the opponents that was his plan. He also got into the second game of the Series as a pinch runner and made a considerable contribution when he stopped a throw with his head to break up a double play. He was knocked cold and carried from the field, but when he came to, he assured everyone that he was not to be done in by a simple "hit in the haid."

Paul Dean (". . . beside Paul, I'm just a sem-*eye*-pro," said Diz) won game number three, despite some free

hitting by the Tigers. He bore down when he needed to, firing his smoking fastball, which may have been the best in the business in that era, past Hank Greenberg two or three times when the bases were full. Big Brother's laughter could be heard all over the park, as Detroit left 13 men on base. But the Tigers won the fourth game and made the score even again. Then they had the audacity to beat Dizzy Dean in his home park and go ahead, three games to two. But Dizzy did manage to strike out Hank Greenberg with runs on base for a brief taste of triumph.

So Brother Paul, with the help of an astounding day at bat by Durocher, the All-American Out (three hits and two runs), pulled the Cardinals back even in the sixth game and left it to Dizzy to tie the final knot in the Tiger's tail. That Dizzy did, in a manner so completely Dean-ish that it seemed as if it had all been made up inside Dizzy's head. Dizzy, first of all, was unhittable. Then he started off the St. Louis scoring himself with a two-base hit in the third inning. After that, just about everyone in the line-up either hit safely or walked. Pepper Martin—practically a forgotten man these days, even though he had played a good steady third base and hit solidly—bunted for a base hit. He and Dizzy both came to bat twice in the inning. (The second time, Dizzy singled and Martin walked.) Altogether, the Cardinals scored seven runs in that inning, six more runs than they needed, for Dizzy allowed none at all. With a seven-run lead, which the Cardinals eventually turned into eleven, Dizzy began to rub the Detroit fans raw with his clowning on the mound. He postured, grimaced, laughed in the batters' faces, and shouted taunts at the

Pepper Martin, in the 1934 World Series, was still playing for St. Louis. Mickey Cochrane, who had had a bellyfull of Martin when Cochrane was catching for the Philadelphia Athletics in the World Series of 1931, was managing Detroit in 1934 when he and Pepper met again. Pepper, playing ''over his head'' as usual, scored once more on Mickey.

enemy, just as if baseball was a kids' game and not a battle to the death.

Frankie Frisch, playing second base behind Dizzy and trying to act the part of the grimly determined manager, threatened to remove Dizzy from the game if he did not settle down and "act serious." "Oh, no," said Diz. "You wouldn't *dare* do that in front of all these folks!" And Frankie didn't dare.

But the Detroit fans exploded at the first real excuse for bloodletting, which came when tough Joe Medwick was threatened with a spiking by third baseman Marvin Owen, and made as if to lay Owen flat. The bleacher bugs howled with rage. When Medwick (called Ducky for a reason that had nothing to do with his lovability) took his place in left field, they hurled every sort of movable garbage they could lay hand to. Fruit, half-eaten sandwiches, cushions, chair slats, bottles, cans, and God knows what showered down on Medwick in such quantity that he ducked right back to the dugout. He came out again, and the barrage was resumed. He ducked back for breath and tried once more. This time, the bombardment grew heavier than ever, for there had been time to rush about and gather up a greater supply of new and more bruising objects. The umpire begged Frankie Frisch to remove Ducky from the game in the name of international peace. Nothing doing, said Frankie. The home club has to keep the peace. So the umpire turned the matter over to Judge Landis, who sat, bareheaded as usual, in a front row box.

Landis listened to both sides of the dispute, with each glowering culprit speaking his peace like a small boy called before the school principal. Then, with more practical sense than evenhanded justice, the good judge tossed Medwick out of the game. The rain of garbage ceased, the game was resumed, and the Cardinals won it 11 to 0 and took home the World Championship. Dizzy, remember, had also won the pennant-clinching game with a shutout—9 to 0.

That whole season had been full of Deans, not only on the pitching box, but on the country's sports pages, in the front office of the Cardinals, and in the bad books of Judge Landis. Once before the judge had had to hold impromptu court to keep peace on the Cardinal club. In the summer the Dean brothers had refused to take part in an exhibition game. (Diz hated those things, for they meant no extra pay and interfered with his leisure. Once he pretended that he had "got on the wrong train" and so missed showing up.) The club had advertised the appearance of the Deans in an exhibition in Detroit. (There was no inkling that before the year was out both boys would be there for real.) But Paul and Dizzy, who had just lost a doubleheader to the Cubs, decided they had either a sore arm or a sore ankle and gave Detroit the go-by. The Cardinals owner, Sam Breadon, promptly called in both pitchers and laid small fines on them. Dizzy, who had never been a man to accept punishment meekly, then refused to take the field again. Paul sat down, too. And when they were suspended, they appealed to Judge Landis for justice, convinced, as no ballplayer with common sense today would be, that the commissioner was beholden neither to ballplayer nor owner.

Instead of summoning the parties before him, the judge hustled down to St. Louis and held court. The hearing lasted four hours, with Dizzy and Paul representing themselves against Frank Frisch, Sam Breadon, and two high-priced lawyers. Just how anyone managed to keep a straight face as Frisch recounted how Dizzy, in response to the fine, had torn up his uniform (and then tore up his traveling uniform so the photographers could get a shot of it) was never explained. But the good judge managed to belittle the whole foolish business, reduced the punishment to a reprimand, ended the suspension, and sent the Deans back to work. Whereupon, Dizzy went out and threw a 5 to 0 shutout against the Giants.

It is ironic that Dizzy Dean should ever have gotten into a hassle with anyone over his unwillingness to play baseball, because his willingness to pitch his right arm out of the socket regardless of rain, shine, aches, pains, spit, snow, or blow was what cut his career in two. There is no question that Dizzy was a baseball phenomenon as great as Babe Ruth, Cy Young, Ty Cobb, or Honus Wagner. He could hit, run bases, catch fly balls, and pitch better than any man who walked the earth in his best days. Had he been able to retain his "fogger" and his "crooky" as long as lesser men had, his records would have mounted so high that young ballplayers would despair of approaching them.

But Dizzy lasted just eight full seasons in the majors. (He had a cup of coffee—or a glass of bootleg beer—with the Cardinals in 1930, and he worked 54 innings for the Cubs in 1940, so those years do not count. Nor do his exhibition appearances with the St. Louis Browns when his arm was dead and buried.) He led the National League in strikeouts for four seasons in a row, won 30 games in 1934, 28 in 1935, and 24 in 1936; had he not gone back to pitching while still favoring an injured toe, he might well have posted another ten years of 20 wins or better. But it was hard to keep Dizzy out of action when there were prizes to be won. And it is always difficult to keep a club owner from letting a ballplayer shorten his career, when there are fatter profits for the taking. But Cy Young pitched for 22 seasons, Walter Johnson for 21, Christy Mathewson for 15 full seasons and 2 partial ones, Lefty Grove for 17, Rube Waddell for 10 and a few small pieces, and Satchel Paige for nearly a lifetime. Had Dizzy been able to hang on as long as any of these, who could have matched him? Certainly no one matched him for getting pure fun out of winning a baseball game. When, in the first game of the 1934 World Series, he cracked a long two-base hit off Firpo Marberry, he stood with both feet on second base, laughing merrily and called out to Marberry: "What was that you throwed me?"

The Waking
of Nicodemus

IN the 1940s baseball, except for the heart-rending run the Dodgers made for the World Championship just before the war began, was mostly wartime baseball. There were fat catchers, one-armed outfielders, sore-armed and one-legged pitchers, diabetic infielders, and many others of the mildly handicapped, valiantly struggling to keep some sort of game alive. But all the big names had gone to war, some of them, it must be granted, to safe rear-echelon posts where no discouraging words were offered and no shots fired in either hot blood or cold. Politicians, as always, seemed bent on saving not simply their own precious hides and sensibilities from war's alarms but also those

of their favorite professional athletes. Army and Navy commanders even vied for baseball and football talent to keep on their bases and "build morale" through victories on the diamond or the gridiron. This was one time when it was the battlefields that fed the fields of friendly sport, rather than the other way around. Indeed, more than one professional player of games who refused to perform for his unit's ball club found himself hustled off into hot action as punishment.

At home during the war there was the usual despair of baseball's future, as there had been in the previous war. (Ty Cobb, leaving for France a few weeks before World War I ended, predicted that he would be far past playing age when he returned, if indeed there was any game to play. He came back to play another ten seasons.) Club owners saw their franchises shrink in value and lay awake nights counting the pitching arms that were hourly exposed to the rockets' red glare. The New York Yankee franchise, along with its stadiums in Newark and Kansas City, were sold to a trio of adventurers for about ten cents on the dollar after one set of investors backed away for fear there would be nothing left before the war was done.

But the war ended and brought with it a surge of prosperity that some had long given up hope for. The new 52-20 (20 dollars a week for 52 weeks) scheme for distributing cash to returning veterans in lieu of the high wages and fat profits they might have missed, provided a reservoir of fans who could afford to come to ball games day after day and consume peanuts, beer, and hot dogs by the trailer-truckload.

The Brooklyn Dodgers, who had set out to dominate the age before the war interrupted them, once again began to fight their way toward a rematch with the Yankees, who had done them down so ignominiously in 1941. They were a patchwork lot, with new owners and a manager who had been made to order for them—Leo Durocher, long the chief gasser of the Gas House Gang. And they had a general manager who was about to turn the baseball world upside down—Branch Rickey, himself a St. Louis graduate, who had raised the previous general manager, Larry MacPhail, by hand. Rickey was brought in largely because a civilizing influence was needed, not only on Durocher but on the whole roster, which had developed into a gang of roisterers who would have made Dazzy Vance's 0-for-4 club look like a conclave of Methodist preachers. The wartime Dodgers were a hot-tempered, hard-throwing, hard-drinking, heavy-betting, and staying-up-late crowd who could not even pronounce the word discipline, much less understand it. It was going to be Rickey's job to enforce the curfews, cut off the phone calls to the bookies, and keep them out of the clubhouse, and put an end to the floating poker game. He also had to stifle a rebellion of sorts, when many of the tougher characters on the club offered to walk out in protest of an "insult" by manager Durocher to old Bobo Newsom, who was stopping on the Brooklyn roster on one of his tours around the leagues. (Leo had suspended Bobo for throwing a spitter and "lying about it.")

Rickey managed to calm the wild waters after a while, keep Leo in his job, shut out the bookies, bring an end to the poker game, ship away some of the horseplayers, and trade off Bobo Newsom. Many of the prewar heroes such as Whitlow Wyatt, Dolf Camilli, Bill Herman, Cookie Lavagetto, and Arky Vaughan had faded, and some had simply gone away. A coach named Charley Dressen, who had been rusticated for being a horseplayer, was reinstated when he proved that he was cured of his affliction. (He went back to his next-favorite hobby—stealing signs from enemy catchers.) And when the war ended, with the Japanese surrender, Branch Rickey, with two partners named O'Malley and Smith, had just secured complete control of the Dodgers, so Rickey could handle the club as he pleased.

One of the things it pleased him to do first was hire a black man to play baseball for him. This move, viewed as "the end of baseball as we know it" by the game's wiseacres and most of the other club owners, was "voted down" in a secret ballot, with every single club owner except Rickey opposing it. But the new baseball commissioner, Albert B. (Happy) Chandler, former United States Senator from Kentucky, who had been foolish enough to believe that the owners wanted another top man as independent as old Judge Landis, gave his approval, and Rickey added the black man to the roster of his minor league club in Montreal.

The solemn warnings of disaster—to the Negro Leagues as well as to the majors—almost drowned out the news of other great doings on the diamond. The return of Babe Herman to Brooklyn (as a pinch hitter), for instance, and the jumping of Mickey Owen, Brooklyn's great catcher, along with Danny Gardella, Sal Maglie, and a few others to the Mexican League, where fans delighted to throw firecrackers at the players and where the Pasquel brothers delighted to pay salaries in high five figures to everyone who would come down from the majors to greet them.

"Baseball as we knew it" obviously had looked different to different people. To some it had been hard work, sweat, daily abuse, and low pay. To some it had been a cozy, white man's world where no lesser breeds intruded to spoil a fellow's lunch by wearing the wrong color skin around.

The idea that black men could play baseball of big league caliber burst on many a sportswriter like the discovery of the Comstock Lode. Yet there had been blacks playing every day of the

Branch Rickey, who put an end to organized baseball's color bar, never attended baseball games on Sunday. A promise to his mother, he said. When he did attend he often had business matters to take charge of, far removed from the game itself.

week, for almost a century, who could outpitch, outhit, and outfield most of the white (or gray) players who had earned star ranking. Indeed, when statisticians averred that "no man ever hit a fair ball out of Yankee Stadium," they should have been amending that to read "no white man," for a black catcher on the Pittsburgh Grays, by the name of Josh Gibson, is reliably reported to have driven a home run clear over the triple deck stands. And long before Josh was born, there had

A convocation of Old Timers at Shea Stadium, New York, includes Lefty Gomez, at the left, star Yankee pitcher of the 1930s; Stan Musial, great Cardinal hitter of the 1940s and 1950s; Mrs. Joan Payson, owner of the New York Mets; Walter ''Buck'' Leonard, greatest black first baseman of all time; Casey Stengel, champion manager and monologist; and Lawrence ''Yogi'' Berra, the only man besides Stengel to manage both the Yankees and the Mets.

been black stars who needed no head-start at all to come in ahead of their more fashionably hued counterparts.

In the 1880s a number of black men played ball with ''white'' clubs, and no harm came to the body politic. The first were two brothers who had played ball together at Oberlin College in Ohio. They were Moses Fleetwood (Fleet) Walker and William Welday Walker, both of whom played with the Toledo club in the Northwestern League and later in the American Association, which rated as a major league in that day. Fleet Walker afterward played for Newark, which carried on its roster one of the greatest black pitchers of all time: George Stovey, who still holds the Newark club record of 35 victories in a single season.

Altogether in the 1880s there were some twenty black baseball players active in the organized leagues. There was a black second baseman named Bud Fowler, who played for Keokuk and Binghamton. In Buffalo another black man, Frank Grant, also played second base. And Charles Kelly, a black first baseman, played for the professional club in Danville, Illinois. But there were already cradle Confederates and others who had adopted their racist creed busily endeavoring to chase the black man out of the baseball parks (unless he paid his way in). One of the most notorious of the white supremacy champions was cross-grained Cap Anson, who even scabbed on the 1890 players' strike because his first loyalty was to himself. Cap, when his White Stockings played against Toledo, spotted Fleet Walker on the diamond and bellowed, "Get that nigger off the field!"

Anson threatened to remove his own hired hands from the field if Walker did not go; the Toledo management, however, insisted that Walker would play even if it had to recruit a team from among the spectators to fill in for the White Stockings. Cap backed down that time, but five years later when he found George Stovey facing his club at Newark, he made the same threat. This time Stovey himself walked off, refusing to play against Anson. Sour-faced Cap was not satisfied with this. When he learned soon afterward that John Montgomery Ward, boss of the New York Giants, had planned a trade that would bring Stovey to the big league, Cap roared in anger. There was a law against that!

There had, indeed, been a number of private agreements in professional baseball to maintain the game's "racial purity." Blacks had been specifically excluded from the National Association in 1867. In 1888 the Tri-State League, among others, had formalized the barring of black ballplayers. But Welday Walker, then playing for Toledo in that league, protested that if they were going to bar the players, they should bar black spectators, too.

"The law," he wrote, "is a disgrace to the present age. . . ." The law in that instance was repealed, but Cap bullied Ward into canceling the deal for Stovey and managed the establishment of an unwritten law that kept black men out of the majors for sixty years.

When Rickey finally defied this ban, there were some who seemed to think black ballplayers just suddenly began to proliferate. But black fans had long watched some of the greatest ballplayers in the land grow up and grow old in the "Negro Leagues," which were often rather haphazard structures yet still provided paydays for hundreds of the nation's best athletes. The very first of the all-black clubs had been hippodroming outfits in which players found more fun than profit. The greatest, perhaps, was that organized around the dining-room staff of the Argyle Hotel in Babylon, Long Island, New York, and led by headwaiter Frank Thompson. They called themselves the Cuban Giants, although most of them had been no closer to Cuba than Charleston, South Carolina.

Like most local clubs of this type, the Cuban Giants began to seek wider and wider pastures in which to operate and needed to recruit ringers from all over the East to enable them to meet stronger opposition. Before long they featured two of the finest ballplayers then active—Sol White, a mighty long-ball hitter, and Shep Trusty, top black pitcher of the 1880s. The Cubans then turned straight professional and paid wages equal to what a man might earn as a waiter in a first-class dining room. They established themselves as a strong attraction in their first pro year (1881) by defeating Bridgeport, champions of the Eastern League. In 1887 the Cuban Giants beat Cincinnati and Indianapolis of the International League and threw a scare into the mighty Detroit club of the National League, which carried on its roster the National League's greatest slugger, Dan Brouthers, as well as Charlie Bennett, named the best catcher in the league, and the king of second basemen, Sure-Shot Fred Dunlap. The final score was 6 to 4 in favor of Detroit.

Stirred by the Giants' success,

Jackie Robinson, turning gray above the ears, returns to Yankee Stadium in his Brooklyn uniform to celebrate Old Timers' day by demonstrating his bunting form.

"Cuban" and "Giant" teams of all sorts began to sprout, a number of them organized and managed by white promoters seeking to cash in on the Giants' success. There were the Cuban X Giants, the Genuine Cuban Giants, the Mohawk Giants, the Elite Giants, the Leland Giants, the Brooklyn Royal Giants (who originated in the Royal Café in Brooklyn), and the Lincoln Giants of Lincoln, Nebraska. By the turn of the century there were several handsomely accoutered teams of blacks on which players could earn a great deal more than dining-room wages and could travel in comfort. The Page Fence Giants, sponsored by the Page Fence Company of Adrian, Michigan, owned their own railroad car and staged a parade on gleaming new bicycles before every game.

But to wring more than a meager living out of the game, the great black players had to play all year round, in Cuba, Mexico, and Central and South America, areas where black skin did not mark a man a subcitizen. Here, and in the big cities where the black population would turn out in numbers large enough to pack a ballpark, the ablest black players established their fame. And every club listed players who could hold their own in either major league, while some were the equal of the very best ever developed by the white world. Before World War I the white press generally acknowledged that there was no better pitcher in the world than Walter Johnson—a gentle, abstemious man who fired a sidearm pitch so fearsome that even he was afraid of what might happen to a man hit by it. Johnson came from Coffeyville, Kansas, and probably grew up, without realizing it, in the same environs as another pitcher who was every inch his equal. For Coffeyville was the hometown of an inordinately skinny and long-limbed young fellow named Wickware, a black man whose skin was more red than black and who, because his joints were so sharp and his bones so meatless, was nicknamed "The Red Ant." In 1914 Wickware, pitching for the Mohawk Giants after the major league season was over (and after Walter Johnson had led the American League pitchers in wins: 28, and in strikeouts: 225), faced a team of barnstorming major leaguers called "Walter Johnson's All-Stars" in Albany, New York, and beat them, striking out seventeen major leaguers as he did so.

The best black team in the country at that time, however, was the Lincoln Giants (no longer home-based in Nebraska). They played most often at Olympic Field at 136th Street and Fifth Avenue in New York City. The Lincoln Giants owned two of the finest black pitchers alive—Ad Langford, a spitball specialist, and "Cyclone" Joe Williams, who was the best of them all, with great speed, sharp curves, and fine control, as well as an arm that never seemed to grow tired.

Joe Williams faced most of the best white players of his age and beat many of the leading pitchers in both leagues. In 1915 he faced the World Champion Phillies with Grover Cleveland Alexander on the mound and beat them. Then he faced them again, or a team made up mostly of Phillies, with crafty George Chalmers pitching, and came in first again. Joe had previously licked the New York Giants, when *they* were champions, and had beat them twice, once with Hooks Wiltse pitching, and once with Rube Marquard.

There was a black shortstop at this time, too, who was every bit the equal of Honus Wagner, still named by some the best ballplayer who ever lived. But John Henry Loyd (he spelled it with one "l") could do all that Honus could do and apparently do it just as well. He was a timely and strong hitter. He had enormous hands, as Honus had, and could smother a ground ball in them and get off a throw with all the deftness and smoke of the great man himself. Loyd was a sight taller than Wagner (6 feet 2 inches) and a shade leaner (185 pounds). He was not so bowlegged as the famous Dutchman, but he ran the bases with equal speed and with a similar loping stride. His most noted physical feature was his oddly out-thrust lower jaw, which earned him, from the fans in Cuba, where he was long a favorite, the name of *La Cucharra*—the ladle. (Corrupted into English, it became Cachatter and was thought to refer to the way Loyd offered constant encouragement to pitcher and teammates.)

An even better black slugger, however, and a forerunner of the matchless Josh Gibson, was Home Run Johnson, who, in the century's teens, when Babe Ruth was just beginning, played second and third base for the Lincoln Giants. There were few fences built that Johnson could not knock a ball over.

Then, to match Roger Bresnahan, "greatest catcher in the game," the black teams could offer Buddy Petway, who was throwing from a crouch long before any white catcher learned to. Indeed, Buddy is reputed to have taught his flat-footed snap throw to Johnny Kline, who called himself Johnny Kling and became a star with the Chicago Cubs. And there were other great hitters, like Pete Hill and Frank Duncan, who could have made room for themselves on any white club in the land, and outfielders with throwing arms as mighty as Bob Meusel's—Jap Payne, for example, who threw a ball with top spin on it, so it would bound long and low, straight into the catcher's glove from deepest outfield.

Between the wars and even through the Depression, organized black teams, playing full schedules in their own leagues, grew apace. But the wages and working, or playing, conditions in the black leagues soon fell to ghetto standards. Transportation was by broken-winded buses, often too small for the whole club to ride comfortably, invariably hot, slow, and subject to breakdown. It was not unusual for a black ball club to pull into a park early in the dark of the morning for a game that same afternoon, and for the players to sleep on their suitcases in the locker room. If they stayed at hotels they were "nigger" hotels, where ants might crawl up a man's leg as he brushed his teeth, where beds were broken, and ventilation dead. If a man earned $100 a month, he was living well. He might even be able to afford to rent a room by himself somewhere and eat something besides hard-fried fowl, stringy pork chops, fat meat, and cast-off greens.

Yet black men still played ball in preference to taking the miserable jobs otherwise offered them. And there were stars in the black leagues who would have set new marks in the majors and earned five-figure salaries. Cool Papa Bell of the St. Louis Stars, who played their games behind the car barn, was an outfielder as fast, graceful, and strong as Tris Speaker. Josh Gibson of

Old Satchel Paige gets a good shove off the rubber to put the buzz into his "bee ball." This is 1951, when Satch had turned forty-five and was still trying to win ball games for the St. Louis Browns.

Larry Doby, first black player in the American League, found himself on the losing side in the 1954 World Series when his Cleveland club lost the championship to Willie Mays and the New York Giants. Here Larry dumps a humpbacked single into right field in the fifth inning of the first game.

the Pittsburgh Crawfords could drive a ball farther than Babe Ruth could.

And then there was Satchel Paige. Satchel Paige did for the black leagues what Babe Ruth had done for white baseball. He did not actually free the slaves, but he sure bettered their lot in life.

Fans who learned about Satchel's existence only after he had been permitted to play ball with the white boys thought of him merely as a sort of geriatric marvel—an old fellow (some said in his fifties) whose fame rested on his ability to throw a pitch as far as the plate despite the infirmities of age. But Satchel Paige was actually the greatest pitcher of baseballs who ever lived. His fastball (and Dizzy Dean himself said this) made Dean's fogger look like a change of pace. It might rip the glove off the catcher and stun him when it struck his chest. And Satchel (he won his nickname carrying satchels as a boy) had almost flawless control. He practiced throwing baseballs

Black was truly beautiful in the first game of the 1952 World Series when Joe Black of Brooklyn held the New York Yankees to six hits, struck out six, and walked only two in beating them 4 to 2.

through a hole—no more than eight inches in diameter—in a board fence, and he could steam them through from pitching distance again and again. He won bets from skeptical observers by knocking off rows of pop bottles set on the baseline, not missing one. When he wanted to hit a batter—and Satch was properly ''mean'' when he was pitching to win—he had to use his change-up or he'd have broken the batter's bones. Wherever he appeared, when he was in his teens and twenties, his frightful speed made spectators gasp, enemies cringe and managers rejoice. It was not unusual for the manager of his club to advertise that Satch would strike out the first dozen men who faced him. It *was* unusual when Satch failed to do just that.

Satchel played semipro ball to begin with, then joined the Chattanooga Black Lookouts, where he lifted his earnings to more than $200 a month. But it was not until he joined the Pittsburgh Crawfords (named for

the Crawford Grill, owned by Gus Greenlee, who ran the club) that Satch really began to alter the whole fiscal structure of the black leagues. Teamed with Josh Gibson (who sometimes guaranteed to hit *at least* two home runs a game), Satch turned the Crawfords into the biggest gate attraction in baseball. He would pitch in some forty games for the Crawfords, and every time he appeared, even in Depression days, the parks would be filled to bursting.

And it was Satch the fans wanted. If he was not slated to pitch, the fans, regardless of Josh Gibson's hitting ability, just would not turn out. Without urging, Gus Greenlee jumped Satch's salary up into the thick-steak neighborhood. And Satch began to drive long, low cars, dress like a barberpole, and scatter his funds about as if they were candied popcorn. His lifestyle only added to his fame. But it was his consistent ability to strike out men, almost at will, that pulled people in to

After this impossible catch by Willie Mays in the 1954 World Series, the Cleveland Indians never had a chance. First Willie, almost at the bleacher wall, runs under a potential home run by Vic Wertz. He gloves it neatly. He turns and fires it into the diamond, losing his cap in the effort.

watch him. There had never been anything like Satch in baseball. Suppose Walter Johnson's speed had, of a sudden, been miraculously doubled, and he could have struck out *everyone* for the first four innings! What sort of crowds would he not have drawn to Washington's ballpark, and how fat would Clark Griffith have grown with the profits Johnson's speed created!

Well, that is about what Paige was doing. His mounting salary and the incredible crowds he drew meant higher wages for even the league's lowliest performers. And the good players sometimes lived as well as white stars of equal magnitude. (Except, of course, that there were no really decent hotels for a black man to live in, unless he traveled to the Caribbean, as Satch and his cohorts often did.)

Satch was not the kindly, old, slow-talking, shuffling "darky" that some white ignoramuses preferred to picture. He was a braggart, a hot-tempered man, and one who was not above jumping a contract in a minute to grab a few extra dollars. And he dissipated as generously as any Babe Ruth ever did—although, like Babe himself, he pulled himself up short when his dissipations began to eat into his playing skills. He was also a born show-off, made to order for a hippodroming ball club. In a fit of temper he once called in his outfield and struck out the side. And once, if you believe what he tells, Satch faced a "strike" of his own out-fielders when he was with a white club in Canada, and he struck out the side then with nobody on the grass behind him.

There were of course many who thought that Satch was strictly a show-boat, that his strikeouts were probably fixed, and that he would not have lasted a week in the majors. But other great white ballplayers besides Dizzy Dean (who barnstormed with Satch for several years) stood up to Satch and were soon convinced. Satch never did pitch to Babe Ruth, although he traveled with Babe Ruth's All-Stars one season, leading a black club to play against the big leaguers. Still, Satch met most of the minor Ruths—including Hack Wilson—and mowed them down with his fastball. Nor was Dizzy Dean the only white ballplayer who, after facing Satch, agreed that Paige was

the greatest he had ever seen. Connie Mack allowed he'd have paid $100,000 for him . . . if he were white!

So when Jack Roosevelt Robinson was enrolled with the Dodgers' farm club in Montreal in 1945, it was not really the first appearance of a star black ballplayer in the land. But some individuals did run to and fro proclaiming the Dawn of the Jubilee and others made ready to hustle down to the gum tree to wake Nicodemus, despite the fact that Nicodemus had long been alive and well and playing baseball in Pittsburgh—and in Baltimore, New York, Chattanooga, Atlanta, and New Orleans on fields where some baselines had rocks in them sharp enough to score a man's hide and outfields with as many ups and downs as an abandoned corn-field.

Robinson was not a "darky" type either, although he was by no means an original like Satchel Paige. He had no Deep Southern accent, displayed a temper as explosive and vocabulary as fiery as old Satch's, behaved with fierce dignity and a sense of his own worth, and once he had served his apprenticeship by accepting all the foul verbal abuse the white world had been saving up for him, he took no back seats to anyone and gave back as good as he was offered, on the bench or on the field.

There was of course an immediate movement among white players to walk off the field, in the Cap Anson tradition, if Robinson appeared. And there were sportswriters aplenty who privately encouraged the ballplayers to resist this threat to "baseball as we knew it." Oddly enough, the resistance to Robinson among the Dodgers themselves was led, not by the players from the Deep South, but by the players of Italian extraction whose own forebears had been ghetto-bound. And the sportswriters who offered the loudest and most mealymouthed protests were men who drew salaries from big Northern newspapers.

Thanks to some very forthright talk by Ford Frick, then president of the National League, the planned strike never came off, and the tide was never turned back. Other promoters were quick to reach for the competitive and gate advantage black players might provide them. And Satchel Paige, at the age of forty-two, finally put on a big league uniform and helped Cleveland win a pennant. Without his fiery fastball, and with free use of the curve that he had long scorned to practice, old Satch still managed to get major leaguers out. "I outcute them," he explained. For he had sixteen different deliveries, making it almost impossible for a batter to time the ball. And he still had the control that few had been able to match.

Black players were recruited with extra heartiness by some club owners through this era, partly because they could be made happy with salaries that white players were able to scorn. But star performers in every position blossomed at once—mighty sluggers like Larry Doby and Luke Easter; steady hitters like Roy Campanella, Monte Irvin, Orestes Minoso, and Hank Thompson; strong-armed pitchers like Don Newcombe and Joe Black; and above all, once-in-a-lifetime stars like Willie Mays.

Some of these men would finally make it to the white man's Hall of Fame. But the great black players who had seen their day, a few of whom had just missed making it into the white man's leagues, were largely forgotten, except in the hearts of the older black fans. Men still wrote columns about Christy Mathewson, but few ever recalled the mighty Rube Foster, who earned his nickname by defeating the original Rube Waddell in a black vs. white ball game, had actually been hired as a pitching coach by John McGraw, and who as pitching coach had taught a few tricks to Mathewson.

Foster was one of baseball's greatest showmen, with an imagination twice as lively as Bill Veeck's and with baseball sense that far exceeded Bill's. When Rube's strong arm grew old, he took to managing and promoting, and he delighted to amaze spectators by putting four or five pitchers in the line-up at once, so he could call in an outfielder to put one tough batter out and then return everyone to his original spot. He was also the only manager who ever used actual smoke signals instead of "signs" from the bench. He called for a bunt, steal, or take, through puffs of smoke rising from his old corncob pipe. He also would sometimes stage a game in which every batter on his club would do nothing but bunt or every man reaching third base would try to steal home until one of them made it.

Foster also organized the Negro National League, and he was the first man to give real stability to black baseball with regular schedules and a "Negro World Series." After Rube's death in 1930, the league came tumbling down. It had taken a man such as Rube—outsized, hard-boiled as McGraw himself, personable, shrewd,

Josh Gibson, top batter in the Negro National League, is the only man, according to some who saw him do it, to hit a fair ball clear out of the park at Yankee Stadium.

aggressive, bristling with self-confidence, and determined to come out on top to hold the operation together. When he was gone, there was no one like him.

One price the black players had to pay for the collapse of a tightly organized league was the lack of official records. While everyone knew, for instance, that Josh Gibson had hit many more home runs in a season than Babe Ruth did, there was no positive documentation. Men were around who had watched him pole four home runs out of Griffith Stadium in one game. But there was no Elias Bureau to guarantee it really happened. And while spectators who saw them all might agree that Satchel Paige, Bullet Joe Rogan, or Chet Brewer of the Kansas City Monarchs could throw as fast a ball as Bob Feller or Walter Johnson, the strikeouts were not set down anywhere, except perhaps by the Recording Angel. Probably a man could find a newspaper somewhere memorializing the twenty-three strikeouts in a single game posted by John Donaldson of the Chicago Giants. But if they were not in the white man's official book, they did not count.

Buck Leonard, first baseman of the Homestead Grays, was perhaps as good a fielder at his position as Hal Chase, and he was surely a stronger batsman, besides being a more wholesome character. Oscar Charleston of the Pittsburgh Crawfords would almost certainly have matched Tris Speaker in center field. Willie Wells of the Newark Eagles may have been a swifter and more surehanded shortstop than Glasscock, Wagner, or Dave Bancroft. But no one ever offered these men a chance to prove their skills where the "right" people could make note of them and mark them down in the sacred volumes.

Organized baseball ultimately was shamed into admitting a few of these great black ballplayers to their Hall of Fame in Cooperstown. But that was only after Ted Williams, in accepting his own election to the Hall, scandalized the gathered stuffed shirts by offering, instead of the standard serving of bashful platitudes, a straightforward wish that the black players be admitted. In keeping with its ancient tradition of lead-footed hypocrisy, baseball first made as if to isolate the black heroes in the back of the bus somewhere—in a "special" section reserved for those who somehow fell short of complete worthiness. Fortunately, the baseball brass suffered a sudden access of shame or good sense or felt the pressure of public dismay and agreed to accept the black heroes on equal footing with the white—not many of whom, it must be said, were any more than just equal to the best of the blacks.

Whether there will now be an Old-Timers Committee to delve into crumbling files and fading memories for confirmation of the qualifications of other half-forgotten black baseball players has not yet been determined. But it may be that ultimately the whole nation, or at least that part of it that is inclined to make much of the games men play, will be able to contemplate the likenesses of the young black heroes who once stirred the hearts of their admirers with their throwing, catching, and knocking of baseballs into the vanished skies.

The Last of the Trolley Dodgers

WHILE Ted Williams was certainly the single figure that dominated baseball, or won its most headlines, in the war years and the decade afterward with Joe DiMaggio running right at his shoulder, it still seems, in looking back to those days, that the era really belonged to the Dodgers. That may well be because the great doings at Ebbets Field during this period were the very last doings of any kind before Brooklyn lost its darling baseball club forever.

Surely, however, Ted Williams' batting averages, so often flirting with .400 and once exceeding it, and Joe DiMaggio's feat of hitting safely in 56 consecutive games are the individual feats that will most mark this period in the game. And the Red Sox-Yankee rivalry that burgeoned about these efforts involved thousands of fans and inspired unmeasured reams of prose.

It was significant, in a small way, that both Ted and Joe began to play baseball in California, where, when they began, there were no big league clubs, although there would soon be a proliferation. California, where boys could play baseball nearly the whole year round if they liked, and where games were seldom called off because of cold weather, had from the earliest days cradled many a ballplayer. Several of them, beginning with Frencesco Pezzola, who played in New York as Ping Bodie, were of Italian orgin, descended from lettuce-field workers, some of whom had come to California a whole century before. And most of them could play half a dozen different positions and had been toughened in the "outlaw" leagues in the Wild West, where men like Hal Chase and the Black Sox had found occasional refuge. So when they reached the big leagues, they were seasoned in every way.

But the Brooklyn Dodgers were still the pride of the motley citizenry that dwelt along the noisome Gowanus Canal, out in the dismal reaches of Canarsie, in prideful Flatbush, and around the green expanses of Prospect Park. Here ballplayers had grown aplenty, too, right from the very beginning when Dickey Pearce and Jim Creighton were abroad, past the days when the great Waite Hoyt (known as Waite Hert to the faithful) had starred for Erasmus Hall High School. But no matter what their birthplace or their derivation or (in this enlightened day) the color of their skin, they were all owned more devoutly by the Brooklyn fans than any fans in any other part of the world ever were devoted to hired athletes.

Thousands of Brooklynites who should have known better—firemen, waitresses, Chinese laundrymen, lawyers, politicians, burglars, prostitutes, priests, cops, schoolchildren, housewives, clerks, actors, doctors, salesmen, swindlers, and idle rich—either crowded into the ballpark to burst the veins on their temples screaming for victory or crouched by the radio until near midnight to learn the Dodgers' fate. And when the club returned from any famous triumph, there were grown men and women by the score at the airport as if to greet the wounded survivors of a great battle.

A volunteer band, or random collection of amateur musicians, serenaded the club from the stands. A lady with a cowbell celebrated every distinguished feat. Men and women who barely knew the English language nonetheless burst into tears when the Dodgers lost.

But the Dodgers won the pennant in 1947, with only Hugh Casey; Pee Wee Reese; Pete Reiser, the ambidextrous outfielder; and Dixie Walker left of the crew that had almost beat the Yankees in the last prewar series. Jackie Robinson, too scatterarmed to hang on at shortstop, played first base that season and stole 29 bases. Tough Eddie Stanky, a real Gas House-type who knew only how to win, had taken over at second. Carl Furillo, one of the original anti-Robinson cabal, had replaced Joe Medwick in the outfield, while Spider Jorgensen had taken Cookie Lavagetto's job at third, and Bruce Edwards crouched behind the plate in the stead of marvelous Mickey Owen, now a refugee in Mexico. Except for Hugh Casey, who saved 18 victories that season while winning 10 on his own, the pitching staff was all new. And new, too, was the manager—or at least he was new in this job. For this was the year when Leo Durocher had been set out of baseball for a year for "conduct detrimental to baseball." There were those in the rival clubs and in the local press boxes who had long believed that Leo had been guilty of such conduct nearly every day of his life. But what the specifics of this charge were, no one ever exactly determined, for Commissioner Chandler, in issuing the edict, had ordered both Durocher and Larry MacPhail, who was

Before she earned fame as the lady who rang the cowbell to urge on the Brooklyn Dodgers, Hilda Chester could be found frantically dispensing hot dogs behind the stands at Ebbets Field.

When the Dodgers won the pennant in 1941 it was Brooklyn's first championship in twenty years. In 1920, the previous championship year, there was no such scene as this, for beer was available only behind locked doors.

It was easy to tell the Dodgers fan from the Yankees fan when the Yankees won the first game in the 1941 World Series.

then boss of the Yankees and the author of one of the complaints against Durocher, to keep details of the hearing, or hearings, to themselves. Durocher had been seen in the company of gamblers. He had lost the support of the Catholic Youth Organization through being named corespondent in a divorce action. He had been charged with assaulting a fan (and later acquitted). And he had loudly accused Larry MacPhail himself of bringing noted gamblers to a ball game in Havana.

So Leo played golf or pool (which he was better at) all season, and the team was run by Burt Shotton, Branch Rickey's old-time "Sunday manager." (Rickey never attended baseball games on Sunday. A promise to his dead mother, he said.) Shotton was a contrast to Durocher, for he did not holler, yell foul insults at the enemy, kick dirt at umpires, or offer to punch anyone in the nose. (Just the same, one of his unhappy charges allowed, he was a "sarcastic Southern son of a bitch!") He was not thought to have a chance to lead that gang to the pennant, with the Cardinals stronger than ever and the Dodgers riven down the middle by the Robinson dispute.

And when Burt Shotton showed up for the first home game against the Giants in the Polo Grounds that year wearing clerical-type spectacles and a long top coat and watched the game from the stands while Coach Clyde Sukeforth ran the club, the sportswriters gave up their last hope. As if to signal the desperation of the Dodger cause, the Giants hit six home runs and won the game, 10 to 4. And even when Shotton took a seat on the bench the next day, and Jackie Robinson, his nerves still

jumping a little, made three hits before the largest Saturday crowd in National League history, the Giants *still* won, 4 to 3. But by the Fourth of July, the Dodgers were in first place, where pennant winners are supposed to be on that magic date. They tightened their grasp on the top rung by beating the Giants in morning and afternoon games (not a doubleheader, but single games requiring separate admission charges at Ebbets Field). The first game, which the Dodgers won 16 to 7, had to be halted after eight innings so the customers could be rushed out of the park and the new ones brought in to see the second game, which the Dodgers took, 4 to 3.

After that only the Cardinals gave the Dodgers competition, and the chief excitement at home and on the road was Jackie Robinson, who was glumly accused of "showboating" by the crypto-Confederates among the Yankee and Giant fans. But all over the country fans turned out largely to watch Jackie in action, to see him cavort on the baselines, driving pitchers to distraction with his false starts and dancing back and forth, and to see him hit. The road attendance that season exceeded the home attendance. And the home attendance set a record for the National League: 1,807,526.

The opponents in the World Series being the Yankees again, the faithful, most of them still nursing sore memories of the 1941 disaster, came out to see the tables turned. This was the first World Series ever to be seen on television, and it was also the richest, up to then, from the standpoint of gate receipts. Obviously being able to watch the game in the living room persuaded no one who might have access to tickets to stay home. To get the juice out of a World Series game, you had to *be* there. No Series ever stirred excitement like a subway Series, with the rival parks just a forty-minute ride from each other.

This was a Series full of portents, not all of them on the field of friendly strife. As so often happens in a World Series, the "heroes" were men of whom no great feats had been expected. And the great men whose very presence there set the crowd to yelling did not always perform according to their reputations. Cookie Lavagetto, who had been shunted to the bench by Spider Jorgensen, ruined a no-hit attempt by Yankee pitcher Floyd Bevens. Al Gionfriddo, who never played major league baseball again, became an overnight sensation when he stole a home run from Joe DiMaggio with a catch that Joe himself would have been proud to tell about, an impossible grab that many people did not believe had happened until the umpire signaled the out.

All in all, the ups and downs of this Series were such as to have caused cardiac arrests throughout both boroughs. Brooklyn's incomparable Ralph Branca, the only real nine-inning pitcher on the Dodger staff, started out as if he would not let a single Yankee get to first base. For the first four innings he put the Yankees down one-two-three. Then, all of a sudden, it looked as if he would put the whole club on base at the same time, if there had been room enough. And when the Yankees got through hitting in the fifth inning, they had five runs; Branca was taking a hot shower; and tough Joe Page, the New York relief specialist, had come to starve the Brooklyn hitters to death. This big-inning business had wrecked

Brooklyn's hopes before, and this, apparently, was to be a repeat of 1941.

The next day the Yankees welcomed left-handed Vic Lombardi, second-best starter on the Brooklyn staff and not much of a finisher. Left-handers were the favorite meat of the Yankees that season. It took them hardly five innings to collect nine hits and five runs. Then they tossed in a "big inning" anyway, when they set upon relief pitcher Henry Behrman to add four runs to the six they had tallied in earlier innings. George Stirnweiss, the undersized second baseman whose diabetes had kept him out of the service, got three hits, including a triple that day. Old reliable Tommy Henrich hit a home run.

So the Series went back to Brooklyn, with the Yankees, led by Bucky Harris (who was called a "four-hour manager" by some of the Yankee brass) prepared to watch the Dodgers roll over. When did anybody ever take the first two games and not win them all?

But the Dodgers, back in the cramped and cozy confines of their own outdated little ballpark (occupancy by more than 33,000, a sign warned, was unlawful!), rejoiced not to have to cope with the strange shadows, the haze, the expansive outfield, and the dizzying height of the Yankee Stadium pitching mound. (A center fielder in Yankee Stadium can see the hitter only from the knees up.) And all the marvels that their fans had expected of them were suddenly within their reach. The Yankees had the consummate gall to toss old Bobo Newsom at them—Bobo, who had been their very own but a few seasons earlier, and for whose honor they had once been ready to pledge their jobs.

Everybody in the Brooklyn line-up

Sandy Amoros, by catching a "sure" home run off the bat of Yogi Berra, broke some Yankee hearts and saved the day for Brooklyn in the sixth inning of the final game of the 1955 World Series.

laid into Bobo to fashion a big inning in Yankee-style that sent Bobo back into the visitors' clubhouse—a familiar place to him, as indeed was almost every locker room on the circuit. The Yankees were not really stunned by this big inning, for they kept picking at Joe Hatten and Ralph Branca for two runs at a time. And an awkward pinch hitter named Lawrence Berra, out of St. Louis by way of the Navy, came up and hit a home run, the first time in World Series history a pinch hitter had thus comported himself. But Hugh Casey, the Brooklyn version of Joe Page, hurried in and held tight to the victory.

The next day was the day of the near no-hitter, when Yankee hearts broke as Dodger hearts had long been wont to do. There was big Floyd Bevens within reach of what passes among sportswriters for immortality, with but two outs left in the ball game and not a hit marked up against him. (The Dodgers had scored one run on two walks, a sacrifice, and an infield out.) Two men got on base in the ninth without a hit—Furillo working Bevens for a walk, as eight other batters had done previously. Then Bevens walked Pete Reiser on purpose to get at Cookie Lavagetto, who was at the very end of his big league career and no threat to anyone, except that he seemed not unlikely to hit into a double play and make Bevens immortal with a miss. But Cookie was determined not to end his days with a whisper. No-hitter or not, he hauled off on the second pitch —which seemed too high to be a strike—and bounced it right off the concrete wall, sending in two runners with the count needed to win the game.

If only the Dodgers could have come up with a *pitcher* who could have provided a swan song like Lavagetto's! But they could find no one in the barrel but Rex Barney, a man with fearsome speed and almost a total lack of confidence, who might have been another Walter Johnson (who was nicknamed Barney after Barney Oldfield, the racing driver) but instead turned into just another wild man. Rex scared the Yankee hitters with the way he sent those baseballs screaming past them. But while he was in there, Rex walked nine batters, and nothing Burt Shotton could invent could get back the runs let go by Barney. Although Shotton used eighteen players and every pinch hitter but one got on base for him, he could not catch up with New York. Spec Shea gave Brooklyn but four hits among them, and four hits divided among eighteen hitters does not make for many runs. The final score was New York 2, Brooklyn 1.

But game number six was the masterpiece, the game that perhaps lived longest in the recollections of those fortunate enough to have made the scene at the stadium that October. Alas, that the Dodgers could not have won *all* their home games, that this might have been their climax! There were 74,000 spectators at the stadium, more than a later law would allow, with men and

women and children clinging to crossbeams, sitting in aisles, and standing along back fences. The nearby rapid transit platform was crowded thicker than it would be at rush hour and every nearby roof held its helping of nonpaying watchers, many of whom could not even tell which team was hitting nor count the score.

This was a game for the hitters. Both Allie Reynolds, the Yankee pitcher, and Vic Lombardi, for Brooklyn, left the game in the third inning. The Dodgers needed three more pitchers to get out of the game alive, and the Yankees used five trying to save their own skins. There were thirty-eight different players involved in the game, including a twenty-eight-year-old rookie catcher who was spending his first year with the Yankees after a stretch in the service—Ralph Houk. He came in as a pinch hitter for pitcher Vic Raschi in the seventh inning and hit a single. But the Yanks were unable to turn it into a run. Their best chance already had been blown in the previous inning, when Joe DiMaggio came to bat with two out, carrying the tying run in his shoes. He had won the previous game with a home run, and he set out to do exactly that with this game.

But Burt Shotton must have anticipated him, for he had just made his smartest—or luckiest—strategic move of the Series: He sent Al Gionfriddo, a potential track star, into left field in place of slow-footed Gene Hermanski. So when Joe DiMaggio picked on one of Joe Hatten's best pitches and sent it whistling toward the left-field boxes, where he had left many a home run ball, Gionfriddo did not deem it out of reach. A left-hander, with his glove on his right hand, he fled for the foul line, his lean arm outstretched. Everyone in the park—except Al—knew the effort was hopeless. It was a sure home run, the score was tied, and this was the championship for sure—for how could the Yankees *not* win in their home park?

Knowing he had put the ball right where he wanted it to go, DiMaggio was already loping toward second in the disdainful manner of the home run hitter who knows there can be no play on him. The Yankee fans had all risen, as if pulled by the same string, to roar their delight at this miracle. And poor Gionfriddo! Well, he seemed bound to cripple himself in a collision with the rail, in Pete Reiser-style. Hardly any of the Yankee supporters bothered to watch him dash himself into a coma. Then all of a sudden there was a scream from somewhere far off. The base runners, who had been trotting happily as boys at recess toward home plate, turned and stood open-mouthed in their tracks. It was utterly impossible! Reaching out at least a foot farther than was humanly possible and timing his final lunge to the tiniest fraction of an instant, Gionfriddo had plucked that ball right out of the air a few inches above the rail and held on to it. Even Yankee fans screamed then. And the pin-striped contingent on the bases glumly reminded themselves that, of *course*, it was not Hermanski out there but that little dirty name of an Italian who ran like a spider and wore his glove on his right hand!

After that the ultimate loss to the Yankees was an anticlimax. How could any club produce more heroics than this? If the Dodgers had had a pitcher or two to spare! Or if Pistol Pete Reiser had not been lamed!

Poor Reiser. Had he not been the sort of man given to stealing home plate

when husky catchers tried to bar his way with their bodies or to catching fly balls when the effort carried him headlong into concrete walls, he would surely have been one of the four or five greatest names in the Hall of Fame. It is more than a possibility that he might have matched Ty Cobb, for he had all of Cobb's fire and determination to win but none of Cobb's cruelty or bitter egotism. Hardly anyone recalls it now, but Pete could throw a ball as hard, as far, and as accurately as any man in the game. Cobb never owned any such arm as Reiser had. And Pistol Pete could throw with either arm! Not just get the ball moving in the right direction with his left arm but sizzle it straight and far to the target exactly as if he were throwing with his right.

As a hitter Pete might have grown into the greatest. Had he not been so often laid up from baseline collisions, outfield near-suicides, and just plain hard luck (he once cracked a bone while merely throwing the ball), he'd have learned to take the measure of every pitcher in the game.

When Pete first joined the Dodgers in Clearwater, Florida, in 1939, more than one or two observers came to the conclusion that this was the young Ty Cobb reincarnated. Of course there had been many a springtime Ty Cobb since the original had faded. But none of them ever had delivered a more substantial performance to base the appraisal on. Pete was only eighteen years old, had never attempted major league ball before, and knew nothing of the pitchers who were throwing to him. In his very first appearance in a spring exhibition, Pete hit a home run. After that came a walk and two singles. In the next game he hit two home runs

A perfectly planned and executed pick-off play by Cleveland pitcher Bob Feller and shortstop Lou Boudreau misfired through an error — the umpire's error. Umpire Stewart called Phil Masi of the Boston Braves safe although Phil was far off the base when Boudreau tagged him. World Series, 1948.

and two singles. In his first 11 at-bats, nobody could put this young man out. A switch hitter who could not be intimidated by a cross fire or fooled by a curve, Pete let no man drive him away from the plate. He was as fast as any man on the squad and had the strongest arm. He stole bases daringly but not with the foolhardiness of a speed-happy youngster. He just grabbed what he could get and hung on to it.

When Pete finally reached the big leagues, after a season in the minors, he took just one year to take over the top spot in batting. Then in 1942 in St. Louis, when he was batting .380 and seemed about to post the best season of his brief career, he chased a long drive right into the outfield wall and cracked his skull. After that Pete tried and tried. And while he was good, and better than many, he was never really Pete Reiser again. Not that he ever flinched, even when he faced another concrete wall. But he suffered from dizzy spells and headaches. And he was taken into the Army when healthier men were being coddled at home.

When Pete came back, he was simply not the same. He had lost a little speed, lost some of his timing, and had lost too much weight. But he had never lost his daring. He continued to make a career (almost) of stealing home and did better at this spectacular feat than Ty Cobb had done. But he never regained the extraordinary skills that seemed destined to make him the leader of them all, and he remained just Pete Reiser, a pretty good ballplayer who could be counted on to give his full skill and strength to the job of trying to win, regardless of what stood in the way.

The really portentous events of this subway Series, however, did not involve Pete Reiser nor any ballplayer at all. And they took place in a midtown hotel, far from the sweat and dust of the diamond. After the Yankees had triumphed and the newspaper writers had been turned loose in the locker room, Larry MacPhail, part owner of the Yankees, was seen embracing a retiring, slightly graying gentleman, who looked as if he would rather be somewhere else.

"Don't congratulate me!" Larry exhorted the sportswriters. "Here's the real hero! I built the losers! *He* built the winners!"

In this wild statement Larry was speaking the simple truth. He had, indeed, done most of the work of putting together the Brooklyn Dodgers, who had belonged to him before Rickey took hold. And meanwhile, the retiring man in the somber clothes, who was named George Weiss, had industriously and unobtrusively gathered together this collection of young men, who had just proved themselves the best in the business. So the writers toasted George, and George, as he often did, blushed scarlet and could think of few words to say.

Then the whole mob began to pull themselves together to go wind up the celebration in style in a hotel ballroom. MacPhail, who had partaken generously of the champagne and other potables traditionally dispensed at all such ceremonies, had begun by this time to talk freely of his plans for rebuilding the Yankees from top to bottom with a wholesale infusion of MacPhail blood, in the person of his sons. George Weiss, having overheard some of those assurances, began to wonder if perhaps he might be needing another job. On the way to the party, he had voiced his misgivings but had been assured by the younger MacPhails that this was just their father's way and that it was really "the champagne talking."

So George was not prepared at all for the dire moment when Larry, red-faced and roaring, having just dealt out a black eye to a sportswriter, burst into the bar at the celebration and, his eye lighting on George, let out a bellow: "You son of a bitch! You're through! My son will take over!" Here Larry beat his breast like no wedding guest of fact or fancy. "My *son!*"

It eventually became apparent that Larry, sober or not, meant what he said, for he was able to tell George quietly just when to pick up his check. This disaster never befell the Yankees, however, for the remaining two of the triumvirate of owners hastily made a deal to buy Larry out—at an incredible profit. And George was rehired and given a title, a rug on the floor, a higher salary—but no part of the ownership, which might very well have been his had he been the type to fight as determinedly for his own interests as he did for those of his boss. And in this failure of George's lay the seeds of even more portentous doings in later years.

There were other excitements in the game, of course, in other cities. In 1948 Bob Feller got into his first World Series game and almost won it. Indeed, he should have won it, except that an umpire was caught nodding, or looking the other way, when a carefully practiced pick-off play between Bob and Lou Boudreau nailed a runner by half the length of his body. The man was hopelessly out. And the umpire called him safe. And so the man eventually

No one in modern baseball ever stole home more often or more effectively than Pistol Pete Reiser, Brooklyn center fielder. Here he grimaces in triumph as Chicago Cub catcher Salvador Hernandez puts on the tag too late. This run put Brooklyn ahead, 2 to 1, and the Dodgers won the game 4 to 3. Ebbets Field, Brooklyn, May, 1942.

All seems happiness and good fellowship as Baseball Commissioner Albert B. "Happy" Chandler and Dodgers' President Branch Rickey welcome Leo Durocher back to his job as manager of the Dodgers, April 1, 1948. Leo had just served a full year's suspension imposed by Commissioner Chandler for "conduct detrimental to baseball."

scored the run that won the game for the Boston Braves.

But Bill Veeck's Cleveland Indians won the championship anyway. And Bill soon sold out for a bigger profit than Larry MacPhail had made and moved on to try to turn other baseball franchises into cash. And the Boston Braves themselves were turned into money by being sold to a convocation of outlanders in Milwaukee, where they found money dropping from the trees.

The sudden discovery that baseball franchises could be made into capital gains and that buyers could then (and until the tax department smartened up) "depreciate" the player contracts over a few years would soon set baseball clubs shuttling about the country-side seeking greener pastures, cropping them close, and moving on to new and lusher spots.

Even more earthshaking was the sudden reversal in 1948 of the leadership of the Giants and Dodgers. In mid-July, when the two clubs were tied for second place, and after Eddie Stanky, one of Durocher's favorites (and another of the antiblack cabal among the Dodgers), had been sold to Boston, Durocher himself suddenly turned his coat. In the morning he had been the beloved field manager of the Dodgers; in the afternoon he had accepted the generalship of the enemy forces and was wearing the uniform of the New York Giants, having been sold off by Branch Rickey without so much as a quiver of the lip.

The blow was too much for many Brooklyn fans, who tried keeping their eyes closed for minutes at a time to see if, when they opened them, they would be truly awake, and the stars would have returned to their assigned pathways in the skies. As for the Giant fans! A few of them swore (and one or two kept their pledge) never to set foot in the Polo Grounds again as long as that fiend incarnate and that apotheosis of all that was unspeakable about the loathsome throng from the borough over the bridge held a place on the Giants' bench. But Durocher and his new wife made the switch as readily as they might have filled in a change-of-address form. Durocher began at once to figure out how to bring "his kind of ballplayer" (including Eddie Stanky) to New York. And his wife just turned the radio dial to another number and laid her heart on the Giants.

Then in 1951 after the Dodgers had finally put together a new and mightier selection of paid ballplayers to carry the fight to the other boroughs and with the Yankees obviously making ready to take the field in a rematch, the skies fell in. In what was undoubtedly the most thrilling and most shattering event

(depending on whether your heart lay in Manhattan or Brooklyn) in local baseball history, the Giants snatched the pennant from the Dodgers in the last seconds of a play-off game that had already been practically won by Brooklyn. The Bobby Thomson home run, resulting from a too-careful placing of a pitch by Ralph Branca (who should have just reared back and fired), turned the baseball game and the city upside down, caused a young Irish nurse in the nearby Columbia Medical Center to burst suddenly into uncontrollable tears, and prompted a Chinese lady in Brooklyn, momentarily forgetting her native tongue, to seize her husband by the arm and cry out, "This awful! Let's go back to China!"

But instead the World Series went to the Polo Grounds, the home of the Chinese home run. And the World Championship stayed in Yankee Stadium.

It was 1952 before the new Dodgers were able to grasp the top rung once more. This time they had an aggregation of mighty hitters such as had seldom graced their home park all at once and had developed, bought, or traded for a staff of strong-armed pitchers, any number of whom could pitch more than seven innings in a row. Jackie Robinson now starred at second base, where Eddie Stanky, the man who delighted to call him "nigger" or some less lovely sobriquet, once used to scramble. From Montreal the Dodgers had brought up and seasoned one of the most agile, hardest-hitting, and strongest-armed catchers in the game: Roy Campanella, a black man with an Italian father.

In the outfield now, besides Carl Furillo of the siege-gun arm, who was suffering from a chronic eye irritation, roamed a young man named Duke Snider, who had been sent back to the minors in the beginning to learn more about the size of the strike zone and had then developed into one of the top home run hitters in the league. The other outfielder was another long-ball hitter, Andy Pafko, a veteran of more than eight years with the Cubs. First base was covered by a reconstituted catcher with the biggest hands in baseball—Gil Hodges, who had appeared in Brooklyn nine seasons earlier as a nineteen-year-old third baseman. A failure as a catcher, Gil in five full seasons had developed into the slickest-fielding first baseman in the league. He was another man who could drive the ball out of the park upwards of thirty times a year. There was no power hitter at third base. But the man who played there, Billy Cox, had been purchased from Pittsburgh (where he played shortstop) because of his agility, his habit of making impossible stops, and his quick arm. With all that power at the other corner and up the middle, who needed another home run hitter?

Where the real improvement took place was in the pitching staff. A black man named Black (Joe) turned out to be as steady a relief pitcher as Hugh Casey had ever been and a good enough starter, too; in 1952 he won an award as Rookie of the Year. There was also lean Preacher Roe, who did not disdain the spitball when he thought he could sneak it by; twenty-five-year-old Carl Erskine, who, in June against the Cubs, had thrown the first no-hitter a Dodger pitcher had delivered since who knew when; and Billy Loes, a lanky, independent young right-hander, who had been born and brought up a few miles away

from Ebbets Field. They would have had another black pitcher (or maybe if they had had him, they would not have brought up Joe Black), but he had been wanted by the Army. And if they had had him—hulking, hard-boiled, rough-and-ready Don Newcombe, who was not afraid of anything in the world except airplanes, they might have beaten the Yankees.

As it was, they had to settle for coming close. Joe Black, with his demon fastball and his dinky curve (a stiff middle finger kept him from closing his hand on his curve properly to give it spin), startled the Yankees in the first game. They made fun of his curve, but they could not hit it. Nor could they hit it much in later games, when they beat Joe.

Poor Joe lost the deciding game of the Series, when the Yankee rookie Mickey Mantle, fast blossoming into more than a replacement for Joe Di-Maggio, put the Yanks ahead and put Joe out with a home run in the sixth inning.

The Dodgers tried again in 1953, with almost the same line-up. They were stronger this year, for an operation had cured Carl Furillo's eye trouble, and Carl had led the league at the bat. A speed-marvel from the Montreal farm, a young man who could outrun Robinson on the bases, a switch-hitter, and a wide-ranging fielder, pushed Jackie Robinson over to third base and thence to the outfield. For Jack could not match Jim (Junior) Gilliam's work on the infield.

By this time Jack had left his honeymoon days far behind him. No longer did he swallow his anger when someone called him a dirty name, nor did he turn the other cheek when he was roughed

The end of a perfect game — perfect that is for everyone but the fans and players from Brooklyn — is marked by this leaping embrace between New York Yankee catcher Yogi Berra and pitcher Don Larsen, who has just struck out pinch hitter Dale Mitchell to make the twenty-seventh out in a row. New York vs. Brooklyn, World Series, 1956.

Ted Williams of the Red Sox and Joe DiMaggio of the Yankees, rivals in t

up on the baselines. If a pitcher threw the ball at him now, Jackie's response was the old Ty Cobb – Leo Durocher stunt of luring the pitcher to the baseline with a bunt and then running right over him. If anyone tried to feed him spikes or an extra-hard tag on the baselines, Jackie had the same medicine to hand back at the next meeting. He shouted back at tormentors, traded insults with Durocher, and let his temper flare when an umpire victimized him.

There was no dissension on the Dodgers now. Carl Furillo and Jackie were teammates first of all, and even though there were still spots where local prejudice might force Robinson, Gilliam, and the other blacks apart to seek lodging, the whole crew mixed together at meals, at card games, and at locker-room roughhousing. And anybody who roughed up a black Dodger on the baselines had the whole tough Dodger crew on his neck. But cohesion was not enough to beat the Yankees, who gave the Dodgers one less victory in the Series this year.

Next year the Dodgers fell short of

40s and 1950s, both used to hit baseballs high into the air. Ted hit them higher.

the flag, as did the Yankees, and the *real* contest was interrupted while the despised Giants, with Durocher calling the plays and a young man named Willie Mays (who had come back from the Army bigger, stronger, and faster than he had been when he went in) performing most of them, carried the flag for the National League. The opponents were the Cleveland Indians, who were favored in many circles because they had on board the American League's top batter, Bobby Avila, and the league's leading batter-in-of-runs,

Larry Doby. Doby, who had been the Cleveland club's first black player and was now a seven-year veteran, had not found his own way made much easier by the pioneering of Jackie Robinson. He had been refused lodging at the Santa Rita Hotel in Tucson, where the Indians stayed in the spring, and when the club came to Los Angeles, had been shunted away from the Biltmore into a "Negro" hotel. But Larry had plugged on without too many complaints and smoothed his own path with his mighty hitting.

But in this Series practically all the Cleveland hitting was done by Vic Wertz, and even he was robbed of an extra-base hit by the greatest catch Willie Mays ever made in a career full of miraculous ones. So the bloody Giants prevailed, and the Dodger fans had to hide their heads and put their hands over their ears for one more season.

In 1955 the Yankee-Dodger series was resumed with a lot of new arms, sharper eyes, and younger legs. It was played under the shadow of a threat from owner Walter O'Malley to shift the club right out of town—this, in spite of the millions of dollars in earnings to which the fans had contributed. The threat had not been uttered in so many words, but it had been implicit in O'Malley's decision to play some of the 1956 Dodger games in Jersey City, as if the club belonged to anybody who would offer it playing room and not to the fiercely loyal subway denizens of New York's busiest borough. When the pennant was won and the Series begun, however, Brooklyn's heart still belonged to the Dodgers. Once more both parks on either end of town were jammed as tight as the law allowed, and uncounted thousands ignored meals, jobs, studies, and the world's alarms while they clung close to radios or sat transfixed before television screens.

What they heard and saw and rejoiced over in their hearts was the most thoroughly transporting of all the World Series to date, one filled with startling reversals of form, heroic deeds by hitherto unknown heroes, portentous sights, and uproarious celebrations. The Yankees came to the battle with a number of faces unfamiliar to the devotees of earlier struggles, including that of Elston Howard, the first black

man to be deemed worthy of wearing the pin-striped uniform. (Another black man had been hired, a remarkable first baseman named Vic Power, but his somewhat checkered private career—no different, really, from that of countless white heroes—was thought to render him ineligible to "represent his race" in this almost last stronghold of racial purity.)

The Brooklyns had a few new faces, too, and one old face that had been much missed in previous Series—that of black Don Newcombe, the overpowering pitcher who had finally paid his debt of service to the draft board. There was a new manager, too, a man who seemed the utter opposite of Durocher or of Charlie Dressen, the merrily egotistical little guy who had led the Dodgers to a pennant and then lost his job because he and his wife decided they *must* have a two-year contract with O'Malley. The new manager, Walter Alston, had been cultivating the Dodger farm in Montreal, where he had trained and sent upstairs a number of Brooklyn's recent heroes. Alston was a quiet man seldom given to loud argument and possessed a countrified air (he lived in a small town in Ohio).

Among the new Dodgers were two infield replacements, Don Hoak and Don Zimmer, a Mercury-footed outfielder named Amoros, and a lean left-handed pitcher named Karl Spooner, who had pitched just two games in 1954 and won them both with twenty-seven strikeouts. (Fifteen of them came in the first major league game he ever pitched.) Since then, Spooner had struggled with a sore arm, had won but eight games, and seemed always just about to recover his original magic. (His earned run average for his first two major league games was a string of zeros.)

The Dodger victory in this Series was made doubly sweet by the fact that the Yankees won the first two games, and won them in World Series fashion with home runs from an unexpected source and first-rate pitching from a supposed has-been. The first game was won for the Yankees by Joe Collins, the good-glove first baseman, who hit two home runs off supposedly invincible Don Newcombe—the man who was expected to tip the scales in the Dodgers' favor. The second game was won by Tommy Byrnes, who had been fired from the Yankees four years earlier when Dan Topping himself ordered his immediate release—because Topping was sick of seeing Byrne hand out bases on balls. Tommy had come back from the bushes with his control improved, his arm just as supple, and his jaw just as loose. He talked almost endlessly as he pitched, to himself, to the catcher, to the batter, to the umpire. In this game, which the Yankees won 4 to 2, Tommy allowed but one extra-base hit and four singles.

The Brooklyn fans, recalling too well that in more than thirty years no club had lost the first two games of the Series and then won the prize, turned out for the third game as if it were the first night of a wake. The pitcher they had to count on now was a somewhat sickly lad named Johnny Podres, who had been celebrating his twenty-third birthday in the clubhouse and was still unable to keep his fastball low. And of course all those Yankee brutes fattened their young on high fastballs. But Johnny promptly set Dodger hearts to singing through exquisite use of his change of pace, which he *could* control.

Again and again, the mighty Yankees stepped into the pitch too soon and feebly popped it up for the Brooklyn infielders to devour. Meanwhile, the Dodger sluggers, led by Roy Campanella, who opened the scoring with a two-run home run, finished off fireball Bob Turley in less than two innings, got rid of Tom Morgan in three, and kept adding two runs at a time to their total until they had eight altogether. All the Yankees could collect was three.

In the fourth game the Dodgers kept on hitting, or at least resumed hitting, just as soon as the Yankees had jumped to a lead. Not the least bit intimidated by a home run from the bat of Yankee third baseman Gil McDougald (the man with the worst batting stance in baseball, who let his bat droop behind him like a banana stalk) and a run-scoring single by shortstop Phil Rizzuto, plus a double by pestiferous Billy Martin, the Dodgers, behind 3 to 1 in the fourth inning, set off all the cannon at once. Roy Campanella, Gil Hodges, and Duke Snider fired off home runs in succession, and the Dodgers would not let up until they had made the score, at the end of the fifth inning, 7 to 3. The Yankees never caught up, although they crawled close. The final score was 8 to 5, and the two teams between them had used up eight pitchers.

The fifth game was a true Brooklyn miracle, for it was won by a beanpole-type right-handed pitcher named Roger Craig, who had started ten games that year, won only five, and completed only three—and who would one day earn a sort of fame working for a new New York team, not yet invented, and losing more games than anybody else alive.

This day Roger looked like Bob

Feller to the Yankees. In six innings (his usual limit) he allowed but three hits. Then, when the Yanks got to lean Roger for a pinch-hit home run and a walk, Clem Labine, who had worked four innings the day before, came in and saved the game. Of course by this time the Brooklyn hearties had counted a few scores of their own. Sandy Amoros, the light-hitting outfielder (.247), hit a home run that scored two runs, and Duke Snider, who had been "recruited" right out of high school by one of Branch Rickey's circular letters, hit two. Ah, that lovely right-field wall!

There was no such inviting target in Yankee Stadium, where the clubs met to play the Series' sixth game. This time the Dodgers, with their pitching down to the nub, closed their eyes and hoped for a new miracle from their mystery pitcher, Karl Spooner, who, like Rex Barney of a few years back, seemed to own all the attributes of greatness except the ability to deliver when playing for real. But Karl Spooner lasted quicker than ever. He was able to get only one batter out from among the first six who faced him. Then, with two runs in and two runners on base, young Bill Skowron (who was called "Moose" at home because he looked like Mussolini) drove a ball into the seats. That gave the Yankees five runs altogether, gave Spooner the rest of the day off, and gave Yankee pitcher Whitey Ford more than he needed for victory.

To the shame of the Brooklyn faithful, they failed to turn out in full array for the final game. It had happened so often before! Who needed to trek all the way to the stadium just to see it again?

But this time the stay-at-homes, who might have been peering at the live spectacle from behind someone's shoulder in the back of the grandstands, kicked themselves for not being there in the moment of triumph. For Johnny Podres, still apparently the birthday boy, did not allow the Yankees a single run, shutting them out in a World Series game for the first time since Preacher Roe had done it in 1949. And the Dodgers got one more run than they needed, even though Tommy Byrnes was as stingy with the hits and as free with the words as ever. But a double by Roy Campanella, plus an infield out and a single, brought in one run; one more scored on a sacrifice fly by Gil Hodges. And the game was yanked right off the lip of the precipice by an impossible catch—à la Gionfriddo—by Sandy Amoros, the substitute left fielder.

Sandy—another guy who wore his glove on his right hand—had cheated toward center field when left-handed Yogi Berra came to the plate with Gil McDougald at first and Billy Martin on second. But Yogi, as he so often did, sliced the ball down the left-field foul line and caught Sandy many strides out of position. Martin and McDougald, convinced that—just as everyone knew would happen—the blow had been struck that would tie the ball game, sprinted, heads down, for home, or for as close to it as they could get. But Sandy was ready to hurl his body right into the rail to save that champeenship. With a final desperate twist of his careening body, and a long, long stretch of his straining right hand, he just managed to trap that ball in the edge of the leather and keep it. Yankee base runners and coach Frank Crosetti were thunderstruck. That made only one out! Desperately Gil McDougald, who was

Charles "King-Kong" Keller, shown grimly belting a baseball into the air, was Yankee General Manager George Weiss' personal choice for the man to match Babe Ruth's records. But a back injury cut short Keller's career.

part way to third, put his head down and dug for first base. But Sandy, who knew exactly what was happening, flung himself into throwing position and let fly with all his young strength. The ball sizzled in to Pee Wee Reese, who relayed it instantly on to Gil Hodges' hands while McDougald was still a few strides short. Two out! Martin, who had been slowed down by cautious Frank Crosetti, made it back to second all right. But the next batter, Hank Bauer, lame from a charley horse, could not get the ball out of the infield. And sud-denly the game was over and the Brook-lyn Dodgers—the *Brooklyn Dodgers* —were Champions of the World!

The screams that arose at the stadium were echoed in every corner of the city, throughout the suburbs, and into New Jersey and Connecticut, wherever two or three were gathered together in the name of the Dodgers. Taverns erupted, living-room windows trembled, sky-scraper towers vomited torn-up paper, and factory wheels stopped turning while men and women ran joyously up and down the aisles.

Ted Williams, after hitting a home run (number 521) in his final game, hangs up his Red Sox shirt for the last time. Fenway Park, Boston, September 28, 1960.

In Brooklyn there had been no such doings since the surrender of the Japanese. As a matter of fact, not even that celebration matched what took place along the streets, down the avenues, and up the alleys of the borough of churches, when the blessed Dodgers, so long denied their due, had finally been declared champions of the subway. And Johnny Podres—well, he was surely the pitcher of the decade, with his best years ahead of him. Hardly anyone recalled the name of that one skinny kid from Flatbush, who could throw as hard as Spooner but was too wild to do any good. Was it Koufax? Cowfax? Some name like that. He had won a couple of games that season, but they didn't dare chance him in the Series.

Nobody really dared take much of a chance on Sandy Koufax for another few seasons. But the pitching coaches knew he had incredible stuff on the ball, if he would just get out of the habit of trying to blast his way out of trouble by throwing harder and harder and hard-er—and getting wilder and wilder.

No prophet knew either that by the time Sandy Koufax developed the control that would make him the best pitcher in baseball, the Dodgers would have moved out of Brooklyn, and the Giants would have fled with them, to renew their rivalries on the other coast. Men were contemplating desperate measures to keep the Dodgers where they had been born. But Ebbets Field was past a joke now, so cramped and dilapidated that it would have been rejected by a club in the minor leagues. Television had cut down on attendance (but not on profits), and there were riches and soft living beckoning from far across the continent. Matters reached such a pass that Nelson Rockefeller even made a try (in vain) to buy the Dodgers and keep them at his side. But the Dodgers sold their park and then leased it until 1959, by which time they hoped (they said) the city would have provided them a new pen to play in.

The Dodgers, however, did not live out the lease. The city fathers could not find any sound reason why they should finance a rich baseball franchise right then. And, anyway, no one really *believed* that the mighty folk whose job it was to keep the world running right would ever permit the Dodgers to move out. The Giants maybe. But never the Dodgers.

So the Dodgers went on and fought it out for still another pennant—the last one they would ever bring to Brooklyn. With big Don Newcombe back in form and winning twenty-seven games, the Brooklyn boys just managed to nose out the Braves, who now camped in Milwaukee, for the right to meet the Yankees again. This time the Yankees had Mantle and Bauer back (Mickey had been crippled with two bad knees in the 1955 Series, and Hank was limping). And they had brought back from Kansas City, where they had shipped him for two half-seasons, 40-year-old Enos Slaughter, who had wrecked the Red Sox ten years before by running all the way home from first on what should have been a single.

But the Yankees were somewhat short of pitchers, with only Whitey Ford having posted a seasonal record anyone would want to brag about. They still had that poor unfortunate who had been bombed out in four innings in the fourth game of the previous World Series, a very tall, broad-beamed right-hander named Don Larsen. But what could you expect from him?

In the World Series, however, you had to expect anything. In the fifth game with the Series tied, 2 games to 2, the Yankees, scraping the bottom of the pitching barrel, started Don Larsen, who had completed only *five* games that season.

This time Don pitched a perfect one. The hulking Larsen looked like a relief pitcher right from the start, for he pitched every time as if he had men on base, without a windup. He never had anybody on base, however, and only a few came close. Only one man got as many as three balls, and only Jackie Robinson came close to making it safely to first. Robinson hit a whistling drive that caromed off the glove of third baseman Andy Carey. But Gil McDougald, the shortstop, shagged the ball while it was still alive and fired it to first base an inch or two ahead of Jackie. It was possible to complain (and a few, including the batter, did) that the final pitch that struck out Dale Mitchell (who was making his farewell appearance in the big leagues) was too high to be called a strike. But the umpire let Don Larsen have it anyway, and Don became "immortal" for a few years.

Even though Brooklyn won the sixth game, back in Ebbets Field, and beat Bob Turley, who also threw without a windup, it took them eleven desperate innings and some great pitching by sinker-ball Clem Labine to manage it. And win or no, the Dodgers, as their old boss, Charlie Dressen might have phrased it, was already dead. They were counting on big Don Newcombe to recover his strength in time to overpower the Yankees in the finale. But Don had spent all his change in the regular season, and all he could throw now, it seemed, were home runs. Yogi Berra got one first time up, then got another next time. And in the fourth inning Elston Howard hit the one that finished Newcombe. The grand-slam home run that Bill Skowron hit in the seventh just made the whole thing ridiculous, for Johnny Kucks gave out only three hits and no runs at all to the Brooklyns.

And that, alas, was the last time Brooklyn was ever represented in a World Series. When next the Trolley Dodgers took the field, they hailed from Los Angeles, where there had been no trolleys to dodge since the memory of television announcers ran not to the contrary. And where, a sports editor charged his minions, they must never, never, never refer to the ball club as Bums.

M & M, M and
M, and Others

IN those sometimes gay and sometimes gray decades after the war, it seemed for a while as if everyone who could hit the ball hard must have a name beginning with M. For there was Stan Musial, the flawed pitcher and sore-arm outfielder, who turned himself into one of the greatest hitters in the game. And there was Mickey Mantle, the painfully shy young schoolboy hero who wept tears of homesickness when he left Commerce, Oklahoma, for his first try-out with the Yankees. And there was Roger Maris, the fretful young man who, in trying to cope with the press that hounded him as he aimed for Babe Ruth's record, worked himself into such a state of nerves that his hair fell

out in clumps. And there was Willie Mays, who, when there was no baseball game to play in, occasionally got himself into a game of stickball on the streets. Of these only Stan Musial of St. Louis ever led the league in batting more than once. (Stan was one of Mantle's boyhood heroes.) Mantle came in first in batting (and in home runs and runs batted in) only in 1956 when he hit .353. (And made 52 home runs). In 1957 when Mickey attained his lifetime high of .365, Ted Williams topped him with a .388. As for Maris, he never reached .300. All the same he twice led in runs batted in and of course led everyone at last with his 61 home runs in 1961. And Willie led his league with .345 in 1954. But Musial six times led the National League in batting and left a lifetime average of .331. He was usually the most feared batter in the league, but especially in Brooklyn, where the fans who feared him gave him his nickname of "The Man." Too often Stan the Man spoiled the Dodgers' chances with two-base hits, in which he seemed to specialize.

Musial in a sense was a synthetic batter, as Mantle was a natural one. Stan had tried to be a pitcher, but an injury had ended that career almost before it began. He turned to the outfield but there, for a long time, needed to have the relay man meet him far out on the grass, for he could not throw as far as the baselines. To hold on in baseball, he had to become a hitter, and he concentrated fiercely on that. Eventually, seeking more power, he adopted the strange stance that became his trademark, his body twisted about like a woundup spring and his head almost hidden behind his shoulder.

But there was another hitter whose name began with M—a teammate of Musial's with the Cardinals for a few seasons—an ex-tennis player who, after he had supposedly finished his career in baseball, became, for a time, the hottest pinch hitter in the game. John Robert Mize reluctantly entered baseball while he was in school; he thought tennis was more fun. But once his coach at Piedmont College in North Carolina had seen how far John Robert could drive a baseball with a bat, he insisted that young Mize devote his springtime weeks to the ball club. John responded by making five hits, including two home runs, in the first two games.

In this era few baseball executives ever paid close attention to the doings on the baseball diamonds at the small colleges. But Branch Rickey of the Cardinals and George Weiss of Baltimore, and later of the Yankee chain, had plucked many a low-bonus prize from those orchards, and they constantly scouted them. Branch Rickey's brother Frank spotted young John Mize in the Piedmont outfield and signed John right out of the classroom to play in the outfield for Greensboro. His first full season with the Piedmont League club (1931) returned him an average of .337. For fourteen more seasons, in the minors and majors, John never hit less than .300.

Mize was a man who liked to choose his pitch. Endlessly patient at the plate, he seemed to swing the bat effortlessly through a smooth level arc. But the strength in those mighty shoulders and thick forearms, plus John's exquisite timing, helped him drive the ball long distances. Mize led the National League in home runs three times and tied for the lead once. His high total was 51 for the New York Giants in 1947, when he tied Ralph Kiner of Pittsburgh.

Mize had been turned into a first baseman by the time he reached the big leagues, and despite his apparent slowness, he was a good one. But he was a man who seemed especially susceptible to injury. Indeed, a hernia suffered while he was with Rochester of the Cardinal chain led to his being fobbed off on the Cincinnati Reds before he ever had a chance to perform for the big team. (Branch Rickey, a notorious horse trader, while he would not actually conceal a man's ailments—he told the Reds they could send John back if there were doubts about his ability to play—had a gift for getting rid of players who seemed destined for short careers.) The Reds gave big John a brief tryout and then returned him for the guaranteed cheerful refund, so Rickey had to put him back in Rochester to ripen some more. And while he was there he had John patched up by a surgeon, watched him a while, and then brought him up and set him roaming in the outfield. A very few games there indicated John was no star outfielder. But he was a hitter. (He batted left-handed, although he threw with his right.) And he soon moved in at first base in place of the aging Ripper Collins. John at this time was twenty-three, Collins thirty-two.

Had Mize belonged to the Yankees at this time, he'd have never made it to first base, for Joe McCarthy, boss of the Yanks, nursed a deep prejudice against Southern ballplayers, especially in the infield. They were all right on the pitching mound, Joe said, and might get by in the outfield, but they were "too slow-thinking" for the infield. (Joe also ruled out pipe smokers from his clubs. "Too complacent," said Joe. "Anytime you get stuck in a line of traffic, nine times out of ten, you'll find the car that is holding everybody up is driven by a guy smoking a pipe.")

But in St. Louis John sparkled at the bag. And he celebrated his promotion by driving out 28 solid hits in 19 games. In 1941, his last year with St. Louis, he played 61 errorless games.

Mize went to the Giants when he was supposed to be on the downgrade, slowing down afield, adding extra baggage to his six-foot-two-inch frame, and even tailing off a trifle at the bat (down to .317 from a high of .364). But Mize went into the Navy after only two seasons in New York, and like Willie

Detroit 30-game winner Dennis McLain and his battery mate, Bill Freehan, were the best of friends until Freehan wrote a book detailing some of Dennis' personal failings. Then Dennis stopped speaking to Bill. Dennis was later suspended by Commissioner Bowie Kuhn for "investing" in a bookie operation.

Mays, he came out of the service leaner, stronger, harder, and sharper. It is said that he used to close himself into an unventilated tin hut on a South Pacific island during the hottest part of every day and do calisthenics on a wrestling mat sweating off every excess ounce and hardening every muscle in his body. No matter how he accomplished it, Mize came back to the Giants in the best physical shape of his career to bat .337, his highest mark since 1939. And the next year he hit his high mark in home runs.

In 1949, however, at age thirty-six, Johnny Mize definitely seemed washed up. The previous season he had fallen below .300 in batting for the first time in his big league career, and he was so slow afoot that, even at first base, he was able to cover only part of the ground he used to call his own. The New York Yankees, this season, found themselves at the end of summer

Ted Kluszewski was never the most graceful of first basemen. But he was aggressive and fearless. Here he dives headlong at Cub base runner Frank Baumholtz to double him off first when Baumholtz tried to get back after a Cincinnati outfielder caught a fly. Chicago, 1951.

desperately in need of a pinch hitter to bring in the runs required to beat the Red Sox to the pennant. So John Mize seemed to be worth the $40,000 asked, even if he did no more than help them take the flag. (George Weiss was forever grabbing up the one or two veterans they needed *now* to accomplish certain needful tasks.)

Slow afoot or no, John eventually paid off his new owners. But he started off as if he were doomed to end his days on the bench. He had hardly become accustomed to his new uniform when he took a tumble on the field and hurt his shoulder so badly that he was barely able to swing his bat. From then

on, Casey Stengel had to use Big John as if he were part of the Sunday chinaware. In the neck-and-neck scramble with the Red Sox, there was little room for experimentation.

Of course, there were those who insisted that the Sox were already dead (even though they grabbed the lead for a moment on the twenty-sixth of September), ruined by a rejuvenated Joe DiMaggio, whose name did not quite start with an "M." Joe, despondent because he was unable to find a cure for the painful bone spur in his heel, had been brooding in the clubhouse or on the bench. But in Boston, someone directed him to a maker of orthopedic

Ed Mathews produced home runs for the Braves wherever they went. But here he is striking out as the Braves, late of Boston and Milwaukee, open the season in their new home, Atlanta.

shoes who, after a couple of tries, was able to fit Joe with a cushioned heel that made it possible for him to play. So Joe went out and really wrecked the Boston club with four home runs in three days.

John Mize, however, saved his hitting until the World Series. Then he "rooned" the poor Dodgers by hitting a sharp single in the ninth inning while the bases were full of his teammates.

He went to bat twice in that Series and hit safely both times. After that John made a specialty of breaking up ball games. His most consistent work was done in the World Series of 1952, when the Yanks once again smote the Dodgers hip and thigh. In the ninth inning of the third game, Mize, batting for Lopat, hit a home run that just fell short of winning the game. The fourth game was won by Mize and Mantle, who hit a home run and a triple, respectively, driving in the two runs that were needed by the Yanks to beat Joe Black. John hit a third homer in the fifth game, but that, too, was wasted when Carl Erskine blew everybody else down. Like so many of the great ones, Mize always responded to the heat of the pennant race.

By 1953 his array of minor injuries had begun to remind John that he would not last forever. And so, his batting

Hardly anyone is watching as Cardinal strong man Stan Musial slides home safely when Boston Braves' catcher Ernie Lombardi drops the throw. Empty stands predict eventual move of Braves to Milwaukee.

average having dropped to .250 (he appeared mostly as a pinch hitter and played infrequently at first base), John gave up his last hopes of hitting sixty-one home runs in a season. (Babe Ruth, who was distantly related to Mize, had predicted that Cousin John would be the man most likely to break his record.)

Also using a capital M to start his last name was a solid young infielder-outfielder who was the only man alive to play regularly with the Braves in Boston, Milwaukee, and Atlanta. He was Edwin Mathews, a right-hander who batted left and twice led the National League in home runs. Eddie was a rookie in Boston, with a club that drew only a quarter million fans all season long. It was no fun playing, no fun practicing, and no fun being on the town. The fact that Eddie hit 25 home runs (and led the league with 115 strike-outs) in his rookie year hardly seemed to make a dent on the national consciousness. Few, indeed, were the Bostonians who cared to come watch Eddie and his mates learn how to play baseball. And the Braves themselves, many of them just starting in the majors, used to pray it would rain.

It might be imagined that Milwaukee, to a boy brought up in Southern California, as Eddie had been, would seem hardly more hospitable. But Mathews thought Milwaukee was paradise. For one thing the fans were nearly numberless, and they were all full of joy at the coming of the Braves. For another, Eddie was learning from Billy Jurges how to play third base, a job that had been a minor mystery to him, despite his having worked at it through several seasons. But the chief benefit to the Braves was the strengthening of the club through the addition of some strong arms, including Bob Buhl's, to the pitching staff, the positioning of Joe Adcock's heavy bat to match Eddie's own at the other corner of the diamond, the sudden increase in team speed by the coming of Billy Bruton, and the lifting of the club's slugging potential by the arrival of Andy Pafko. Overnight, or over the winter, the Braves turned into winners. And every ballplayer finds it easiest to play his best with a winner.

Eddie promptly led the league in home runs with 47 and drove in 135 runs, to come second to Roy Campanella in that department. The Braves made a run for the pennant, missing it by plenty, but only because the Dodgers were so incredibly strong that season (1953). Next season, his third in the majors (he was now twenty-two), Eddie fell off to a mere 40 home runs. But he suddenly started fielding like a real third baseman and cut his errors down by more than half. The Braves, who had brought in a soft-spoken twenty-year-old from Mobile named Henry Aaron to replace ancient Sid Gordon in the outfield, were still in the pennant race most of the way, although they dropped a notch in the standings.

In 1955 when the Braves came in second again, there was Eddie with 41 home runs and once more fielding his position like a demon. Eddie was a big man for a third baseman, a job usually filled by barrel-chested sluggers or small, scrambling types who can get right down in the dirt. But Eddie tried for everything he could reach, and he could reach a long way. In 1954 and 1955 he led all third basemen in the league in the number of assists, and in 1954 he started more double plays than any other hot-spot man on the circuit.

Milwaukee, led by Eddie's long home runs, kept getting closer to beating the Dodgers to the top of the league. In 1956 they missed by only one game, and in 1957 they made it. Eddie, who had batted .292 that season and hit 32 home runs, set no records in his first World Series, but he won the fourth game with his two-run home run in the last of the tenth inning, after pinch hitter Nippy Jones had talked his way on to the bases by showing the umpire the shoe blacking on a ball that proved he had been hit with it. Nippy's runner, Mantilla, scored the tying run when Johnny Logan doubled. And Eddie Mathews brought Johnny home with his homer. Eddie also went a long way toward settling the Yankees' hash in the final game, when he drove in two runs with a double.

After that victory the merry Braves flew home to the wildest celebration young Eddie had ever seen. The heroes were met at the airport by a screaming mob which acted as if the rest of the world had surrendered to Milwaukee. The main street of the town was closed to all traffic so that barrels of beer might be rolled out for all to dip into. The singing, the playing of music, the clashing of metal against metal, the squawking of radios, the drunken yelling and dancing and dumping of paper into the street went on all night, and Eddie vowed he had landed at last in the nation's greatest baseball town.

In the next World Series when Milwaukee met the Yanks again and really should have beaten them (they led the Series, 3 games to 1, when it came back to Milwaukee), Eddie made hardly a splash. In the regular season his batting average had dropped off to .251, the lowest it had been since he left Boston, and his total of 31 home runs (good enough to place him third in the league) was also his low mark since he hit 25 in his rookie year. Next year Eddie took a grip on himself and had one of the best seasons of his life, with 46 home runs and a batting average of .306. The Braves, however, fell two games short of taking the pennant. And Eddie began to find a few worms in the Milwaukee apple. An arrest for speeding got more attention from the press than he thought it merited. And then a "misquotation" in a Milwaukee paper, or the quote of an idle, offhand remark to a newswriter, put Eddie in bad odor with *everyone* for a while. (He said, "I guess we're pretty tired," to a sports reporter and the reporter made it sound like an abandonment of all hope of winning.)

So Eddie, who was no griper or sourpuss, made a habit for a while of not talking to sportswriters at all—and that's about the worst crime any athlete can commit. So, despite his steady beating out of long base hits and his slick labor with his glove (he kept on showing the way in starting double plays), Eddie, for a time, was no hero at home. Not being the blowtop or the brooding type, however, Eddie did not turn his irritations into a grudge fight, nor did he grab headlines with public tantrums or wholesale accusations.

It was an oddity of the 1950s and early 1960s that the two top personalities in the game—Ted Williams and Mickey Mantle (Joe DiMaggio having faded quickly after the war) —should be men whose self-esteem required constant violent protection through assaults on water coolers, slamming of bats, kicking of helmets, and loosing of foul words upon the circumambient air.

Eddie Mathews was no such type as *that*, nor was he quite in the Mantle-Williams league as a hitter or a public personality. Never in his career did he attain a higher average than .306. But he remained a good, reliable worker at the plate and in the field, a man on whom you could anchor a solid infield, and a hitter who was always a threat to drive in all the runs on base or win a game with one swing.

And speaking of hitters whose names begin with M, no one can ignore that long-legged, sad-faced, and gentle-mannered young man who, like Hank Aaron, grew up in Mobile, Alabama—Willie McCovey, sometimes called "Stretch," who might have been a basketball star if he had not hurt his knees. Big, broad-shouldered, and strong, Willie was sometimes considered slow and a poor fielder, but he was neither. A bad knee and foot cut down his mobility in mid-career. And he had a manager who accused him of dogging it when he was really injured. But Willie could dig hard throws out of the dirt with the best of them, and he saved many an infielder from an error through his skill at reaching a long, long way for a bad throw. And Willie, before he hurt his knee, could do the 100 yards in 10 seconds, in his baseball togs.

But Willie would have held a job on his hitting, regardless. When he joined the Giants in midseason 1959, after four years in the minors, he made four hits in his first game. His batting average that season, when he was named Rookie of the Year, was .354. He hit 13 home runs.

Willie had smashed up his knee while playing in Dallas two years earlier, trying to score from third on a slow ground ball. After his first season with the Giants, the club had his knee operated on and shipped him to Tacoma so he could work himself into shape. The Giants already had a 1958 Rookie of the Year, Orlando Cepeda, playing first base. Willie came back to San Francisco, split the first base job with Cepeda, and did a lot of pinch-hitting. His average fell off from that big first season, but he knocked in 51 runs.

From then on Willie made a sort of career out of almost being a hero. Hitting ahead of Willie Mays he was not often awarded a walk. In the play-offs with the Dodgers in 1962, however, with the clubs tied at two games each, Willie came up in the ninth when a home run would have won the pennant. But Willie got a walk, and Mays hit a homer to drive him in with the score that took the prize.

Then in the World Series against the Yankees, McCovey again qualified as a hard-luck hero, when he came to bat in the ninth inning of the seventh game with two out, two runners on base, and the Yankees leading 1 to 0. With the count on Willie one ball and one strike, he hit "the hardest drive I ever hit in my life"—a "game-winning blow" for certain, well over the second baseman's head, and destined for deepest right-center field. But Bobby Richardson, in a leap that just about every other infielder in the league would have found impossible, rocketed himself into the air at the precise moment, flung his glove up as high as it would reach, and brought it down with the third out and the World Championship in it.

Earlier Willie had walloped a ball high and far toward the right-field barrier that would have turned the ball game into a tie. But there was a high

Johnny Mize, counted as all through in the National League, was hired by the New York Yankees chiefly to do this job: pinch-hitting a home run to put the Yankees ahead in a World Series game. New York vs. Brooklyn, 1952.

Yankee hero Mickey Mantle uses every muscle in his body as he drives a ball into the outfield in a game with the California Angels in 1968.

wind beating in off the bay that took hold of the ball and hung it up in the air like a seagull until the steam had gone out of it. Then the ball dropped on the field for a triple.

Willie's hard luck extended to his physical condition, too. His knees continued to betray him, until he had enough calcium deposits in both to lay bricks with. In 1965 he banged up a knee again and found his speed and range cut down further. Before long he had developed a painful inflammation in his left foot. But nothing could keep McCovey sidelined for long. A special ripple sole was created to make it possible for him to play without pain, and Willie went right on driving in runs— more than 100 a year for three years in a row.

Hard work, discipline, ambition— these had been built into Willie's style of life from his earliest days. His father had not been an athlete; indeed, he cared nothing for baseball or sports of any kind. (Willie was the only real athlete in the family.) But his father had been a strict man, who accepted no back talk and saw to it that every member of the big family carried his proper share of the load. Like Willie himself, Willie's father was a man of relatively few words. But when he had words to utter, the children listened.

And Willie learned early what it meant to work for a living. He won letters in three major sports in high school, but he also won minor letters—had such things been awarded—in delivering newspapers after school and in working as a dough-roller in a cracker factory. Willie had just about given up hope of getting into professional baseball when he finished high school. He pitched and played first base for an organized softball team in Mobile. Then having graduated from high school, he took a trip to Los Angeles to visit his brother. He had made up his mind that he would never go back East, when he got word from home that the Giants wanted him to come to their tryout camp in Florida. Willie refused to believe they meant it, until they sent him his plane ticket. Then he went back and became a ballplayer for life.

Gimpy legs, bad foot, injured hand and all, Willie consistently hit home runs and cleaned runners off the bases. In 1969 with 45 home runs, 126 runs batted in, and an average of .320, Willie became Most Valuable Player. In 1971 when the Giants were headed for the play-offs, Willie was nursing a new knee injury. His average fell off to .277 and he could manage only 18 home runs. But in the play-offs with the Pirates, Willie again just missed dragging his club by main strength over the finish line first. Willie's long home run in the fifth inning of the first game put the Giants so far ahead (5 to 1) that the Pirates could not match them. But the Pirates took the next two games. In the fourth game Willie struggled to keep the Pirates from taking the pennant. He drove in the first Giant run in the first inning. Then in the second inning, with the score tied 2 to 2 and two runners on base, Willie brought everybody home with one of his long, long home runs. (It looked, some said, not as if it was merely going out of the park, but out of town. It landed among the workmen who were building the stands a little higher.) This put the Giants ahead 5 to 2, but the Pirates then collected 7 runs and took the flag. Altogether in the play-offs, Willie, in 14 times at bat, made 6 hits and drove in 6 of the 15 runs the Giants scored.

How great McCovey might be if he were always sound, there is no knowing. He surely would be more mobile without the brace he has to wear to keep his knee from collapsing. And he might possibly have played with a better heart, if for four seasons he had not had to suffer the prejudices of a Southern-type manager, who assumed that Willie, like all "darkies," was just pretending to be hurt so as to get more time to loaf on the bench. ("Imagine my not wanting to play!" Willie would comment quietly, in later years.) In the early weeks of the 1973 season, McCovey, physically sound again, hit 4 home runs in 7 games, and drove in 7 runs.

If a man were to check back in the alphabet to count the hitters whose names began with K, for example, he would have found, through the 1950s and 1960s, an array of sluggers of fame almost as mighty as the Ms. For there were Kiner, Kluszewski, Kaline, and Killebrew, any one of whom could scare a pitcher out of his pants. Of these all but Al Kaline had a crack at leading their leagues in home runs. And Kaline, who suffered as many injuries as McCovey did, once led his league in doubles.

Ralph Kiner, who became a broadcaster for the New York Mets, had a relatively short career—only ten years. But he crowded a lot of action into that period. After joining the Pittsburgh Pirates in 1946, he led the National League in home runs for seven seasons in a row. It is true that the Pirates' owners had "adjusted" the dimensions of the park a little by moving in the left-field fence to provide a garden where home runs might grow. But Kiner still drove some mighty good pitches on some mighty long rides. He also drove in 100 runs or better in six different seasons. Twice he hit more than 50 home runs (51 in 1947, 54 in 1949). The fact that his batting average never exceeded .313 and only three times exceeded .300 did not trouble him. "Home run hitters," he once said, "drive Cadillacs."

As for Al Kaline he may have driven a Cadillac on occasion (although he did once turn down a raise in salary), but he hit relatively few home runs, and the Detroit management never found itself ordering the builders out to bring a fence in closer for Al's sake. Kaline, a Baltimore boy who started his major league career in Detroit, was more interested in base hits. In his second full year with Detroit, when he was twenty-one years old, he won the league batting title with an average of .340. He also drove in 102 runs. But he has never hit more than 29 home runs in a season.

Kaline also has always concentrated on fielding his position with skill and speed. Most sluggers of the postwar era had no fielding pretensions at all. Al Kaline won the Golden Glove award for his fielding skills ten times. (Some rival batsmen often looked as if they had borrowed one of the metal gloves to field throws with.) Al owned one of the strongest throwing arms in baseball and long stood among the leaders in throwing base runners out from right field. In 1958 he even beat out Roberto Clemente in that department.

In 1971 despite the fact that Kaline had not been as strong at the bat as usual, the management, conscious of his many years of unremitting and unprotesting effort and his willingness to play wherever the boss might decide to send him (even third base!), offered Al a contract with a $100,000 salary attached. Al said no, he did not deserve it—yet. Then he led his club in batting that season and agreed to take the higher salary for 1972.

Al Kaline's only World Series to date came in 1968, the year he missed six weeks because of a broken arm. As the end of the season approached and the World Series seemed a possibility, Al did not feel he "deserved" a chance in the Series. The other guys had been going so well, while he had been riding the bench. But in the final week of the season, Kaline came back to run pitcher after pitcher right out of the park. He made at least two hits a day, sometimes four. He decided then that he did deserve a shot at the Series and went in and led both clubs at bat with an average of .379—six runs scored and eight runs batted in. He was then very close to his thirty-fourth birthday and had completed sixteen seasons with Detroit.

Harmon Killebrew, when he entered baseball (having been "scouted" by his state's senator), looked like a throwback to the days when home run hitters were all chest and shoulders and thick arms. The Killer was not a short man, but he was so solid and so broad that he gave the impression of being somewhat squat. (When he started at Washington, he was 6 feet tall and weighed 195 pounds.) It was also assumed that he was not much of a fielder, nor did anyone expect him to be. In his first full season, 1959, he managed to lead the league in errors at third base. (He also led the league in home runs.) Before he was much older, however, he had turned himself into a better than adequate infielder, partic-

ularly at first base. And he was the sort of player who would take any job that was thrust on him. No one else in baseball has yet played, as Killebrew has, three different positions in three different All-Star games.

Other hitters have sometimes seen their hitting decline when given a new job to learn. Not Killebrew. Always calm, willing, and determined, he has consistently placed himself among the home run leaders, with 40 home runs or better in 8 of his 9 years in the major leagues.

Ted Kluszewski may not have had mightier muscles than Killebrew, but he had more of them, and he had them sooner. His arms were so enormous that it was almost impossible to fit him to a shirt that would not split at the seams when he swung his bat. So the Great Klu used to chop his sleeves off at the shoulder to give his biceps a chance to breathe. A left-hander who stood 6 feet 2 inches and weighed 225 pounds, when he was trimmed down, Klu never matched the home run production of Killebrew or Kiner. But he did dent fences and break seat slats with the force of his wallops often enough to make National League pitchers all wish he would go work off his frustrations in some other yard. He also got a piece of the ball more often, for example, than Killebrew did, for he usually managed to collect fewer strikeouts than bases on balls. Killebrew once led the league in strikeouts, and in his first dozen seasons, he almost always struck out more times than he walked. (Ultimately, he learned to lead the league in walks.)

Klu became a home run hitter so suddenly that it startled him. He had long made a study of batting, particularly his

own. With an almost religious devotion, he would pore over films his wife
had taken of Klu in the batter's box.
And when he went into a slump, as he
often did, he would study these films
minutely until he saw what he was
doing wrong. But then, one season,
instead of going into a slump, he went
into sudden orbit. In 1952 he hit 16
home runs. (In 1950 he had hit 25, tops
for his six seasons in the majors.) Then
in 1954 he hit 40. The next year he
hit his league-leading 49, and in 1956
he hit 47.

What happened? Klu asked himself.
He hadn't been doing anything different
that he knew of. He had always hit a
lot of two-baggers, and one season
made 11 triples. But when he started
putting balls out of the playing field,
his doubles fell off, and his triples
shrank to zero. And no amount of
studying of his films ever revealed the
secret. Klu was not a wrist hitter, like
so many of the new era sluggers. He
was almost too musclebound to get that
kind of quick snap into his forearms.
But he turned himself partly away from
the pitch, with his forward foot almost
on the plate and got his pulling power
from the fierce pivot of his body as he
swung his front foot around into the
pitch.

Klu got his growth early and might
very well have been a football star of
the Nagurski type. He was attending
Indiana University on a football scholarship, won by his great deeds as
a high school end, had already won a
place on the All-Big-Ten team, and was
playing baseball chiefly to stay in condition when Bill McKechnie, manager
of the Cincinnati club, saw him driving
baseballs out of sight and signed him
to a contract. Klu left college at the end

of his sophomore year and joined the
Columbia club in the South Atlantic
League, for which he played first base
and outfield and led the league in hitting. Next spring he showed up at the
Cincinnati training camp and gave Bill
McKechnie a few bad moments by
catching a throw to first in his bare
hand. He had not learned how to shift
his feet and get his glove hand into position. But before the season was over
(he spent most of it in Memphis), Klu's
fielding had become slick enough to
win his manager's admiration. And his
batting in the Southern Association was
good enough to lead the league. In ten
at-bats with the Reds, he made one hit.
But next season he made more than 100
and the year after that, he batted .309.

Ted put in eleven seasons with Cincinnati and won many ball games there.
He never did quite attain the spectacular
heights he reached in the minors, where
he once made eleven hits in thirteen
successive times at bat. But he was
tough enough so that he was sometimes
given a base on balls with the bases
empty. Perhaps his greatest moment in
the majors came after he had been
traded to Pittsburgh, then to Chicago,
and got into his first World Series in
1959.

In 1959 the Dodgers were again in
the World Series. But now it was the
Los Angeles Dodgers, who had left
their fans forlorn beside the Gowanus
Canal, requiring them to sit up until the
smallest hours of the morning sometimes to follow the doings of their
absent heroes—Duke Snider, Carl Furillo, Gil Hodges, Junior Gilliam—on
the midnight radio. And the enemy
in this Series was the Chicago
White Sox, a club that most Brooklyn
fans would once hardly have allowed

The other ''M'' in the New York Yankees M & M combination, Roger Maris, puts one more home run into the right-field stands at Yankee Stadium, to move him closer to his record-setting 61. New York, 1961.

to share the same thought wave with their heroes. But the Brooklyn fans knew Ted Kluszewski and knew little good of him, for he had been wont to rattle hits off the concrete walls of Ebbets Field in his greener days. And in this Series Ted very nearly did their vagrant heroes down.

Kluszewski, in 1959, was thirty-five years old, still suffering, some thought, from the back injury that had turned him into a part-time performer in 1957 and prompted his being dealt off to Pittsburgh. After that injury he never hit .300 again. He was mostly a pinch hitter now, and his home run totals had

shriveled nearly out of sight. But when the first game of the World Series between Los Angeles and Chicago was played in Comiskey Park, Ted promptly turned the game into a laugher, which seemed to foreshadow humiliating defeat for the pride of the National League.

This was the first World Series in Comiskey Park since the Black Sox Series of 1919, so White Sox fans were ravening for just such a slaughter as this. And they rejoiced especially in Big Ted, who had been rescued from the other league just in time to become eligible for the Series. In the first in-

Juan Marichal, big man of the San Francisco Giants' pitching staff, rears back like the walking-beam on a riverboat to strike fear into the heart of a batter. Second baseman Ron Hunt, in the background, experiments with bubble gum.

ning, against rookie Roger Craig, Ted warmed up with a single that drove in a run. When he came up again in the third inning, big Ted whistled a home run into the right-field stands to drive in two more runs and make the score 5 to 0. The White Sox then followed Klu's example by destroying a succession of relief pitchers. In the fourth inning, the club having batted all the way around, Ted got another time at bat. And he improved this one by sending a longer, harder, higher blow deep into the upper tier in right, to make the score 11 to 0.

Happily for the Dodgers the Sox had only one Kluszewski, and so the Los Angeles club was soon able to get back on the track, thanks partly to a bit of mistaken strategy on the part of White Sox manager Al Lopez. For after big Klu had started the second game right off with a single again and had scored a run and had singled once more to put another run on base, Lopez let a man run for him. Klu's runner scored easily on a double by Al Smith. But the man who had singled behind Klu was another slowfoot, catcher Sherm Lollar, and he was thrown out at the plate. *He* was the man who needed the pinch runner. And now there was no Klu in the game to get that run back.

The third game was played in Los Angeles, where Klu and his mates performed before the biggest crowd (to that time) that had ever watched a baseball game—92,394. (Even bigger crowds saw the next two games.) And once more Klu got on base and scored (this time without the help of a pinch runner). The rest of the Sox hit hard enough to have won the game, but they did not hit at strategic intervals, so not enough runs were fashioned.

In the fourth game Klu once more drove in a run with a single in the seventh inning and once more he scored—this time with a Sherm Lollar home run to propel him along. But once more the rest of the White Sox failed him. The Sox pitchers, however—three of them, not one of whom allowed a run—took the fifth game all by themselves and needed no help from Klu in the building of the only run the White Sox scored.

The sixth game was played in Comiskey Park again, before a horde of fans who had only a faint hope to sustain them. Klu was wound up for this game and ready to win it. But the Sox had no pitchers left who could stay the Dodgers. When Ted came to bat for the second time, the Dodgers were already ahead 8 to 0. Seeing two men on base ahead of him, Ted dutifully drove a pitch into the stands to make it 8 to 3. But it availed the Sox nothing for Walter Alston brought in Larry Sherry, who had saved all the other games, and he saved this one, too.

Ted went on a couple of seasons later to play in Los Angeles for the expansion team that became the California Angels. Here he played with somewhat more regularity and got his home run total back into double figures (15) again. But the Chicago World Series had marked the true finale to his days of glory.

It might be argued that there were Ms among the pitchers, too, who threw with as much power, through the 1950s and 1960s, as some of the great sluggers swung their bats. For these were the days of McDowell, Marichal, and McLain, to say nothing of Dave McNally.

Sam McDowell pitched in Cleveland,

where Robert Feller worked and won for so many years, and where since the days of mighty Cy Young, high-speed pitchers had long been a specialty. McDowell started with the club in 1961, when he pitched part of a ball game, just ten years after Bob Feller had pitched his last great season there. (Bob hung on until 1956, not having laid up a stake large enough for him to lie back on, but he never again approached the 22 wins he posted in 1951.) There were those among the day's great hitters who declared that McDowell's fast ball would have beaten Feller's to the plate. But not many of them had known Bob Feller when he was pouring in the pitches that set strikeout records for him. Still, McDowell was whistling fast and so was the man who came between Feller

and McDowell, Herb Score, whose ability was lamed when a line drive took him in the eye and started his career downhill. McDowell came closer to Feller in number of strikeouts in a season. But neither McDowell nor Score ever approached gentle Robert in the number of times they sent the enemy home without a single run.

Juan Marichal, from the Dominican Republic, later a teammate of McDowell's on the Giants, was, for a time, the highest-paid pitcher in the game and for a time, too, he looked like the best. He has not attained the staggering strikeout totals that Feller posted, nor even matched McDowell there. But he is close to Feller in shutouts and far outshines Score and McDowell in control. Despite the tremendous stride he takes and the lifted

Left-handed pitcher Dave McNally of the Baltimore Orioles, whom his former manager Hank Bauer named the best curve-ball pitcher in the league, is shown here trying out his fastball. Baltimore at Kansas City, 1969.

front foot that seems to reach higher than his head and even shut out his view of the batter, Juan invariably strikes out many more than he walks and keeps the baselines scantily populated. By the end of the 1971 season, he had thrown 50 shutouts in a twelve-season career. (In 1965 he shut out the New York Mets five times.)

Marichal does not throw as fast as a few of his great contemporaries. But he throws hard enough to unsettle most batters, and his high kick, developed after he signed with the Giants, keeps the hitter from getting his eye on the ball until it is sizzling toward the plate. Juan's real strength lies in his ability to control a whole cupboard full of pitches—fastball, sharp curve, slider, and change-up. His weakness, and the weakness that has kept him from

becoming the ultimate pitcher, is his proclivity for getting hurt. He has had a groin injury, a sprained ankle, a bum leg, and once had a finger jammed in a car door. And big Juan may be the only pitcher who had a season spoiled when he injured somebody else.

In 1965 when the Dodgers faced the Giants at Candlestick Park on the twenty-second of August, after a day of high-pitched bench-jockeying that had both sides burning, Marichal came to bat and swapped rude remarks with John Roseboro, the Los Angeles catcher. Roseboro, Juan insisted afterward, made as if to leap upon Juan.

And Juan simply swung down with the bat and raised a lump on Roseboro's skull. The screams that arose from the field and bench would have frightened off a squad of Martian invaders. Everybody in a Los Angeles uniform converged on Juan to take his bat away and beat him with it. But Willie Mays, who is about as strong a man as the game has seen, pulled enemies apart and kept Giant and Dodger from laying about each other with 35-ounce maces.

No one, however, was in a mood to forgive Juan Marichal for having been so lost to the traditions of the game as to attempt to break a man's skull, rather than his jaw. The umpire damned Juan in his report, whereupon the league fined him more than $1,500 and kept him off the diamond long enough for him to miss a turn or two on the mound. When Juan came back to work, he seemed to lack a little of his competitive zest, for he lost games with leading contenders, the very enemies he had always handled most easily. And it was his failure that seemed to cost the Giants the flag.

Men wondered aloud then if perhaps Juan had had his self-esteem shaken by this eruption of what, in this country, was deemed a most unmanly impulse (unless, of course, it was unleashed against long-haired peaceniks, homosexuals, or other obviously noncombative types). Juan laughed almost merrily when he heard this. In the Dominican Republic, where Juan had been bred, a man was *expected* to defend himself with whatever weapon came to hand. But when, in later games with the Dodgers, Juan was roughed up a bit on the baselines in memory of the Roseboro battle, he began to wonder. He loved baseball all right. But some-

Harmon Killebrew's level swing earned him two home runs in this 1959 game between Killebrew's Washington Senators and the New York Yankees. The dust spurts as Harmon attacks the pitch with a forward stride.

times, he allowed, "It is not so much fun."

Juan soon recovered his appetite for outwitting batters. (He had, perhaps, a better "book" on all his opponents than most catchers owned and seldom failed to feed a batter the pitch he was most likely to go out on.) And he retained his determination to earn the highest salary in baseball. And he also retained his skill with the bat, which often made him a better run-batter-in than some of the top outfielders.

As for Dave McNally, he was no fireball specialist either. But he, too, owned an assortment of pitches and could put them all through the strike zone, if not exactly at will, at least often enough to keep him winning more games than he lost each season. His best pitch was his curve ball. He was, said his one-time manager, Hank Bauer, the best curve-ball pitcher in the American League. At least he was in 1966 when the Orioles won their first major league pennant since the previous century, when they—or a team with their name—had adorned the other league.

As for Dennis McLain, he seemed to have assured himself a twenty-year career in the major leagues by winning 31 games for Detroit in 1968. (He also made good in the traditional American way by marrying the boss's daughter—except that it was the wrong boss. His father-in-law was Lou Boudreau, former manager of the Cleveland

Indians.) Dennis, a young man of great personal charm and unstable temperament, threw a baseball with about as much velocity as any pitcher living fans had ever seen. He was reputedly as fast as Bob Feller or Lefty Grove. In 1968 he struck out 280 batters.

But Dennis was no strong-armed country boy who lived from one pitching chore to the next. He squeezed all the income he could out of his pitching arm and packed all the excitement he could manage into his off hours. He moonlighted as a nightclub musician, bought himself a private airplane, and always seemed to be hastening from one emergency appointment to the next —forgetting all the appointments in between. More than once friends and family had to enlist outside aid to run Dennis down, occasionally finding him several hundred miles from where he was supposed to be. Once he abandoned a teammate at the airport, after promising the man a ride home in the McLain jet. Dennis sought the extra dollar wherever it grew, not always recking where his search would lead him or among what strange company. While his fame still echoed through the land, he found himself near bankruptcy from trying to make three dollars grow where there was scarce room for one. He also found himself disgraced and suspended after it came out that one of his "business" projects was financing a bookmaking operation. (On the basis, apparently, that he had not made any profits on the deal, McLain was merely suspended by Commissioner Kuhn for a misdeed that might have meant life-long ineligibility for a player of less renown or less gate appeal.)

After his downfall McLain seemed to lose his pitching skills, or his concentration, and seemed ready to tumble out of organized baseball for good. In 1971 he put in an unhappy and unsuccessful year with Ted Williams' Texas Rangers (they had been the Washington Senators when Dennis came aboard). He lost 22 of the 32 games he started, completing only nine of them. Dennis was not a man to nestle comfortably under the wing of as tough and intractable a bird as Ted Williams, particularly when he was falling so far short of what the boss had expected. It seemed like the dawn of a new day for Dennis when he was traded to that swinging outfit in Oakland, where Charley Finley may have dreamed McLain would turn Vida Blue into a faded memory. But Dennis just could not find his groove there at all. He won a single game, lost two, posted an earned run average in excess of six runs per nine-inning game, and was summarily shipped to Atlanta, where he did little better. As the season ended, however, Dennis was assuring himself and others that he had grown up at last and would soon have that ball humming in a style befitting the only thirty-game winner the majors had known since Dizzy Dean. Alas, hardly anyone outside of Dennis and his immediate family really believed him. Before the 1973 season began, Dennis had been awarded his unconditional release. He was twenty-eight years old.

Seemingly ageless Al Kaline, Detroit's $100,000 outfielder, shows his age as he raises his hands to ward off a wild relay from the outfield while scoring on a fly. Yankee Stadium, 1968.

Concerning Old Men, Miracles, Some Orioles, and a Crow

THE 1960s were full of portents. First of all, the invincible New York Yankees, having won their twenty-fifth pennant, lost a World Series (1960) on a crazy bounce—a World Series in which they had set new records by scoring 55 runs against only 27 for the Pittsburghs, making 91 hits against a Pirate total of 60, and posting a top team batting average for a seven-game series: .338. The Yankees also set a new "slugging" mark of .528 with 10 home runs and 17 other extra-base hits.

Bobby Richardson, veteran New York second baseman, long an exponent of a clean life and a modest batting average (he had hit .252 that season), turned tiger in the Series and set some marks of his own: He batted in 12 runs in the Series and pushed over 6 in one game. In game three he hit a home run with the bases full. Yet despite all this, the Pirates won the Series when an obvious double-play ball, hit straight at Yankee shortstop Tony Kubek by Pittsburgh's Bill Virdon, hit a pebble, the devil's toenail, or some such thing, and struck poor Tony right in the throat, knocking him out of the game and placing two men on base, who soon came in along with three others to put the Pirates ahead when they should have been out.

On their way home from Pittsburgh, after glumly watching Bill Mazeroski win the championship for Pittsburgh with a ninth-inning home run, the Yankee brass decided between themselves that *somebody* was getting too old. It couldn't be themselves, for they were in the pride of their middle age. So it had to be Casey Stengel, the man who ran the club on the field, and George Weiss, the man who ran the operation from the inner office. So these two old men were fired—and remained in New York to haunt the Yankees almost clean out of existence. Fortunately, the Yankee owners, who felt sure they had now got the hang of running the team themselves, did not follow their first impulse of also trading off pitcher Whitey Ford, who had won two games in the Series but had also been carrying the pitcher to the well for a good many years and perhaps could be traded off for a whole trainload of rookies, who would guarantee another dozen championships.

But championships, the Yankees learned, are not always so easily contrived. With the players Weiss had gathered for them, the Yankees won four more championships, then abruptly came apart. They had dropped out of immediate contention before, but this time they dropped right out of the first division and wore the look and posture of cellar-dwellers throughout the rest of the decade.

Elsewhere, while balls still took bad bounces, there were brighter signs in the heavens. Expansion of the leagues brought new clubs to California and Minnesota, where for the first time since anyone could say different, baseball teams were named after the states. And in Baltimore, where major league baseball had come back after an absence of more than fifty years, a new set of champions appeared and looked,

for a time, as if they might assume the Yankee scepter.

Old Yankee fans drew some comfort from the fact that this new flight of Baltimore Orioles was led by a former favorite, Hank Bauer, of Prairie Village, Kansas, who had long worn the pinstripes of New York. Hank, a tough-looking, softhearted, and gentle-mannered man who smoked cigarettes by the ton as a player, had often sat growling on the Yankee bench when he had been "platooned" out of the outfield, for he loved the game with an old-fashioned devotion and counted every minute lost when he was not out trying to do down the enemy. He may not have been sharp-tongued enough or sufficiently iron-fisted to whip a band of high-salaried stars into line. But in 1966 he was exactly what the Orioles required to set them all winning together.

They were not, however, supposed to win the World Series. Instead, they were counted lucky to be on the same field with the Los Angeles Dodgers who, everyone granted, had the best team in baseball—and certainly the best pair of pitchers in Koufax and Drysdale. And while the Orioles may have had the best curve-ball pitcher in their league, Dave McNally, they had no 20-game winners. And their bullpen consisted of somebody's next door neighbor named Moe Drabowsky, or was it Grabowski? Hardly anyone knew for sure. On the strength of their pitching, the Dodgers were odds-on favorites to win the Series and were given a strong chance to take it in four games. As for the Orioles, the odds were 20 to 1 against their winning four in a row. "But *our* pitchers," Hank Bauer kept protesting, "are not all that bad!"

(When it was over, Hank was heard to mumble, "I didn't think our pitchers were all that *good!*")

As a matter of fact, all the pitchers were good. But none was better than Moe Drabowsky, who walked practically unheralded into the first game in the third inning, struck out eleven men (a new World Series record for a relief pitcher), allowed but one hit, and gave up no earned runs. Moe, who had been passed from club to club in the opposite league in previous seasons like a jobless and aging uncle, had not even figured in the pregame expert analysis of the opposing forces. He was pictured as the guy who might come in and hold the franchise for an inning or two while Koufax or Drysdale was throwing a near no-hitter. Instead, he looked like the class of both leagues.

And the Orioles, like the Yankee clubs Hank Bauer had played on, drove the baseball out of the lot often enough to keep their side ahead. In the first game, played in Los Angeles, the Orioles scored five runs—more runs than the Dodgers had given up in all the home World Series games they had played in 1963 and 1965 together. And both of the home runs were hit by men named Robinson; one, Frank, a castoff from the National League, where he had once been Most Valuable Player and then exiled for setting too high a value on himself. In the American League, where he was supposedly ready to rust away quietly and then drop to the grass, he drove himself as if he were doing penance, carried his bat with him nearly everywhere he went, and studied ways to make himself Most Valuable Player in the new league. In this aim he succeeded, as he succeeded in adding the power and punch a club needs to fight its way to the pennant.

The other Robinson, a slender, balding fellow named Brooks, hit hard, too, and performed miracles of agility at third base. But the Series was not a hitter's one. Even the Dodger pitching was thrifty, with low-ranked Claude Osteen allowing the Orioles but three hits and one base on balls in the third game. Baltimore's Wallace Bunker, however—rated even lower than Osteen because he had toiled all year with an injured elbow—still managed to keep the Dodgers from crossing the plate. Bunker could not throw a curve. But whatever he did throw was a mystery to the mighty men from California, who did not score a single run after the first game was over. And the winning club achieved a team batting average of .200. Hank Bauer had never seen the likes of that with the Yankees.

There must have been some eerie influence at work other than hitters and pitchers in this Series, however. The second game, lost by sore-armed Sandy Koufax, who gave up only six hits, was thrown away, 6 to 0, by the Dodgers because reliable Willie Davis lost *two* fly balls in the sun in the same inning. The October sun is always a menace in the World Series, for it shines low and straight into outfielders' eyes. But surely Willie had seen it before and caught flies in it. He stood there, all the same, the sun glinting off his dark glasses, and let both flies strike him somewhere near the hands. And then, to make it clear that some malign spirit was busy such as had misdirected the ball that struck Kubek's Adam's apple in the 1960 Series, reliable Willie let fly a throw that almost carried into the stands. Other Dodgers also sought out ways to give unearned runs to the

Orioles. In addition to the three contributed by Willie, Jim Gilliam, Ron Fairly, and Ron Perranoski each added an error. Gilliam might easily have been charged with two, for Jim fought a silent battle with the very first hit in the game, beating it about as if trying to stun it and then letting it run free. The official scorer generously overlooked this interruption and called it a hit.

The Dodgers, and the semiprofessional seers of the sport, never gave up hope. How could a great Los Angeles team lose to a bunch of untried, sore-armed, or outworn pitchers such as this—to the likes of twenty-year-old Jim Palmer, twenty-one-year-old Wally Bunker, and one-hundred-year-old Moe Drabowsky? Dave McNally, the prize of the Oriole staff, had been touched for two runs by the Dodgers. When they got him back home, for the seventh game, they'd score a bushel. But in his second outing Dave had his fast curve working better than ever, and the Dodgers could scrape off only four hits among them and no runs at all. So the Dodgers, too, set a record for the Series, thirty-three scoreless innings in a row. Not since the days of Christy Mathewson and Iron Man McGinnity in the World Series of 1905 had any club gone through three full games in one World Series without scoring.

But this Miracle of the Birds was soon diminished by the Miracle of the Resurgent Red Sox. The Orioles had been given a chance for the 1966 pennant. The Boston Red Sox, at the beginning of the 1967 season, were given no chance for the championship at all. Indeed, more than one reader of baseball rolls had picked them to finish last. And the club itself, it seemed,

fought hard against coming in first, backing away from the flag like a bashful freshman at the door of the senior prom, until the other contenders simply outstumbled them.

The Red Sox grew stronger in the mid-1960s through the promotion of several able rookies from their Toronto farm club. In 1967 they brought Toronto Manager Dick Williams up to take charge of the brood he had hatched. And in the long line of Red Sox managers, some of whom had tried the job twice, and some of whom had been fired or run away to hide in mid-season, Dick was something else. He was sharp-tongued, sarcastic, given to open faultfinding, threats of condign punishment, and rather reckless name-calling. In short, he was exactly the type the romping Red Sox could cotton to the least. The Boston clubhouse had always been one where ballplayers felt safe from harsh criticism or generalized whip-cracking. Managers who had dealt too harshly with some of the Boston stars had occasionally found their whip hands restrained by Papa Yawkey, the kindly club owner, a man who disliked controversy, loved baseball players, and never wanted to see one of his heroes put down. Dick Williams also acquired an unhappy habit of blaming the sportswriters for misquoting him whenever one of his more intemperate observations was printed as it stood, so there were mutterings against him in several quarters early in the year. For all these reasons, plus the fact that some of the 1966 stars showed up overweight, the Bostons seemed less likely than ever to climb higher than ninth in a 10-team league.

The Sox began the miracle year in "the best physical shape ever," accord-

Ballplayers who faced Cleveland left-hander Sam McDowell said he threw gumballs or aspirin tablets. Here he is on the way to 15 strikeouts in a game against the Chicago White Sox in 1970. Cleveland still lost the game 2 to 1.

ing to Dick Williams' coaches. The nine men who started the first game of the regular season averaged just twenty-four years of age, the youngest crew any local fan could recall. They were also just about the most fleet of foot. While the training season had not been entirely full of promise (the "big" pitching prospect of the spring, Jerry Stephenson, was an early flop), there had been intimations of championship all the same. A tall kid named Lonborg had pitched seven great innings in relief against the Yankees in an exhibition game. (He had also driven the umpires half bughouse with his sinker ball.) And the "kid shortstop," Rico Petrocelli, was rated no less than "superb" by the self-assigned appraisers of baseball talent. A youngster named Billy Rohr, in an exhibition game against Detroit, surprised everyone—and particularly his own manager—by pitching the whole game and beating Detroit, 4 to 1. So he was chosen to open the regular season against the Yankees.

After a sleepless night, Billy thereupon won his first major league start with a one-hitter, was immediately acclaimed best in the league, and collected a fat fee for exhibiting his shy countenance on the "Ed Sullivan Show." The Boston newspapers (there were still several alive in that city) thereupon proclaimed in front-page streamers that "*This* is next year!"

Within a few weeks most of the sportswriters agreed they had celebrated too soon. If there was such a thing as playing an entire season in one month, the Red Sox managed it. A few of the lean and well-trained rookies, notably a big first baseman named George Scott, began to pack small extra amounts of fatty tissue around their middles, as Red Sox players had long had the habit of doing. Joe Foy, the third baseman, weighed in 10 pounds above his ideal figure. And Jerry Stephenson, the no-longer-promising pitcher, took 18 pounds extra out to the mound (and also resumed his annoying habit of "running off to Anaheim" whenever he had a few days off).

The great hitters did hit hard occasionally, but they did not win. In an eighteen-inning game against the Yankees, Carl Yastrzemski and Tony Conigliaro collected five hits apiece. But the club still finished one run behind. Dick Williams promptly blasted every man in sight—and repeated to the sportswriters every angry word he had uttered. He scolded Jim Lonborg for throwing the ball "right down the pipe" with a two-strike count and the bases loaded. He allowed that Scott had cement in his head for swinging at a pitch after being given the "take" sign. But Williams was not exhibiting much genius himself. For obscure reasons he had played George Scott in the outfield, where the big man had nearly ended his career by running full tilt into a fence. And he had insisted Reggie Smith was a second baseman, even though Reggie came out of every game looking like a loser in a $50 preliminary fight, from getting banged in the head by those sliding base runners.

After everybody had been called names by the manager and most of them had called him a few back, Williams put Scott back at first and Smith in the outfield, where they belonged. ("I never meant it to be *permanent!*" he explained.) Then the Sox began to win. Lonborg stopped "thinking too much," struck out thirteen batters in one game, and made up his mind to win them all.

Yastrzemski and Conigliaro continued to drive baseballs out of everyone's reach. And Dick Williams laid his rasping tongue, not on his own players, but on umpires ("Incompetent!"), the league president ("That guy Cronin can't even be bothered to stay in the park until the game is over!"), and on Cal Hubbard, the gray eminence who had charge of all league umpires ("Hubbard must have watched with his earflaps on!"). And he quickly accused sportswriters of having invented all those quotes anyway.

Inspired by all this earnest character-building, the Sox wound up the month of April tied with the Yankees for first place. The fans were in ecstasy, and the ballplayers, having dropped from the heights to the depths and climbed back again in a single month, saw nothing but glory ahead, maybe even a third-place finish. (No one at this time, outside of the confines of some obscure home for the mentally unbalanced, seriously counted the youthful Red Sox as contenders for the flag.)

It was a bit of good luck for Williams that the club found itself all pulled together so suddenly, with hope of first division money in every heart. For he imposed a regular jailhouse routine on the club, insisting that *everyone*—big batting star or no—should turn out every day for morning practice, obey strict curfew, and submit to bedcheck. There was grousing at this and even talk for a time of open rebellion. But always a string of victories united the club and aborted the creation of those poisonous "factions" that had been to blame, said Williams, for all previous failures.

But still there were ups and downs for everyone. Even Yastrzemski put in time on the bench. Russ Gibson, the promising young catcher, ran out of promise. Reggie Smith struck out 13 times in 25 visits to the plate. Tony Conigliaro had to play soldier for two weeks. Petrocelli was lamed by tendonitis. Catcher Bob Tillman accidentally beaned pitcher John Wyatt. (Big John had creased a couple of his own teammates in practice.) Joe Foy's house burned down.

Still reeling, one presumes, from the shock, Joe Foy, the night after his personal disaster, hit a bases-loaded home run against the Yankees and started the club off on another string of victories.

Some observers did say that the man who inspired the sudden spurt was not Joe Foy at all but Eddie Stanky, who had offered, without being asked, his personal assessment of Boston's Carl Yastrzemski: "Maybe an all-star ballplayer, but only from the neck down." When Stanky led his team into Fenway Park shortly afterward, he was awarded a shower of beer cans, paper cups, and assorted garbage. Whereupon doughty Ed wrote to his wife (and told the writers about it) that should he meet his death at the hands of the Boston assassins, she should "sue Tom Yawkey and Marvin Miller for a million dollars each!" (Why Marvin Miller, a few people dared to wonder. He was simply the new director of the Major League Players' Association and had never thrown a paper cup at a ballplayer in his life. Well, Stanky elucidated, with characteristic clarity, Miller was "always popping off about how much he did to help the ballplayers.")

Or perhaps what brought the pennant to Boston was the trade that lifted Elston Howard (and briefly broke his heart) out of the Yankee locker room and made him a Boston boy. Ellie,

Pitcher Ed Connolly of the Boston Red Sox was waiting to back up a throw from the outfield in this game against the Yankees, but Yankee third base coach Frank Crosetti wasn't waiting. He flopped out of the way and protected his skull.

slowed down even more than he had been to begin with, and no longer getting all the way around with his batting swing, was still crafty and cool enough to coax winning games out of Boston's unsteady pitching staff. And before anyone knew what had happened, the club was most of the way through the season and still on top.

Now, indeed, Boston went mad, in the manner that only a winning baseball club seems to prompt. Sober citizens, staid businessmen, and semiprofessional grouches stuck bumper and window stickers on their cars beseeching the Red Sox to Go! and Go! and Go! And bewildered visitors from the outer reaches might expect to be importuned by Boston cab drivers, hotel clerks, and even cops to explain what they "thought about the Red Sox."

It was possible to think almost anything about the Red Sox and be half right. They were the best of teams; they were the worst of teams. They charged for the pennant; they stumbled and fell back. In the final few weeks of the 1967 season, they abandoned hope and renewed it more times than some fans could keep track of. Just as they were about to be knocked completely out of contention, one of their rivals would lose a game he was supposed to win, and fortune would flicker to life again. On the seventh of September there had been four clubs in a virtual tie for first place: Chicago and Minnesota shared first place, while Boston and Detroit, just one percentage point behind, were tied for the next position. Boston was favored because they would play most of their remaining games at home. But their pitching staff, according to the game's deepest thinkers, was simply not strong enough to win the flag.

Rival clubs, however, insisted that the Boston pitchers, lacking skill, had found other ways to win. Said Joe Pepitone of the Yankees, "John Wyatt has so much Vaseline on him that if he should ever overslide second base he'd keep right on going to the fence." (So constant were the protests against John Wyatt's Vaseline ball and other Boston men's spitters that one day umpire Hank Soar asked to examine a ball for still another time, found it wiped clean, then in resignation spat on it himself and returned it to the pitcher.)

The Red Sox won one "crucial" game with the Yankees when the Yankee catcher, after tagging a runner out at the plate, dropped the ball and made him safe. And when they suddenly lost three games in a row in mid-September, they rose up from despair, beat the Tigers twice with the help of a wild pitch and then beat Cleveland on another wild pitch to lead the pack once more. They beat Cleveland again when the Cleveland right fielder dropped a line drive that had struck him right in the hands. But they soon fell back to second and had to wait for the other clubs to beat themselves. They took the pennant in a burst of glory, however, when they trimmed their chief enemy, the Minnesota Twins, with a wild pitch once more contributing to the victory.

The delirium in Boston, so long in coming and so heartily relished through the nights and days preceding the Series, seemed almost enough to carry the club to the World Championship. But, again, as in 1946, the enemy was the St. Louis Cardinals. And the Cardinals *had* the pitching they needed, nor could any Vaseline nor any saliva ball deny them. And so once more the Red

Bud Harrelson of the New York Mets demonstrates perfect bunting form: knees bent, bat at eye level, arms extended full length toward the pitch. Atlanta catcher Bob Didier's form is less than perfect. His extended fingers invite a fracture if the ball is tipped.

Sox fans had to cling to their memories of the miracle season and try to blot out all recollection of the World Series.

A greater miracle still, because it was so utterly unforeseen and followed so quickly on some of the most disastrous years in baseball, was the winning of the pennant by the incredible New York Mets, who had been laughed at so long that wiseacres were still making jokes about them when the season opened. Indeed, by this time one or two sportswriters had worked out a theory to prove that the Mets were loved by the New York fans *only* because they were losers. But the New York fans, many of whom had been first drawn to major league baseball by the appearance of the Mets, had always rejoiced in the team's victories and never aban-

Casey Stengel, who earned a reputation as a clown and a master of double-talk while playing for and managing New York, could speak straight and talk seriously when the occasion required.

doned hope. A victory by the Mets—some young, some spavined and cast-off, and some trailing clouds of ancient glory—seemed like a public doing-down of the Establishment, and so it always gave heart to the young.

Not that even the young were predicting at the start of the 1969 season that the Mets would actually come in first. But they would, many were saying, do *better* this year. Even George Weiss, the patient aging genius who had built champions wherever he worked, had handed over the presidency of the club with the feeling that he had finally got some guys out there who would "win games for you."

The Mets also had gotten themselves a new manager: Gil Hodges, once the darling of Flatbush fans, who had ended his playing career with the Mets, had been traded off for a nominal price so he could manage the Washington Senators, and was now allowed to go back in the final move of what apparently had been an only half-articulated gentlemen's agreement. There were those among the fans and writers who openly mourned the passing of Casey Stengel, whose rubber countenance and carefully cultivated double-talk had won fame for the Mets in every town in the land. (There was hardly a ball-park anywhere that could not produce, when the Mets were scheduled there, a contingent of young people bearing banners with the familiar device, "Let's Go, Mets!") But the mourners did not include the Met brass, who had been secretly hoping from season to season that some way might be made manifest for them to retire the old man, then find a manager who would stay awake through all the games, giving as much attention to the doings on the

diamond as to the direction the television lens was pointing.

Casey had come home very late one night, as had long been his wont, climbed out of his cab, and found the sidewalk so elusive that he fell and broke his leg. On this excuse he was retired, and at his own behest, his coach and former Giant catcher, Wes Westrum, a young man who practically admitted the job was too much for him, took on the managership. Wes marked time with moderate success until Gil Hodges could come over. But even when Gil came in, there were many who held that the Mets, who had never got halfway up the hill, were already over it, that even their losing had stopped being funny, and that no one was going to come see them anymore.

But more people came to see them than had ever crowded into a New York baseball park before—because the Mets, having found a catcher who was not ashamed to come to the plate with a bat in his hand and having—through the luck of an informal lottery—signed a pitcher named Seaver who knew only from throwing strikes, suddenly turned into winners. Gil Hodges was no lovable old gnome or even a sarcastic son of a bitch. He was a man whose face during a ball game seldom showed emotion, but one who paid close attention to what was happening on the ball field—and who spoke up when he saw something that distressed him.

Gil had suffered a heart attack at the end of the 1968 season, so it seemed possible that, despite his studiously unruffled exterior, he was no man to relax or cut television capers when his club was losing. Some blamed Gil's heart attack on his suddenly increased consumption of cigarettes—he was smoking as many now as Hank Bauer had when Hank's club was headed for high ground. But the smoking itself must have been a symptom of tension.

Back at work in 1969 Gil had stopped smoking, seemed cooler than ever, but soon made it clear that he had not taken on the job to chuckle himself into retirement. He reamed out his whole ball club when he found them accepting defeat too joyfully. He actually walked out on the field during a game against Houston at Shea Stadium, hands in pockets as if he were going to talk to his pitcher, and removed from the game the best hitter on the club, left fielder Cleon Jones, who had played a fly ball lackadaisically and then had lobbed the ball back into the diamond. (Gil insisted that Cleon had a sore leg, but few believed him.) When some of his young players celebrated an unsuccessful trip to Houston by buying cowboy hats, Gil quietly told them to put the hats away. He surprised his players by actually enforcing the curfew with $50 fines. (Under Stengel a player just had to be careful not to do his drinking at the same bar Casey frequented.)

So the ball club, which had been restless and divided because of a spring season strike (which some players honored and some did not) and which still retained some of the publicly fostered loser tradition, pulled itself together first against their common enemy, the manager. Then they found themselves winning and began to love each other —and the manager—because of that. Starting at the end of May the Mets ran up a string of eleven victories in a row, with pitcher Jerry Koosman striking out batters by the dozen along the way.

The winning spirit may also have been fanned by the rivalry with the Chicago Cubs, who seemed to take it for granted that *they* would win the flag in their division this year. (The new twelve-team league, expanded by the addition of San Diego and Montreal, had been split into Eastern and Western divisions, with play-offs scheduled between division winners to decide the league championship.) The Cubs were led by that master of offensive tactics and language, Leo Durocher, and they were cheered on by a rowdy coterie of young men in yellow plastic helmets who infested the Wrigley Field bleachers, tossing dirty names and small hard objects at enemy outfielders. These Bleacher Bums (who may have been, in a sense, inspired by the organized cheering section the Mets had spawned, led by a yellow-slickered young M.D. from Flushing, Queens) seemed to take special delight in tormenting the Mets. But they also helped inspire such fury in other clubs that the enemy would sometimes outdo themselves against the Chicagos.

The Mets were intimidated neither by the Bleacher Bums nor by Durocher. They threw the obscenities back twofold, pounded the hell out of Leo's best pitchers, and mocked the bush league heel-kicking that Cub captain Ron Santo liked to use to celebrate a victory. And the Cubs had their own troubles, what with their aging manager taking off on spasmodic honeymoons with his new bride, and the ballplayers concentrating on their ingenious scheme of hustling for extra "endorsement" money and pouring it all into a team pool that was to be split, presumably, when the pennant had been safely secured to the mast.

But the Mets had *their* eyes on the

Sandy Koufax, the finest pitcher of the 1960s, pitched in constant pain in his last two seasons with the Los Angeles Dodgers. But he kept on winning.

pennant, too. In early September they found themselves in second place with only Chicago in front. And they were meeting Chicago in a two-game series with the Cubs, dragging a four-game losing streak into the park. In the first game Jerry Koosman struck out thirteen, the Cubs and Mets threw baseballs at each other, and the Mets won 3 to 2. The next game was an easy one for Tom Seaver as Art Shamsky and Donn Clendenon (a wayward soul who had been talked out of retirement by the Commissioner himself) drove fair balls out of the playing field. This sent the Cubs away with just a half-game lead, which was wiped out the next day when Durocher's lads extended their losing streak to seven and the Mets took two games from Montreal.

For the first time since the Mets had

been created in the busy brain of Branch Rickey, the New York National League club was in first place. And they decided to hang tight. On the twenty-fourth of September they took the title at home by beating the St. Louis Cardinals 6 to 0, with Donn Clendenon providing another home run and Ed Charles, the aging black third baseman who had spent his best years walloping baseballs in the minor leagues because his club—the Milwaukee Braves—did not want too many of "them" on the club at one time, hitting one of his own. Charles clapped his hands happily all the way around the bases.

The celebration at Shea over winning this half-a-championship was like the storming of the Bastille, with one young fan actually breaking a leg when he fell off the scoreboard. Fans tore up handfuls of the sacred sod, set home plate adrift, and stole every cap off every Met head that they could reach. The ushers and cops tumbled before them like kids in the Coney Island surf. Everyone who dared enter the clubhouse was laid hold of, be he sportswriter, politician, or other type of stuffed shirt to be shampooed with champagne, thrust fully clothed into the shower, or both. No one had to beg the players to repeat their antics for the television camera. They even doused the camera crew with bubbly and let it splash right into the dread eye of the network itself.

But this was only part of it. The Mets still had to beat the club that won the Western title. In baseball geography, which puts Atlanta in the West and Chicago in the East, the Western winner could have been Atlanta, Los Angeles, Cincinnati, or San Francisco. The Mets were hoping for Atlanta, and they got their wish. Not that they felt utterly confident that they could knock down Henry Aaron and his mates. But they had no real stomach for a series on the other side of the continent, where wild winds blew and mighty men threw baseballs at fearsome speeds.

The sign of a championship club, it is said, is an ability to win even when the club is going badly. Seaver pitched the first game in Atlanta and did not do well. Although he had steamed confidently to the flag, with one scoreless inning after another, Tom looked shaky indeed when the pennant series opened, almost like a kid pitcher making his first major league start. But he escaped from Hank Aaron alive, after all, and his teammates scored a lot of runs while the Braves were committing a few mistakes. (A throw to pick Jones off second just gave Cleon an opportunity to steal third. And a throw to hang him up on the baselines between third and home bounced away and let him score.) The score was 9 to 5.

In the second game the men who threw the baseballs to the plate were again the least of it. Jerry Koosman had no more strikeout strings to unravel. But the modest Met batters outdid themselves, as low-average batters sometimes do when there are great prizes to be won. Even Ken Boswell hit a home run that scored two runs, which was one more than Henry Aaron got for his, and the Mets, who had hoped to take one game in Atlanta, took two, the second one by a score of 11 to 6.

At home in Shea Stadium, with their fans in near-delirium, the Mets kept on hitting home runs. Boswell got another and Wayne Garret, who could barely recall when he had last hit a ball out of the park, hit one out to score two runners, including pitcher Nolan Ryan, who had just produced his fourth hit of the whole extended season. Ryan, a man who toughened his pitching fingers by dousing them in pickle juice, entered the game in relief of Gary Gentry and struck out seven batters to help win this deciding game, 7 to 4.

The fans were thereupon constrained to leap on the field in a second frenzy, once more extracting home plate from the ground and again uprooting sections of newly laid sod. This was the *real* league championship, the old-fashioned pennant victory. But the celebrating in the locker room all seemed synthetic. Some of the players, who had gotten sick on the champagne the time before, wanted none of it. Hardly anyone could put his heart into pushing guys in civilian clothes into the shower—although someone did manage to saturate New York's mayor, John V. Lindsay, to his own obvious delight. And most of the players had their minds on the World Series, where the big money grew. Would they be playing Baltimore or Minnesota?

They would be playing Baltimore, which took three straight from Minnesota, and all the tea-leaf readers agreed that Baltimore would tie a can to the Mets' kite, maybe even in four straight games. Because Baltimore had *everything*—pitchers, hitters, and sensational fielders.

The Baltimore Orioles, however, did not have manager Gil Hodges or the Mets' inspiration, which prompted Boswells, Garrets, Swobodas, Rod Gaspars, and Art Shamskys to play like all-stars. They did, however, own reputation enough to give the Mets a slight attack of the shakes in the beginning. Some said Tom Seaver slipped out of his groove, because he missed breakfast in Baltimore that first meeting. But it looked more as if he were still suffering from the sort of stage fright that grabs even the coolest of customers by the guts when their first World Series opens.

The Baltimore batters had Tom staggering by the end of the fourth inning, what with a home run by Buford and other indignities. The Orioles were leading then by 4 to 0, and big Boog Powell and Frank Robinson had not even begun to hit. It was obvious, said Frank Robinson and other Baltimoreans, that the Mets had finally run out of gas and were back playing under their heads, as usual.

But Jerry Koosman bred no but-terflies in his stomach. When he faced the Baltimores in the second game, he like to starved them to death. For six innings he did not give them any safe hits at all. Then, when the Orioles, thanks to a stolen base by Paul Blair, managed to scratch out the one run they needed to tie, the Mets "nobody" brigade, led by Al Weis, who had batted .215 that season, rode up to the rescue. Weis, with Ed Charles on third, hit a single to left field to put the Mets ahead. They stayed that way until the final out.

The ultimate miracle, then, had to be fashioned at home, before the eyes of the half-mad multitude that still thirsted to scratch up more sod. And at home, the spirit that had driven mediocre fielders to feats of agility that should have been beyond them and had turned slap-hitters into home run heroes, visited the Mets once more. This time it was Tom Agee who caught two long drives that should have been extra-base hits—one backhanded in the webbing of his glove, after a frantic run, and the other while diving headlong across the out-field sod, reaching for a ball that had, everyone supposed, gotten away from him. These two catches, plus the hard throwing of Gary Gentry, deprived the Orioles altogether of runs and allowed the Mets to win the third game, 5 to 0.

Tom Seaver thereupon returned to the battle with a good breakfast in his stomach, the butterflies having folded their wings, and his control as sharp as need be. Up until the ninth inning, he gave the Baltimores just three hits. The Mets, from Donn Clendenon's having hit a home run his first time up, were leading 1 to 0. But in the ninth, two

Carl Yastrzemski, the man the Red Sox fans once dreamed might replace Babe Ruth, is greeted at home plate by Reggie Smith and Mike Andrews, teammates who scored ahead of him when he hit a home run against the Yankees. Yankee Stadium, 1970.

hits put the tying run on third and the lead run at first. Everyone seemed to crowd in toward the plate to stop that tying run from crossing. But Brooks Robinson looped a fly out to right field, obviously out of reach of Ron Swoboda, who was not much of a man to catch fly balls anyway. But Ron, who knew only that it was catch the ball or kiss the ball game goodbye, dived headlong at it, just barely snagged it in the webbing of his glove, did a complete somersault on the turf, digging up divots as he did so, and sat up without his hat, but with the ball still in his hand and the batter out. Robinson, the base runner, scurried home with the tying run. But the Orioles could not bring the other run over.

The Mets then won this, too, on a freakish bit of luck, plus some hasty judgment by the umpire, when a thrown ball hit pinch hitter J. C. Martin on the wrist as he was pounding down the first base line arms out and spreading himself as wide as he could manage. He was called safe at first, but he should have been out, because the runner when the ball is behind him is supposed to stay *off* the baseline, to run outside it, on his way to first base. But it is a "judgment" call, and the umpire's judgment, once expressed, altereth not. So Martin stayed safe and Rod Gaspar, after some prodding by his coach, carried the winning run across the plate without any effort by the Orioles to throw him out.

In the final game the fates once more stuck their hands into the machinery and made it disgorge the proper number. The Orioles, in regular Oriole-

Even umpires become infected with souvenir fever at World Series time. Here one of the honorable men in blue gleefully grabs and stealthily makes off with two baseball caps while the St. Louis Cardinals crowd around winning pitcher Bob Gibson. Bob has just won the final game of the 1967 World Series at Fenway Park, Boston.

style, took a quick three-run lead on a single and two home runs. But in the sixth inning, a pitch by Baltimore's Dave McNally hit the dirt at the plate and rolled off into the Met dugout as Cleon Jones, the batter, did a brief dance in the batter's box, pointing at his foot. The umpire called the pitch a ball. But Gil Hodges calmly carried the baseball back to the umpire and showed him that it wore a smear of black shoe polish. The umpire, Lou DiMuro, noted the mark, knew it could have come only from a freshly shined shoe, and awarded Cleon Jones first base. (In the 1957 World Series in Milwaukee, another man named Jones, Nippy Jones of the Milwaukee Braves, was awarded first base on an identical appeal. That time, the batter had

extracted the ball out of the hand of Yankee catcher Yogi Berra and showed it to the umpire himself. The umpire changed his decision, and the Braves won the ball game.)

After that bit of ghostly interference, the Orioles had no chance to win the game, even though they were leading 3 to 0. Clendenon immediately drove Jones home with a home run. Al Weis, the phantom hero, tied the score with another home run in the seventh. Then Cleon Jones doubled, and Ron Swoboda brought him home with the lead run when his hump-backed liner got away from left fielder Buford of Baltimore, who had been playing it "safe." The Orioles could not score when their last turn came. Cleon Jones caught an easy fly for the final out, and he had hardly snuggled the ball in his glove when people boiled out over the front walls of the stands and ran screaming to embrace him, pound his back, and deal likewise with any Mets not quick enough to have escaped. The police and ushers merely stood and watched, for their tiny complement could no more have turned back this tide than it could have overset the grandstand. More sod than ever was clawed up to wither in someone's trophy room. But this time the rejoicing spread all over New York in a wild bacchanal such as had not been witnessed since St. Louis kranks had set off cannon in the streets some three quarters of a century before. Men and women who had never set eyes on each other before joined hands in the streets and romped in crazy circles. Ecstatic fans opened strange doors to scream to those inside "The Mets won!" Denizens and employees poured helter-skelter out of taverns the city around. Automobile drivers set up such a honking that all thought was drowned. And, of course, a blizzard of paper—rolls of toilet tissue, ticker tape, torn up foolscap, and newspaper pages—fell softly as snow and gently as a blessing on the crowded streets until it seemed to be dropping without letup from the very skies.

There were less disorganized celebrations, too—fireworks and speeches, a showing of faces on television and in nightclubs—and many a happy thanksgiving at home when the World Series players' share was parceled out. Most experts in the matter could not see what was to keep the Mets from going on and on and on, as the Yankees had done. Among the few sour notes was a grumble from Baltimore sources that

Ron Swoboda's headlong catch that had kept the Orioles from scoring a hatful of runs in the third game was "stupid" and "bush"—that he should have played it "safe," since had he missed, everybody in sight would have crossed the plate. But a man named Weiss, who had seen more championships won and lost than even Casey Stengel had, would not agree. There is no tomorrow in the World Series, he allowed, and a man must be ready to live or die on every play. (Buford had played a ball "safe," and it had brought across the run that put the Mets ahead in the final game.)

With all the wonders that filled the skies in the 1960s, it is not strange at all that hardly anyone noticed the disappearance from New York of a man who alone was left of all those who had known the days of the city's greatest baseball glory—from the time Babe Ruth teamed his open touring car like a runaway dragon up Riverside Drive to the days when Mickey Mantle and Roger Maris set out together to capture and call their own the home run title the Babe had created so long before. This was lean Frank Crosetti, the beloved and balding Crow whose intricate and portentous fidgeting in the third-base coaching box had bemused baseball fans at Yankee Stadium since some of them were small boys.

Crow or Cro, as he always signed himself, was unquestionably the best coach in baseball—the one man who held the respect and the faith of the Yankee regulars through managerial shift and ownership change. (One great Yankee star, enraged when a new manager had jumped to his feet to "wipe out" one of Cro's signs to a base runner, declared, "Cro will be here

Met first baseman Ed Kranepool (right), who played a rather small part in the triumph, leads the cheers as the Merry Mets race off the field after winning the World Championship, 1969. Catcher Jerry Grote is followed by Jerry Koosman, Gary Gentry, and Ken Boswell.

long after that son of a bitch is *gone!*")
Were Baseball's Hall of Fame truly
concerned with memorializing men who
had done great service to baseball,
it would long ago have built an alcove
for Francis Peter Joseph Crosetti of
California, for he turned as many recruits into baseball stars and helped
fashion as many championship clubs as
any man whose likeness is preserved in
that hall now.

Cro, having served a long and glad-
some apprenticeship himself, replete
with scars, injuries, errors, bitter
defeats, and precious victories, could
offer to nervous rookies the down-
to-earth, profane, and finger-by-finger
advice they needed to help them gain
perspective on the job and begin to find
their way out of their stupidities without
embarrassment. He was patient, soft-
spoken, endlessly knowledgeable about
the game, and full of small tips about
fielding ground balls, making tags,
catching flies, wielding a bat, and running bases. Cro was never a man to
peddle gripes in public or downgrade
his mates. He was loyal to his club and
worked hard to keep spirits high and
the infield moving.

Of late years Cro was known to
grumble privately over the brevity of
a ballplayer's apprenticeship or the lack
of intensive coaching in the minors. He
shook his head over basemen who did
not know enough to turn the back of
the hand when applying a tag to a sliding runner (the inside of the wrist bleeds
too easily), or who accepted short sacrifice flies with both feet planted
stolidly in the turf, instead of maneu-
vering to take the ball while moving
toward the diamond so as to give
impetus to the throw to the plate. Too
many pitchers, he complained to his

intimates, pitched "too quick"—did
not reach back far enough to get body
as well as arm into the pitch; too many
batters tried to bunt without flexing
their knees. And sometimes Cro would
sit in a corner and express disgust over
a ballplayer who had just put on a bit
of schoolboy playacting—kicking up
dust in a fit or pounding the ground in
self-disgust after a misplay, instead of
scrambling after the errant ball. He also
grew more impatient in his later years
with players who staged childish pranks
in the locker room. But none of this
attitude ever surfaced publicly. Cro was
a team man, out to win, out to have
fun on the diamond, and willing to do
his own job with thoroughness and
devotion.

Crosetti did have fun on the diamond, too, openly rejoicing at winning hits and clowning mildly when the
moment seemed appropriate. One time
he deliberately threw a star base runner
into confusion by putting on steal signs
and taking them off almost as fast as
his hands could move. Cro actually had
only three basic signs—finger to cheek,
fingers plucking at shirt front, hand
brushing the thigh, any one of which,
on any given day, might mean bunt,
or steal, or take. (Yankees always went
to the plate "hitting"—that is, free to
swing at any pitch they liked—and
would let a good pitch go by only when
they had a sign to "take" it.) But these
basic signs were so intricately woven
into a series of twitches, hitches, adjust-
ing of belt and clothing, cries, hand
clapping, and foot movements that
there was no sorting them out unless
you knew them. Cro's movements in
the third base box were often as
enthralling as the play.

Cro himself had been a great infielder

After the shouting had died, the turf had been torn up, and the uniforms had been half torn off, Met pitchers Tom Seaver and Gary Gentry, like two schoolboys after a wrestling match, check over the damage done by celebrating fans. Last game, World Series, 1969.

who made his way to the Yankees in the days when few men dared dream of breaking into that championship infield. He was hailed, when he did appear, as one of the "California Italians" who had come to give strength to the Yankees—the others being DiMaggio and Lazzeri. But Cro was as American as anybody. His father and mother had labored heroically to save men and women in the 1906 California earthquake, and his grandfather had been a California goldminer in the Gold Rush days.

Like so many great athletes, Cro had been "sickly" as a child. As a four-year-old in San Francisco, he managed to contract whooping cough, measles, and pneumonia at the same time and came out of it pale, skinny, and delicate. His parents thereupon moved to Los Gatos, out in the Southern California sun, and gave little Frankie a big outdoors to play in. Frankie and his older brother chose to play ball, with any sort of ball they could find. And while brother John often knew of other things he would rather be doing, he still, in the manner of big brothers everywhere, took pains to cater to "sickly" Frankie and would throw the baseball to him hour after hour, as long as there was light to see it by. Frank played for his grammar school team in Los Gatos and promptly became a star. When he reached high school age, the family moved back to the city. By this time Frank had had enough of school but not nearly enough baseball, and he sought out ways to spend the daylight hours with the gang at Funston Square, where there was always a ball game going. After young Frank and the truant officer had held a brief discussion on the folly of writing "excuses" for his innocent mother to sign, Frank devoted

more time to his schooling. Eventually, he arranged to attend classes at night so as to be able to attend to his infield work during the daylight hours.

When he was sixteen years old, Frank, through a neighbor, received an offer to play in the industrial league in Butte, Montana, where the copper companies hired extra help in the summer to play baseball while pretending to work in the mills or mines. (Frank actually did cut a few lengths of copper pipe.) Frank's pay was $200 a month, which was rather more than he would have made had he really been working in the mill.

The Butte Mines League was a tough one. The infields were baked hard as concrete. The players were far more skilled than those Frank had dealt with in San Francisco, where he had sometimes earned $3 a game as a "semi-pro." The pitchers threw hard. And the fans, many of them hard-rock miners with a day's pay riding on the game, were tough, loud, and belligerent.

Frank was nervous, short on experience, and overanxious. His first chance at third base rocketed off his toe. So they tried Frank at first base, then at short, and second, shifting him every time he booted a ground ball. Eventually he settled in the outfield, clinging to his job through his steady work at bat and his fiery determination to get into every play. Frank was enormously agile, quick to pounce on a ball that had eluded him, quick to get off a hard, low throw, and quick to grab an extra base on a slow outfielder or an absent-minded pitcher.

This was the sort of apprenticeship most young ballplayers had to serve in those times—not coddled and bonused to death in the minors, nor rushed through an "instructional" league—but

schooled in actual competition, with screaming fans, sweating teammates, and angry managers to point out their faults.

In the winter there was the winter league, where Frank played for the Young Men's Institute, a sort of Catholic YMCA, and where the play was the equal of much minor league ball. There was no Little League for Frank to dawdle in, where twelve batters in a row might get a base on balls, before the kid pitcher could deliver anything that even his doting father could call a strike. And there was no Babe Ruth League either, with subsidized uniforms and baseballs to throw away. In this league the players were out for blood, and the lad who could not deliver was chased back to the spectators' seats. Frank learned his job by digging countless ground balls out of the dirt, by standing up to pitchers who were trying to scare him back to the bench, and by daring the bumps and spikes and hard tags on his round of the bases.

This was American baseball, where the so-called semipros played largely for love, where kids would skip breakfast to get first to the diamond, where the players themselves must needs mow the outfield grass and rake the infield clean, and where there were always kids bigger and older than yourself to try to beat you out of the prize.

The North Beach section of San Francisco, where Frank's family dwelt, spawned ballplayers as plentifully as the old Kerry Patch in St. Louis had or the rowdy West Side dumps of Manhattan when baseball was still named the New York Game. Baseball filled every boy's heart the whole year round, whether he was strong and quick

enough to make a place for himself on a club or could merely play in pick-up games and join the crowd of kids that lived and died with the doings of the San Francisco Seals.

The Seals, whose minions had seen young Frank perform his acrobatics on winter league infields and admired his aggressive way with the bat, signed Crosetti to a contract when he was only seventeen. And when he appeared at their training camp in Monterey, there were coaches and fans who observed that Frank had "nothing to learn" about infield play.

By this time Crosetti had developed the instinctive dogging of the ball that became his trademark. If a ball caromed off his glove, he wasted no time in cursing the luck. Rather he pounced on it like a cat who has let a mouse out of its paws. And Frank could release a throw so fast and fire it so hard that he put out many a runner who had counted himself safe on an error. Crosetti made a religion of keeping his eye on the ball every moment that it was in play. When a ball got away from another infielder, Crosetti, if he had half a chance, would be after it. And he could fling his lithe body in so many directions and with such lightning reaction, that he kept watchers cheering to see the stops he made.

The Seals eventually turned Crosetti into a shortstop, where his wide range, his baseball knowledge, and his strong arm could do them most good. At this position he quickly became the best in the Pacific Coast League—as good, most baseball men agreed, as the Coast League had seen since Swede Risberg, the Black Soxer who had been barred from the game in 1920, and better than Bancroft, or Peckinpaugh, or Buck

Pittsburgh right-fielder Roberto Clemente watches the flight of his home run that won the deciding game of the 1971 World Series for Pittsburgh over Baltimore.

Weaver—another Black Soxer who had become a third baseman in the majors. Young Frank sometimes made errors wholesale, as he tried for ground balls other men would not have waved at. But then he would put on a display of acrobatics that would leave old-timers gasping. Early in his first season at short, he suffered a long letdown, missing chances in the field and swinging vainly at the plate. He broke out of the slump with a day when he made four hits, including two doubles and a home run, and nailed at least one sizzling blow to deep short that should have been a base hit, to throw out the runner by a step. He made three other defensive plays that sent fans home talking about him. After that no one doubted that young Frank would soon be in the majors.

The Yankees bought him for what was reported as $100,000 but really added up to $75,000 and they left him one more season with the Seals before taking him to spring training with the big boys. Just turned twenty-one, Frank was no more nervous than he had been when he first took over third base for the Seals. Indeed, on his first day of the regular season with the Seals, everyone had remarked on his coolness, as he bounced a two-base hit off the wall, calmly worked the pitcher for a walk, and then hit a single. With the Yankees, Frank took over the shortstop job as if he had always been there. In spring training he ranged all over the infield, grabbing ground balls behind second base or in the hole near third and racing in behind the pitcher to grab up slow rollers and throw out runners. He also demonstrated an ability at hitting a ball where it was pitched, and he dropped safe hits all over the field,

to lead the club in batting during the exhibition season.

While his first full season was not as sensational as his work in Florida had promised, he clung to his job despite an early season slump when everyone expected Manager Joe McCarthy to ticket him "to the tube"—meaning the Hudson Tubes that led to the Yankee farm club at Newark. In Frank's second season Bill Werber showed up as a shortstop prospect, and this exceedingly fleet-footed and solidly self-confident young man looked as if he would take Crosetti's job. But Joe McCarthy chose Crosetti and kept him on the bench to fill at third and short. Next year his rival was Red Rolfe, but Crosetti landed the job when Rolfe's ailments kept him idle. Having hit a few timely home runs in his first seasons, Crosetti had gone into a batting slump as he tried to hold his own with his slugging teammates. But Joe McCarthy talked him into cutting down on his swing to concentrate on meeting the ball in front of the plate. After that Frank regained his consistency as a hitter, and no one could move him out of his job.

Crosetti became lead-off man after an injury to Earl Combs. In keeping with his lifelong philosophy of doing the job he was expected to do, Frank concentrated on getting on base to such an extent that he often led the league in being hit by the pitcher. He developed a real skill at twisting his body slyly into a soft pitch and taking a bruise in exchange for a base. And Crosetti ran the bases with great craft. His habit of keeping his eye on the ball enabled him to take many an extra base on outfielders who failed to come up cleanly with balls hit on the grass.

But Cro's true contribution to his

Rookie shortstop Mickey Mantle, fresh out of Commerce, Oklahoma, admires his new glove with Yankee coach Frank Crosetti. (Crosetti paid for the glove.) Casey Stengel made Mantle into an outfielder.

Bowie Kuhn, newly appointed Commissioner of Baseball, sits with president of the National League, Warren Giles (left), and Joe Cronin, president of the American League (right). Kuhn had been attorney for the National League.

club and to baseball came after he had retired as a player and took over as coach. In many respects Cro became the true field manager, for he gave many of the signs on his own. No manager was shrewder than Cro at scheduling a steal or a sacrifice bunt, and the best managers let him make many of his own decisions. Cro also knew the rules of baseball better than many umpires and watched the flight of every batted ball as intently as any man on the field. If a ball caromed off a fielder's glove and into the stands, Cro knew it was a home run, even if the ball bounced out again. Sometimes the umpire did not agree, and Cro would earnestly undertake to persuade him. Cro was alive to the myriad possibilities of every play at the plate and kept his base runners ready to take advantage of any misplay.

But Cro also made baseball a sort of religion—not just in trying to bring his club in first but in helping young players improve themselves. Because he was always in bed betimes, he arose every morning at six or sooner and would meet a young player at the park at any hour of the morning, ready to slap out fungoes or even pitch batting practice without letup, meanwhile patiently illustrating to the recruit his precise failings. He could teach pitchers and catchers, coach base runners to use their speed sensibly, and school overeager infielders in taking ground balls on the short hop. It is doubtful that any man in the game ever instructed more major league recruits than Cro did or helped turn more minor leaguers into stars.

Mates and writers used to ridicule Cro for his parsimony, insisting that he still had a few dollars left of his very first salary check. Cro did, indeed, conserve his nickels and dimes and invest them shrewdly. He also guarded the club's baseballs as if he were assigned to see that they hatched. But there was one teammate who would never agree that Cro was a miser. When Mickey Mantle first appeared on the Yankee practice field in Tucson, still half-choked with homesickness and clinging to the beloved scuffed "fielder's glove" he had used to help his semipro team win a championship, Cro took note of him. On Mickey's second day out he handed the boy a shining new big league glove, fresh out of the box. Mickey did not learn until much later that Cro had paid for the glove himself.

Cro did win security from baseball, for he took no part in celebrations and saw to it that his World Series checks (of which he earned twenty-two) went directly into the bank. Crosetti made no public appearances, gave no interviews, attended no banquets, and sought no acclaim. Victories, he insisted, belonged to the team and not to any individual player. Still it would become the National Game to honor this modest man who provided the backbone to the greatest ball club of the century and became its greatest coach.

The Latin Invasion

THERE had been Latin Americans in baseball for more than forty years before anyone ever heard of Roberto Clemente or the Alou brothers. But they had been mostly from Cuba, carefully selected for the pallor of their skins, and often treated as faintly comic characters. Of those who penetrated to the major leagues, only Adolfo Luque of Havana, who pitched for twenty seasons for Boston, Cincinnati, Brooklyn and New York in the National League, and Mike Gonzales, Cuban-born catcher for Boston, Cincinnati, St. Louis, and New York, attained even a modicum of fame. And not until just before World War II did Clark Griffith, the thrifty owner of the Washington Senators, in search of ballplayers who had not been corrupted by high wages, begin to reach into Venezuela for men who could play the American Game. Even then, most fans were amazed that the likes of Rene Montelguado could actually play baseball like an honest-to-God stateside native.

In 1947 when it finally became forgivable to accept men into the leagues whose skin was unfashionably tinted, a whole sea of talent lay unplumbed before the ravished eyes of baseball's talenthunters. Then it was revealed that boys had grown up playing baseball not just in Cuba and Venezuela but in Mexico, the Virgin Islands, Puerto Rico, and nearly every sunbaked isle in the

Pittsburgh ballplayers were often airborne as they flung themselves into the fight in the World Series of 1971. Here Nelson Briles, engaged in delivering a pitch to the plate against Baltimore, flies right off the mound.

Caribbean. Resembling California in offering year-round opportunity to play the game, these lands brought their players to maturity sooner and offered them to the leagues almost before they had a chance to distinguish between a peso and a dollar bill. Beginning in the 1940s and continuing to the present day, club after club has signed Spanish-speaking players to their roster and sometimes has added functionaries to their staffs just to change the players' gibberish into understandable English.

By 1970 there was not a club in all major league baseball that had not owned at least one young man who had been brought up in the heresy that Spanish was a civilized tongue. And as the number of players increased and their skills developed, sportswriters had to learn a whole new concept of sportsmanship. Latin boys had never been taught to cultivate the "Gee, fellows, I was pretty lucky" brand of manly self-depreciation. The *machismo* tradition inculcated a decent self-respect that prevented a man from pretending he was but a frail creature of fate when he knew a damn sight different. So when old-time writers and commentators asked a Latin hero how he rated himself against the great men who had gone before, they were often abashed and even outraged to hear that the young outlander thought he was just as good and maybe better.

In the 1970s the late Roberto Clemente of Pittsburgh was certainly as good a baseball player as any living fan had ever set his eyes on. If ever there was a man in modern baseball to match Cobb and Wagner, it was Clemente, who could hit, run, field, and throw as well as any and far better than most. He lost points in the books of some of his examiners, however, when he unashamedly professed that fact. He did not do it in the manner of a Muhammed Ali or other professional braggarts. He simply allowed, without compunction, that no one *he* knew of in the game could hit, run, throw, or play the outfield any better than he could. This simple fact stood uncontroverted, yet there were people who resented Clemente's pointing it out. The real oddity, however, was that so few others had made note of it.

Had young Roberto played in New York, where Marvelous Marv Throneberry, Jim Bouton, Ed Kranepool, Joe Pepitone, Al Jackson, and other names of equally ripe renown

had like to drowned in gallons of printers' ink, his name, too, might have echoed from coast to coast. But Clemente had played in Pittsburgh for ten years before his fame began to ring in any halls outside of his club's hometown. And often then Roberto would earn newspaper space because he never concealed his hurts.

It has long been deemed subversive, on this nation's fields of play, to admit to any pain, even if blood be dripping. The batter who takes a fast pitch in the neck may fall down, and even wince a little. But should he play so false to the traditions of his fathers as to rub the spot where it hurt, he will be ticketed to the Ladies' League, where it is all right to scream and dance around when something really stings you.

Clemente did no screaming or dancing about in pain. But if asked how he felt, Roberto might frankly list a dozen areas where he had just as soon it stopped aching. He had played far more baseball games than any other man of his era, what with all he worked in in Puerto Rico and in the minor leagues before he came to Pittsburgh in 1955, so it was no marvel that his body sometimes signaled mild distress. But pain or discomfort did not always keep Clemente from playing. Nor did it ever cause him to ease up during a game. There is no player in the majors who runs as hard to first base as Clemente did, no matter how "sure" it seemed that he would be put out. Great heroes by the dozen have played in pain, of course, as every professional athlete must. But the New York heroes who gave the club their all despite wounds and bone spurs often wrung sodden poetry from the pens of the infatuated sportswriters, while Clemente earned

In the 1971 World Series, catcher Manny Sanguillen takes to the air to grab a high throw that just failed to catch Baltimore base runner Frank Robinson at the plate.

sarcasm and occasional disbelief.

Roberto's aches and pains may indeed have been partly psychosomatic. And it is true that he often performed most spectacularly after he had confessed to being off his feed. (Bob Feller once threw a no-hitter when he "didn't feel right.") But be they in his body or merely in his mind, Roberto *felt* his ailments. And he played on and on despite them—stiff neck, aching arm, sore shoulder (which he rubbed with gasoline), head colds, and stomach upsets. In 1972 he collected his 3,000th hit. He had led his league four times in batting. In right field he acted the part of a fifth infielder, with buzzing long throws to cut down base runners who dared to try for one more base. Clemente once even charged in from the outfield to field a bunt, and he threw a man out at third base after he fielded it.

Any baseball fan could list two or three "greatest" players whose names, thanks to all the press wordage they have been awarded, win instant recognition everywhere—and who have not put their bodies as wholeheartedly into the fray as Clemente always did. Who has not seen a great Yankee slugger slow to a walk halfway down the first baseline when he hit into an "easy" out? Who has not moaned inwardly to observe the game's "finest hitter" take a fly ball on the bounce instead of catching it? But no man lives who ever saw Roberto Clemente dog it.

When his foot hurt in one game, Roberto scored all the way from first on a single. "I wanted to get home and rest my foot," he explained. Roberto never was a great breaker-up of ball games, because he felt that trying for base hits rather than home runs made him more valuable to the club. (Ty Cobb was another exponent of this theory.) So perhaps he did miss many banner headlines that accrue to those who send their fans home in dazed delirium by one mighty blow. But there were times when he seemed to have been robbed of decent recognition through some inexplicable bias. And his outrage at this downgrading of his talents marked him immodest and thus unworthy of enshrinement. (When his name was far down the "Most Valuable Player" list in 1960 after leading his club in batting, Roberto's roar of protest was heard clear from Puerto Rico.)

But Clemente's demeanor was far more modest than that of many a punctiliously "shy" hero. He did not brush off autograph seekers, and he thanked fans graciously for their attention to him. He was also a naive man who dared admit out loud that sometimes he took batting practice, not because he needed it, but so the other players could see him hit. Were he a symphony string player, no music fan would belittle him if he admitted to playing the fiddle sometimes to show his mates how it could be done. But in professional sports, where the schoolyard traditions still persist, such a comment undoubtedly cost him votes toward the MVP title.

The frequent references to Clemente's "imaginary" ills sometimes turned his own fans against Roberto when they saw him sitting on the bench at times they thought he should have been playing. But gradually over his seventeen seasons, Clemente won a larger and larger following. What if he did not join in club celebrations or demean himself with proper humility in front of the press? What if he did not try to drive balls over the impossibly distant fences of old Forbes Field? What if he did not nurse his batting average by maintaining a studiously shrunken "strike zone?" (Roberto could snatch a bad pitch out of midair and drive it 350 feet.) He *did* win ball games. He won the 1961 All-Star Game with his nineteenth-inning single. And he won the 1971 World Series almost by himself, with a .414 batting average and at least one hit in every game. (He hit in every game in the 1960 World Series, too.) He also hit two home runs, barely missed another, made two nearly impossible catches in the outfield, and scared the great Baltimore base runners into stagnation by the strength and accuracy of his arm.

In December 1972 Roberto Clemente died in the crash of a plane that was carrying relief supplies to earthquake victims in Nicaragua. To the end he remained a rebellious man at heart—indignant at the continued peonage of baseball's contract arrangements and angry at the smug discrimination still practiced in the fringes of professional sports against Latins and blacks. He did not laugh at having his mispronunciations given phonetically in the press for a joke. And he refused to agree that malaria, bone chips, and a bacterial infection in his stomach were psychosomatic.

Sportswriters in 1973 voted almost unanimously to waive the usual five-year waiting period and admit Roberto Clemente to the Hall of Fame. A few muttered that this was "setting a precedent" but if so, it was a precedent baseball could profit by. To honor a man who proved his greatness off the diamond as well as on ennobles the Hall of Fame itself and enhances the value of a membership there.

As in the earliest days of the game, the sudden influx of working class Irish and Dutch added ferocity, excitement, and uninhibited joy to what had started out as a rather stately pastime, so today's Latin invasion has begun to invest the National Game once more with recklessness, fierce desire, and a certain elemental rowdiness that always belonged to American sport. Irishmen in the 1860s and 1870s, along with second-generation Dutchmen, had practically demolished the British upperclass traditions of "playing the game" without having to be reminded of the rules. Later on the Italians came in to return the game to the city-dwellers. Then the blacks rescued it from degeneration. And now the Latins have restored to it that inextinguishable urge to come out on top that has long been the heritage of this country's poor.

Unfortunately, there have been hardly any sportswriters able to deal with the Latin newcomers in their native tongue. As a result, many of them have been celebrated as unwitting comedians who do not even know how to say "baseball" in less than three syllables. And the quality some of them own—the boyish desire to whack any pitch they can reach just for the fun the deed provides—is occasionally cited as a "racial" characteristic that is removing all science from the game. But Ed Delahanty, Louis Sockalexis, Joe Medwick, and Yogi Berra used to slash at bad pitches, too, and no fan was ever driven out of the park in disgust from watching them. Indeed, this willingness to risk going out rather than letting runs die on the basepaths is sometimes of more worth to the team than a cozy concern with one's batting average.

Many of today's baseball Latins have, of course, adjusted completely to the native ways and comport themselves with all the seemliness of a young man assigned to a swivel chair in Wall Street. But happily, there were a number of lads from the Caribbean who brought with them the appetite that first led them into the game when there was only one baseball among two dozen of them. The Pittsburgh club, which seems to make Latins most welcome, carries one of the happiest souls from under the subtropical sun—Manny Sanguillen, a native of the Republic of Panama, fastest-running catcher in the game, and now apparently destined to be Clemente's successor in right field. Manny Sanguillen finds it hard to believe that Roberto is really dead. "I dream of diving for his body," he says. "Diving and diving and diving."

Sanguillen relishes the joy of clouting a moving baseball to such an extent that he will almost never let a pitch go by if he can reach it. He grins happily if he gets good wood on the ball and even chuckles when he misses it, because it feels so good to swing. An incurable first-ball hitter, Manny received only six bases on balls in 1971, one walk in every 89 times at bat. (Another Latin, Tony Oliva, the 1971 batting champion in the American League, received 25 walks—about one in every 20 times at bat. Bill Dickey, in his best year, 1936, when he hit .362, walked 46 times—about once in nine at-bats.)

There are league managers who deplore all horseplay or any public illustration that the game of baseball is fun. And often, indeed, fans can be turned off by merry clowning when the home club has just blown a ball game. But open celebration of victory, or even a mighty hit, helps remind everyone that the game is essentially for enjoyment. The Pittsburgh Pirates, when they win a big game, whoop it up like happy boys. And the Latins lead all the rest in exhibiting their delight.

Pittsburgh, one of the few clubs in baseball where no conscious effort is made to keep "them" from outnumbering "us" on the roster, is the only major league club so far ever to field an all-black nine. It is also the club on which hitting is supreme, and so it offers the most satisfaction to its fans. In beating the unbeatable Baltimore Orioles in 1971, the Pirates relied largely on pitcher Steve Blass, who had won only 15 games during the regular season, while losing 8, and had completed only 12 of the 33 games he started. Steve was second-best on the staff in number of victories; Dock Ellis had won 19. Matching this pair against the Orioles' staff of four 20-game winners and one who had won 19 seemed like playing the freshmen against the varsity. Jimmy the Greek, the deity who sets the national gambling odds, thought so, for he proclaimed the Orioles almost 2 to 1 favorites to take the Series.

The first two games of the Series, played in Baltimore, merely underlined the odds. One or two sportswriters even suggested that the Pirates would do well to stay home from the ballpark, while one merry soul predicted "The Orioles in three!" For the Orioles, after treating the Pirates to three runs in the third inning of the first game, choked them off without another hit and beat them about the head and ears with home runs by Frank Robinson, Don Buford, and Merv Rettenmund. Then, in the second game, the Orioles produced an old-fashioned "laugher," with 14 singles off six Pirate pitchers that resulted in 11 runs. "This," said one columnist,

Roberto Clemente, his eyes still sighting the spot where bat met ball, drove this pitch by Baltimore Jim Palmer into the far outfield for a triple. Next time up he hit a home run. World Series, 1971.

"is no longer a contest, it's an atrocity."

At home, however, the Pirates, with Steve Blass pitching the entire game, suddenly took on the appearance of a major league baseball club. Even the things they did wrong turned out right as they brought an end to the Orioles' 16-game winning streak (eleven at the end of the season, three in the play-offs, two in the World Series). When Bob Robertson, ordered to bunt in the seventh inning to advance the two base runners, missed the bunt sign, he drove the ball out of the park instead and gave

Steve Blass more runs than he needed to win, for Steve allowed the mighty Birds but three hits and struck out eight. And in the second game at home—the first night game ever played in the World Series—the Pirates squeezed out the victory despite a "lost" home run—a long drive by Clemente that hooked around the foul pole to land in "foul" territory outside the playing field and so was called a foul. In the fifth game the Baltimore club began to look as if it had got into the Series by mistake. They found it impossible to score a run off Nelson Briles, a pitcher who had won only eight games all season. And they collected only two hits. They also tossed in an error by Brooks Robinson, for a total of five errors in the three games played on foreign soil.

Danny Murtaugh, ailing Pittsburgh manager, had used five different starters in the first five games, while the Orioles had started McNally twice. For the sixth game Danny came up with a sixth starter—Bob Moose, one of four "Bobs" on the pitching roster and a winner of eleven games during the regular season, mostly as a "long" reliever. The Orioles began with Jim Palmer, who had won game number two. Palmer won this one as well, to keep the Orioles respectable. But by this time, even the Baltimore fans had begun to suspect that the Orioles were dead. Even while losing, the Pirates had looked like winners, with Clemente hitting a home run and a triple and the Birds scratching out the victory by means of a wild dash home by Frank Robinson on a short sacrifice fly.

Danny Murtaugh made the World Championship certain by letting Steve Blass pitch another game. Steve won the seventh by granting the Orioles but four hits and one run. Roberto Clemente had already matched that run with a homer, and José Pagan, who had been playing big league baseball for thirteen seasons and had been in the game for money for five years more than that, won the championship with a long double to center field that permitted Willie Stargell to score from first base.

The bliss and brotherhood engendered on the Pirate club by the sweetness of this come-from-behind victory was not exactly endemic to professional baseball in the 1970s. Indeed, it seemed for a time that hard feelings, rebellion, bitter personal feuds, and litigation would turn the Great Game into a free-for-all in which every man was out to do dirt to his neighbor. Much of the hard feeling developed between owner and player, as the Major League Baseball Players' Association exhibited unexpected strength and began to demand a better deal just as if it was the players' due.

The Association had been set up, or at least reestablished, in the 1960s as a company union, or at least as a thoroughly domesticated beast that would be led by one Robert Cannon, a Milwaukee judge who had been serving as the "volunteer" counsel for the organization of players (actually, he received $15,000 in advance each year as "expenses"). In secret meetings attended only by Cannon, by counsel for the club owners, by the part-time director of the Association, and by one or two player-representatives who had exhibited a proper concern for the owners' interests, a plan had been drawn up to finance an office, with a full-time, salaried director, and to assure constant "cooperation" between Cannon and the owners. The director's salary and expenses were to be paid for out of the pension fund—money derived largely from All-Star Game income and player contributions.

This cozy scheme blew higher than Killian's kite when Judge Cannon, with the instincts of a club owner, insisted that the Association office be moved to Chicago (where he could make the scene without having to move his home or abandon his sources of side income) and that he be guaranteed a fat pension. The players, who had been docile enough up to now, were repelled by this and voted the deal down, deciding instead to hire their own director from among several applicants, none of whom could be described as a *persona* thoroughly *grata* among the club owners. As a result, the carefully conceived plan turned on its conceivers and like to have eaten them up, for they had laid out a perfect blueprint for a fully blown union that could be immediately financed out of available funds and be ready for business overnight. There was much frantic scurrying in and out of the commissioner's office as the schemers tried to unravel their scheme. They grew especially frantic when it became clear that the most likely candidate for office of director was one Marvin Miller, a bright and knowledgeable fellow who had learned his grammar as an employee of the United Steel Workers.

Desperately the conspirators endeavored to board up the windows they had just opened. The commissioner, pretending a sudden coincidental access of benevolence, suggested to the owners that they halt the players' contributions to the fund and make all contributions themselves. Then, one noted, the money would be "management money" and so ineligible, under labor laws, for use in financing a union. But, to make a long and sordid story short and clean, the players promptly voted to kick in the necessary funds through a check-off system, elected Miller to the job, and began at once to gird themselves for battle.

After a few skirmishes the major battle was joined in 1972 when, for the first time since the Great Brotherhood Rebellion of 1890, the baseball players walked out in a body and refused to report for duty until their demands (which were modest, indeed) had been met. The owners, who had provoked the strike by refusing to accept the figures of their own actuary proving the pension demands could be easily granted, sat smugly down and waited for the players to chuck Marvin Miller into the street and return as penitents to endorse Judge Cannon, or his like, as their future leader.

The players, however, proved even more militant than Miller. Despite the confident predictions of several highly paid (and unionized) sportswriters who bemoaned the "greed" of highly paid athletes, the players *did* stay out on strike and sacrificed real money to make their point.

This indication that the players were not going to purchase the notion, earnestly vended by club owners, sportswriters, and hired publicists, that Miller was really the players' enemy, went down some throats only after much choking and writhing. A few of the owners, loudly averring that they had "had it" with Miller, were all for canceling out the entire season to teach the hired help a lesson. But there were few indeed among the owners who could stifle their own devotion to a ten-dollar bill for that length of time and ultimately, after the chilliest part of the overlong season was done with, play resumed. The schedule was shortened, salaries were proportionately docked, and public relations men were set to dreaming up imaginary quotes from Marvin Miller such as, "I stuck out my neck for you, now it's up to you to stick yours out for me!" The fact that no such idiotic charge ever issued from Miller's lips, and that his own salary ceased the moment the strike began was noted in few places but remembered in none.

Bitterness between individual owners and players bubbled spasmodically

Dick (Don't call me Richie) Allen, once Philadelphia's bad boy and now Chicago's best, shows some admirers how to drive a baseball a long distance. Chicago, 1972.

through this era, much of it prompted by the pervasive and unacknowledged race prejudice that helped make the lots of blacks and Latin players miserable. There was not a club owner or manager in the game who would admit to the mildest sort of bias against blacks or Latins. But in the deceptive coziness of impromptu "press conferences," there were one or two of the baseball brass who would bemoan the fact that this or that ballpark was "in the middle of jigtown" or snarl that "some nigger's funeral" (i.e., that of Martin Luther King) had disrupted the schedule. And nowhere in the lily-white echelons of the league offices was there ever any acknowledgment of the fact that black players, despite fat salaries and even-handed treatment in the clubhouse, still had special obstacles to overcome and humiliations to cope with, such as white players knew not of. Even getting a haircut in spring training might require a morning's travel for a black man. Latins were expected to join the laughter when their mispronunciations were made fun of. And black outfielders in some cities, from having to range so close to the fans, often had to learn to close their ears to racially flavored obscenities and dodge small missiles.

Richie Allen of Philadelphia ("Don't call me Richie," he will say, "it reminds me of Philadelphia") earned a reputation for being hard to handle because of his special sensitivity to racial abuse. Allen is anything but the white man's ideal of a thoroughly tamed and unobtrusive Negro. In his independence, his urge to sell his services for the top dollar, his occasionally reckless off-diamond behavior, and his respect for his own skills, he is the equal of most white stars. But when he

played minor league baseball in Little Rock, he was the first black ballplayer to appear on that roster. Allen thought he should have been brought straight up to the big club, after hitting .317 and .329 in Williamsport. Instead, he was sent for extra "seasoning" into Faubus-land, and the hazing he received almost ended his career. "Nigger-go-home" signs on his windshield were the least of it. There were obscene telephone calls after midnight, threats of death and disfigurement, and a bombardment of epithets on the field. There was not a decent restaurant in town that would serve him.

Allen lived through it, dreaming of the big money ahead, and came to Philadelphia at the age of twenty-one, hungry, like many another highly paid youth, to savor big-city temptations. Despite his unabashed addiction to the fleshpots and his intense involvement in the handicapping of racehorses (a Rogers Hornsby weakness) Allen was all baseball at the park. He batted .318 his first full year and led the league in runs scored. (He also led in strikeouts, a habit that earned him a persistent following of hecklers.) Allen disliked spring training, dodged out of batting practice to escape the boss, and sometimes was to be discovered at a Florida racetrack when his teammates were dutifully sweating themselves into condition at the training camp. He kept on batting .300 or better, however, and in 1966, hit 40 home runs. Even this sort of performance was not enough to make the Phillie fans forgive him, for they sensed in Allen something less than the grim devotion to the well-being of the ball club that fans expect in a highly paid player. As a result, Allen had to take to wearing his batting helmet at all times to avoid being skulled by some heavy object. Rocks were tossed through his window at night, and his lawn was deliberately cut into tire tracks. Fans even followed him down the streets to call him names.

Allen responded by devoting less and less of his time to the interests of his employer, sometimes "disappearing" completely when he was wanted at the park. He acted this way, he said, so he would be traded. Local sportswriters said he was a damned liar, that he just faked injuries or went into hiding to escape work. But Allen had his way finally, and he was shipped to St. Louis, where he thought he had found a permanent home. But Allen's reputation followed him, and despite 34 home runs and 101 runs batted in, he was quickly shipped off to the Dodgers. In Los Angeles he was, he declared, made less welcome than a hijacker. Manager Alston apparently could make little room for Allen in his heart. There was even a rumor that Alston would quit baseball if he had to keep Allen in his club. (The Cardinals had described the shipping-out of Allen as a means of "improving team morale.") But Alston signed a new contract, and Allen stayed—and found that Dodger morale had pretty well disintegrated before he got there. Nobody, he recalled, ever talked baseball in the locker room, what with all the guys who were trying to be actors or hot rock musicians. And Richie was ready to quit the game for good when he was swapped at last to the Chicago White Sox.

In Chicago he became Dick Allen, a team leader despite his apparently having scabbed on the strike by signing his contract just as all the other players were walking out. His appearance at the park provoked wild enthusiasm among the fans, this in spite of the fact that he stayed out of training camp to "think about his future." (His private belief is that spring training is too long anyway, far more than a hitter needs. And he stays near top condition the year around, despite his unconcealed devotion to the grape, or its distillate. He never, he insists, drank as much as people said he did. Certainly his trim and solid body is not that of a sensualist.)

Dick Allen, in 1972, earned every dollar of his more-than-$100,000 salary by leading the league in home runs (37) and in runs batted in (113), finishing third in batting average (.308), coming in fourth in runs scored (90), and earning the Most Valuable Player title. There was not even a whisper in Chicago of letting Dick Allen go anywhere else. His employer, foreseeing a lifetime for Allen in Chicago, vowed that he would go "right from the White Sox into the Hall of Fame." But wherever he went when his career was over, Dick Allen knew for sure it would not be Philadelphia.

Perhaps the most bizarre of the several minor rebellions and altercations that marked the early 1970s was the off-and-on flouting of authority that grew out of the emotional difficulties of Alex Johnson, outfielder of the California Angels. Johnson's troubles began in the early spring, when he was reprimanded or fined so many times that the club nearly lost count—some 35 times, at least—without in the smallest degree diverting him from the course of what his defenders named his eccentricities. He was accused generally of not giving his best efforts to the club, of failing to run out ground balls, of

Federal mediator J. Curtis Counts is calling for peace between John Gaherin (left), attorney for the club owners, and Marvin Miller (right), executive director of the Major League Baseball Players' Association, during the players' strike in 1972. Miller won his major points.

ignoring fly balls that came within his range, and of proceeding from base to base at a rate of speed far below his capacity. He was also found guilty of carrying his bat with him wherever he chanced to roam on the practice field (once he hitched it to his belt as he ran laps around the park), and of taking an improper position in the outfield during a game at Yuma, Arizona.

Alex explained that he carried his bat because a newspaper guy from Los Angeles had hidden it on him once for a joke. (Alex retaliated by putting coffee grounds in the man's typewriter, but the reporter did not lug *that* with him when he wandered the field.) As for Yuma, Alex said all he did was stay in a narrow strip of shadow cast by a nearby structure—the *only* shade on the field, in a place where only mad dogs and club owners went out in the midday sun.

Eventually, after a teammate allowed that Alex had "pulled a gun" on him in the locker room, Alex was suspended. And when his suspension ran out (thirty days is the maximum permitted under the players' agreement), he was put on the "restricted list," so that his pay could still be withheld. At this point the Players' Association stepped in. The restricted list was meant only for men who failed to report, and its use to keep a player bound to his club without paying him and merely for disciplinary purposes was too obvious a dodge. The matter was submitted to arbitration: it was brought out that Johnson's behavior had not been affected in any way by the attempts at discipline and that most observers had known almost from the start that the lad was not himself. Alex had always had his own way of doing things, such as refusing to accept congratulations for a home run. ("Don't congratulate me for doing what I'm paid for," he would say.) But his recent behavior had been indicative of mood swings far more marked than normal. The arbitrator, to his own credit, and the dismay of the management, ruled that a sick man was sick, whether his ailment were physical or emotional, and that Johnson had his salary coming to him. Two or three white players in the history of the modern game had been subject to emotional breakdowns, and they had been tenderly treated by management (although not always by fans), even to the extent of being hospitalized at the owner's expense. But this new ruling established the fact that black players, too, were entitled to emotional disturbances and that they were not necessarily recalcitrant, stubborn, lazy, ungrateful, mutinous, or "crazy-acting" by nature. So the Alex Johnson case might be rated a milestone in the tedious process of educating white club owners in the uses of the real world.

The Johnson case also underlined the strength of the Players' Association and the importance of the new grievance machinery it had fought to create. But it also strengthened the resolve of one or two club owners to rid themselves of Marvin Miller and his cohorts as rapidly as might be. In this, they had the earnest, and sometimes uninformed cooperation of a number of widely read sportswriters. These writers made Miller out to be a self-seeking, power-drunk labor faker, who had disrupted the cozy father-son relationship that had so long rendered owner-player relationships in professional baseball so fragrant. Among the ballplayers, however, Miller's popularity had taken such deep root that not all baseball's money nor all of its hired men could unfasten it. And when the 1972 season ended, negotiations were beginning on the fateful reserve rule that had been the key provision in the standard contract since Ty Cobb was slicing up second basemen.

The Supreme Court had helped create a sort of dreamworld or fools' paradise in which the club owners slumbered. In a confused and confusing decision, featuring some of the most fatuous prose ever to emanate from that high bench, the Nixon Court ruled that, even though the law was being violated by baseball, the violations were of such long standing that it would be vain to try to correct them now. And so baseball's club owners tucked themselves back into bed and smiled as visions of television contracts danced in their heads.

Meanwhile, Congress had set to work on a law to permit basketball to merge itself into one under certain restrictions, most notable of which was a provision limiting the length of time that a club could "reserve" the services of a player who had not signed a contract. The limit was one year. And lower courts elsewhere seemed inclined to put some time limit on the length of reservation, so there were strong signs that the reserve clause might be "interpreted" out of existence while the owners clung pathetically to a Supreme Court decision that said vice was virtue if it had been ripening long enough.

Over the Hill
to the Gold Mine

SURELY the season of 1972 was the year of the has-been, the cast-off, the dispossessed, and the forgotten—in professional baseball, that is. A pitcher whose "best days" were far behind him, an outfielder who had been deemed "too old" a season or two before, an infielder old enough to be the batboy's father, another pitcher who had been "at his best" with a far-off club in a different league four years earlier, a left-hander who had been consigned to a cellar team to wind up his days far from the scenes of his glory, another left-hander who had been waived out of the league he had started in, a veteran shortstop who had worn out his welcome in Texas, and a giant

first baseman who was playing his fifteenth season in the league and had been given up on by his previous manager—all these won banner headlines in 1972 with deeds beyond the reach of most men or records thought impossible for them to attain. A few of them even combined to win a divisional championship for the Detroit Tigers, who had been deemed dead before the season was well begun. And the cast-off and forgotten pitcher Luis Tiant came close to bringing in the Red Sox first of six in the East, and *they* had not even been counted in the spring reckoning.

Ultimately, however, it was youth that came in first. The best club in baseball, the Pittsburgh Pirates (named

281

According to Detroit Manager Billy Martin and Baseball Commissioner Bowie Kuhn, when Oakland batter Bert Campaneris in the 1972 play-offs threw his bat at Detroit pitcher Lerrin LaGrow, forcing LaGrow to duck in this manner, Campaneris was guilty of the most dastardly crime in the history of the game. Kuhn promptly suspended Campaneris for thirty days (later reduced to seven). But in the Federal League fifty-eight years before, Chicago pitcher Ad Brennan slung his bat in anger at Brooklyn pitcher Ed LaFitte. LaFitte was not hit, the umpire kept peace, and no one was suspended. Likewise when Detroit hero Ty Cobb, in the 1916 American League pennant race, threw his bat at Boston pitcher Carl Mays (and missed), there were no suspensions and no fulminations in the press.

Vida Blue refused to change his middle name to True, even though his boss, Oakland club owner Charles O. Finley, offered extra inducements. But he looked like the best pitcher in baseball in 1971.

best by manager Sparky Anderson of the Cincinnati Reds, who beat them out of the National League pennant) missed the World Series by the width of a wild pitch. In the redundant and overextended play-offs, invented to invest the game with extra days of World Series excitement and World Series gate receipts, the Pirates, who had outrun their "division" by several leagues, were paired with the Reds, who had surprised themselves by struggling to the top of their own division and staying there.

What the Reds had that Pittsburgh could not match was mostly speed —speed in the feet of their base runners and speed in the outfield. But the Pirates owned some fast feet, too, notably the pair belonging to catcher Manny Sanguillen, along with bats heavy enough to make base stealing irrelevant. But the Reds had a man who ran at top speed to first base on a base on balls—Pete Rose—and another man —Joe Morgan—who had a base-stealing glove he put on whenever he reached first base. And they, too, had catcher Johnny Bench, who was not above stealing a base when the pitcher let him get a start. They also owned confidence, good luck, and a young pitcher named Grimsley who came into the play-offs "itching to pitch," after having started the season with the farm club in Indianapolis, where he threatened to quit baseball for good. Grimsley also snarled a little at having to "sit around" until the fourth play-off game before being given a start. But when he came to work in the do-or-die game—number four—with the Pirates ready to grab the pennant in one smashing victory, Grimsley was more than ready. He pitched one of the best games of the whole season, throwing just 84

pitches at Pirate batters, allowing them two hits, one run, and never a chance to come in first. He struck out five and did not walk anybody.

Still, it took Pirate pitcher Bob Moose to grant the pennant to the Reds. Moose was not a wild man by any means. In 1971 he had allowed only 35 unintentional bases on balls. (San Diego had *two* pitchers who allowed 103 apiece, and Montreal had a man who gave up 146.) He had not even put the runner on base who came in to score. Moose entered the game in the ninth in relief of Dave Giusti, who had given up a homer to Johnny Bench and a single to Tony Perez. Sparky Anderson sent George Foster in to run for Tony Perez and urged Dennis Menke to push George on to second with a bunt. Dennis tried twice and missed. So he advanced George with a single.

Then Bob Moose took over. He put Geronimo out on a long fly. Foster took third after the catch. Moose then persuaded Darrel Chaney to pop out. Hal McRae then came to bat. Moose, preparing a special dish in the presence of his enemies, made ready to feed McRae a curve. He made a little too ready, for he pulled down too much and bounced the ball on the ground in front of the plate. The moment the ball skipped out of reach of catcher Manny Sanguillen, McRae took off straight into the air like a spring-bok—a leap of ecstatic joy such as has become the standard gesture in sports to illustrate a triumph. Sparky Anderson rushed out of the dugout and greeted run-scoring George Foster by grabbing him around the ears to hold him close, just as if George had opened the road to victory by some deed of his own, other than trotting from base to base as opportunity knocked.

In the other league, the lesser one,

This bit of Boston ballet was not choreographed by George Balanchine. It was entirely impromptu as John Briggs of the Milwaukee Brewers slid into second; Red Sox shortstop Luis Aparicio made one out and threw to first for a second out; second baseman Doug Griffin backed up Aparicio, and umpire Larry McCoy signalled the out at second. Aparicio's feet are high off the ground in his own version of a pas de deux.

according to all who were learned enough to judge such matters, the play-offs were marked by moments even more weird and portentous. These play-offs, too, stretched through the full five games, pushing the season deep into the chilly end of the month, so that men gave silent thanks the World Championship games would not involve Boston, or Minnesota, or God help us—Montreal! In those towns when World Series time came around, the nights were cold enough to freeze the puddles in the dugout solid or burst a bottle of Pepsi-Cola.

Most memorable of all the dire and disgraceful deeds that marked the American League play-offs was the flinging of a bat by a struck batter at the man who pitched the ball that struck him. In baseball since before your Uncle Pete was old enough to buy his own beer, batters had flung bats at pitchers who hit them or nearly hit them with pitched balls. But the flinging was always, by tradition ''accidental''—as was the thorough carving up of a pitcher on the baseline, after he had been drawn into range of the runner's spikes by a deliberately placed bunt. That is, the batter would swing hard at a pitch and "accidentally" let go the bat at the end of the swing, so that it rocketed out, like a flung mace, toward the head of the enemy or toward his tender shins. To kneel on the ground, however, as Bert Campaneris of Oakland did, to seize the bat by the knob in one hand, and to take good aim and then to let the weapon fly at the head of the pitcher—that, according to Billy Martin, Detroit manager, a man thoroughly grounded in deeds that were vain and ways that were rowdy, was the part of a sniveling coward, a man too craven to share the earth with Billy and his boy athletes. But Campaneris had not learned that one must never let the left hand know what the right hand was throwing. To Bert, throwing a baseball at a man or throwing a bat at a man were deeds equally dark or equally valorous, depending on one's loyalties. "I did not try to hit the pitcher," he vowed, "just warn him what might happen." And the pitcher, a man named Lerrin LaGrow, vowed that for *his* part he had never meant to damage Bert's ankle at all. The Commissioner of Baseball, however, was sufficiently outraged to remove Campaneris from the play-offs and promised to keep him off the diamond for the first thirty days of 1973. American League President Joe Cronin, a man who always liked to temper the wind to the shorn lamb or unshorn ballplayer, talked the commissioner into lowering the term to seven days.

Another strange aspect of the American League play-offs and one that persisted to bemuse the huddled masses at the World Series games was the manner in which Dick Williams, leader of the Oakland Athletics, shuttled second basemen in and out, so that he might use as many as three pinch hitters in the game without having to reach into his meager cupboard for an extra pitcher. It looked for a time as if everyone on that club must play second base. And one time, when he had a catcher playing the position and the catcher dropped a wide throw that a seasoned second baseman could have caught in his sleep, Williams may have had a moment of doubt. But he never owned up to it and kept right on "overmanaging" to the open delight of his cheerleading club owner and the hometown fans.

Charlie Finley, the Oakland club owner, in the fight for the championship after years of frustration, was perhaps the first self-made man since Chris von der Ahe of St. Louis to operate a baseball club strictly as an ego trip. Finley interfered almost openly in strategy and in trades, and, with an Oakland pennant in either hand, led the cheers for his club as it stumbled and scrambled toward the championship. When Campaneris was suspended, Finley invited Bert to come sit beside him in his box right next to the Oakland dugout, inasmuch as the league president would not permit the player to sit on the bench. (Finley's wife, one supposes, would have had to move back one seat.) President Cronin dissuaded Finley from this provocative move, presumably on the grounds that Detroit fans might be prompted to do Campaneris injury.

When Finley's prize pitcher, Vida Blue, Cy Young Award winner in his

Catfish Hunter of Oakland, sporting the whiskers that owner Charles Finley paid him to grow, serves a home run to Cincinnati batter Pete Rose in the 1972 World Series.

lasted well into the season) and disaffected ballplayer. But he had had his way. And his way, he was persuaded, led on to victory.

Victory was hard to come by in the play-offs, thanks largely to the inability of a part-time second baseman to hold on to that low throw. But Vida Blue, after an unsuccessful season, showed up as a relief pitcher in the final game and threw nothing but sizzling strikes. This game, like the others, was replete with unseemly events, including John (Blue Moon) Odom's sudden attack of nausea, after he had allowed Detroit only two singles in five innings. ("The pressure got to me," said John.) But his leaving the game just meant that Detroit had to face the fastest pitcher in the league, and they could not come close to scoring on him.

Still, Detroit fans and players went home feeling they had been robbed by umpire John Rice, who called Oakland's substitute shortstop, Dick McAuliffe, safe at first when the throw had clearly beaten him. Norm Cash, the Detroit first baseman, had taken his foot off the base, said Rice. First basemen frequently take the tagging foot off the base on a routine play before the ball gets there and no one complains. But on a close play they have to keep contact. Big Frank Howard, Detroit's imported substitute first baseman, acting as first base coach, argued this point at great length with the umpire. "They *never* call the man safe on that play," Frank bellowed. "It's automatic! He's out!" John Rice soon had enough of that talk and directed Howard to remove himself from the playing field altogether. "In 150 years," Frank growled, "they've *never* called the runner safe." Well, 150 years earlier,

first full year in the majors, held out for a salary commensurate with his skills, Finley balked and refused a compromise, apparently less to save money than to show Blue who was boss. (He had previously asked Blue to change his middle name to "True" to make him a sort of sideshow attraction. There were observers who doubted that Finley would have made such an outrageous request of a white man.) After the struggle was over, Finley wound up with a poorly conditioned (the holdout you would have had to hit the runner with the ball to make him out, so Frank may have been right. As for Norm Cash, the first baseman involved, he allowed that he kept his foot on the base, risking a spiking, longer than any other man in the game. "I *never* cheat unless I have to," he vowed. The umpire decided that this time Norm did not have to.

The outcome, therefore, remained Oakland 2, Detroit 1, and Oakland had won the right to go out and subject itself to decimation by the Reds, chosen by all pollsters to win the World Series handily.

But the pollsters and pundits had made no account of the weather or the season or the fact that the first two games were going to be played on a living-room carpet built to look like grass and clay. The paving-like substance that covered the infield in Cincinnati caused balls to rocket away as if they had landed on concrete and moved infielders to play part way into the outfield, lest they be decapitated by a daisy-cutter. This, presumably, offered extra aid to the Reds, whose Mercury-footed base runners were thus given extra time to beat long throws to the bases. But Oakland had wing-footed ballplayers, too, including one "pinch runner" called the Panamanian Express, who had been added to the roster *only* because he could run. And the Oakland pitchers solved the problem of coping with rapid base runners by just not allowing any of the Cincinnati hotshots to set foot on the baselines. As a result, Johnny Bench, the cleanup batter who was wont to drive men home from first base with any sort of safe hit, found no one awaiting him on the bases when he stepped

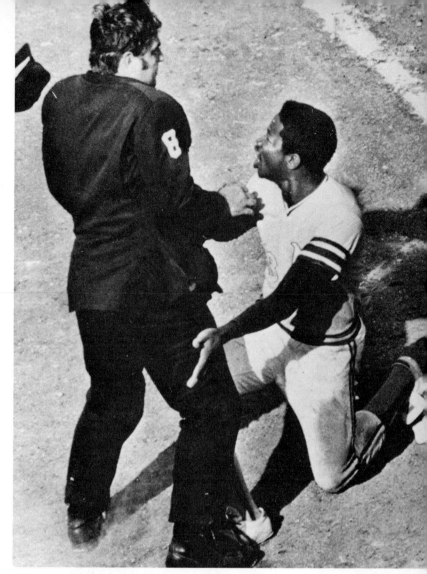

Oakland pitcher Blue Moon Odom, thrown out when attempting to score on a very short foul fly, did not really mean to knock umpire Bob Engel's hat off. He just did not realize the man was so close. World Series, 1972.

to the plate in the first two games. Not Joe Morgan, the man who wore a base-running glove, nor Pete Rose, who started his running the moment he received ball four, nor Bobby Tolan, who figured he was on second base any time he reached first; ever made it to scoring position. Four times in the first game big John led off an inning, facing empty bases because pitcher Ken Holtzman had set down numbers one, two, and three without harm.

In the second game the Oakland neck

More than one observer called this the greatest catch ever made. Oakland left fielder Joe Rudi hung himself on the wall in Cincinnati to grab this fly by Denis Manke of the Reds in the 1972 World Series. But Joe said he had made a better catch in Baltimore.

was saved by a regular World Series-style catch in the outfield (''greater than the catch by Gionfriddo'' and ''the greatest catch ever seen'' according to biased observers) when left fielder Joe Rudi of Oakland seemed to suspend himself four feet off the ground, one hand against the fence, and the gloved hand, turned backward, placed just right to snare a certain extra-base blow by Dennis Menke. (Rudi suggested later that his catch of a fly ball off the bat of Terry Crowley of Baltimore might have been a better one.)

Oakland, then, before anyone had had a chance to reappraise the line-ups, had a 2 to 0 lead in the Series. And *no* ball club had ever lost the first two games in its home park and gone on to win a seven-game Series. And yet Sparky Anderson, dauntless, set the slughorn to his lips and proclaimed that the Series would go seven games and his Reds would win. That may have been before he got a look at the ballfield in Oakland, fashioned as it was of a strange substance called sod, which absorbed rainwater and held on to it. And it had rained in Oakland three whole days together and seemed like to rain three more. The crowd turned out for the first game nonetheless with the rain still falling and a treacherous rainbow in the sky. And it was not until the commissioner himself, with his blue-clad retinue, had walked almost ankle-deep through gathered rain and declared it wet that the players gave up and went home.

It was still wet when the third game was finally played. It was also dark, for the game was played at night. Not the night that you and I know but television night, which is twilight on the West Coast and only black-dark in the East, where the advertising budgets bloom under the stars. In the twilight batters had one hell of a time seeing the baseball, with the result that people who never did such things kept striking out. The Oaklands, led by a relief pitcher with the typical Dick Tracy comic-strip name of Rollie Fingers and a catcher with the front name of Fury, fought valiantly to put the Reds down three to nothing. But Fury, who had hit two home runs in the first two games (he had hit only five all season) could hit none in game three, and instead, threw the game away with a wild heave into center field trying to nail a Red base runner. Rollie Fingers, whose $300 moustache gave him the look of a riverboat gambler, contrived a trick deal on Johnny Bench that struck Johnny out but could not win the game. In true sandlot (or riverboat) style, Rollie gave a broad acknowledgment of his manager's "put him on" gesture as he faced Bench with the count three balls and two strikes. Fury Gene Tenace (his name would have been Tenacci, but his family had changed it long before to make it sound like "tennis") held his right hand out at full arm's length in the intentional-walk pose. Then Fingers tucked a quick slider right into the strike zone, and Johnny Bench, after a grimace of disgust, made his way to the bench.

But even that trick could not score runs for Oakland, what with Jack Billingham striking squinting batters out right and left; Mike Epstein, the Oakland first baseman, having to aim a toss at nobody in the fifth inning; and Bert Campaneris, the rehabilitated Oakland shortstop, never noticing that the man who carried the winning run in his feet had fallen flat on his face on the wet grass outside the third-base line. In keeping with the whole proceedings,

this third game, which the Reds won, 1 to 0, opened with a wild pitch—by California Governor Ronald Reagan who, putting on a real he-man show for the television cameras, heaved the first ball far over Gene Tenace's head and had to run a retake.

Game number four also was played in the dusk, by authority of NBC. This game was won by the manager of the A's, who filled the park full of pinch hitters in the ninth inning and saw them all hit safely. He had help from the old-time vaudeville act of Fingers and Fury once more, with Tenace sending another home run into the suburbs to put the A's ahead in the beginning and Fingers mopping up in the final inning after Vida Blue had let the Reds get a run ahead.

The fifth game, beginning at sunset again, was relatively free of freak plays and devious machinations, but the two managers, in a game that lasted two and a half hours, used 38 players between them in trying to outthink each other. The home run hitters did all the scoring to begin with, Pete Rose losing a ball for the Reds and Fury Gene Tenace driving in three runs with his fourth home run of the Series—a mark set and tied years ago by some of the game's most renowned sluggers. This time, however, the one-two-three men in the Cincinnati batting order performed as they were paid to, so that there were runs for the taking. And Catfish Hunter and Rollie Fingers between them could not stay the Red huntsmen. In keeping with the general tone of the Series, a spell did seem to settle on the A's that helped do them down. Rollie Fingers, for example, craftily conspiring to turn a pop bunt into a double play trapped the ball, instead of catching it, so that the runner on first would be an easy out at second. But then, seized by God-knows-what petty dementia, Fingers picked up the ball and nervously threw it neither to first nor to second but somewhere in between, so that Geronimo, who was to score the winning run, advanced easily to second base just as the batter had intended.

The final out, too, had a Little League flavor, with Blue Moon Odom, abandoning the safety of third base, attempting to score on a short pop foul to second baseman Joe Morgan. Joe Morgan, not being blind to the goings-on 110 feet away, managed, despite a slip on the soggy turf, to get off a throw that reached catcher Johnny Bench in plenty of time. Bench had Odom completely blocked off from the plate with one solidly planted knee. He had to reach down to tag him, but the umpire decreed that the tag had been made before Odom could battle his way through the block. Odom did not think so, and he stumbled wildly to his feet, staggering right into the umpire as he howled in protest. Umpire Bob Engel, like all the umpires throughout this Series, was a model of cool deportment; he merely walked off, unperturbed and unpersuaded.

It began to look as if the A's could win ball games at home only if the lights were out, and Anderson's quiet prediction gave some men to wonder: Would *this* be the time that a team lost its first two at home and still won the Series? The sixth game, in which the Reds broke loose at last with long blows and scary baserunning indicated that this might indeed be the year that would set old men to mumbling for centuries to come. For this was the only game of the lot that showed more than a one-run difference in the scores of winner and loser. The Reds scored six more

runs than they needed in this game, making it, in the sports lexicon, a laugher. Nobody on the Oakland bench, nor in the Finley box, was laughing. The Cincinnati top three got on base six times, stole two bases, and scored four of the eight runs. The Oaklands scored just once.

Vida Blue, simmering with anger over not being slated to start a game (he had refused even to join in the general rejoicing when the pennant was won), got his start and his finish in this game. Weary as he must have been from too much going to the relief of other weary pitchers, Vida did not make it to the end. He granted but four hits and three of the eight runs, but he got the official blame for the defeat. Vida kept the ball low, as he was supposed to. But some of the sizzle was gone from his fast ball, and Johnny Bench, who can deal with a low pitch as well as any man alive, picked one off his knees and put it in the stands, just as his mother had kept urging him to do. After Vida had been replaced, the Reds sent the whole club to bat in one inning and wound up with five more runs, on four hits and three walks. There was nothing freakish at all about the scoring, just solid hitting and fast running. There was a bit of overmanaging, as usual, when Dick Williams changed pinch hitters before the first guy had had a chance to swing. But this time Dick's genie refused to come out of the bottle, and the second pinch hitter, catcher Dave Duncan, struck out.

Aside from the wintry temperature in which it was played—and the fact that NBC had not allowed the clubs a day for traveling, and so Blue had to pitch without the rest he needed—the only truly weird aspect of the game was the arrest, outside of the park of a man with a loaded gun. He was out to put a hole, police said, in Gene Tenace. As it turned out, there was no need, for Tenace was no menace to anyone in this game, his only hit being a tame single that never counted. Better the man should have come around for the seventh game, when Fury Gene played first base and Dave Duncan, after a long exile, resumed his rightful spot behind the plate and began to shoot down Cincinnati base runners.

Sparky Anderson was right about the Series going seven games. But he and the odds-makers, whoever or whatever they might have been, were wrong in picking the winner. The team that had the least going for it, the club with its best pitchers already beaten, its best hitter, Reggie Jackson, on crutches, and its best second baseman not yet decided on, went ahead and won the prize anyway. They demonstrated very early what they meant to do to the Reds. When hot-foot Joe Morgan got on base, John Odom, the Oakland pitcher, threw eight times to the base to keep Joe leaning the wrong way. Then when Joe did set off he got no ''jump'' on the pitcher at all, and Dave Duncan's cannonshot beat poor Joe to second by two or three strides. Bert Campaneris brushed Joe ever so gently with the ball, the umpire punched his fist upward to indicate Joe was out, and Joe trotted meekly back to his warm spot on the bench.

Later on manager Dick Williams showed his contempt for the percentages or his respect for Johnny Bench by walking John and thus, in defiance of all decency, ''putting the winning run on base.'' The A's at the time were two runs ahead, and there were already two runners on base. But said Williams, ''I wasn't going to let Bench beat me.

Gaylord Perry of Cleveland, top pitcher in the American League in 1972, was accused of throwing a ball doctored with some greasy kid stuff, if not with spit. But no umpire could ever find a slippery substance on the ball or on Gaylord's person.

Sparky Lyle, New York Yankee reliever, favors eating tobacco over bubble gum.

Orlando Cepeda, too lame to hold down a regular job with the Atlanta Braves, found a happy home in Boston where he became the first "designated hitter" for the Red Sox, batting for the pitcher under a new rule that allowed a hitter to take the pitcher's place at bat without the pitcher having to leave the game. This rule, many observers cried, would mean "the end of baseball as we know it." Long-forgotten was the fact that Ban Johnson, president of the American League, likewise foresaw the doom of the game if the rulemakers did not put an end to the practice of pinch-hitting. That was before World War I.

I won't do it for anyone else." Perez hit a long fly to bring in one of the Cincinnati runners, but the other two died on the paths, so Oakland remained one run to the good, and the Williams' brilliance rested untarnished. And one run ahead was all Oakland needed to be.

When it was over and Sparky Anderson had used up nineteen players in search of victory and Dick Williams had cashed in his only pinch runner, Charles Finley jumped atop the Oakland dugout, screaming. He kissed his wife, and he kissed manager Dick Williams. Then he did a jig of triumph. At home plate Reggie Jackson, the A's crippled slugger who had missed out on the Series, and Johnny Bench, the Cincinnati slugger who had missed his chance to drive in all the runs his club would have needed, put their arms around each other, while each told the other how great he had been.

But the season's really great players, according to the figures, had not shown up in the World Series at all, not even on crutches. Roberto Clemente was, for all I know, home in bed. Rod Carew, of Minnesota, the best batter in the American League, was watching television in Golden Valley, Minnesota. Pitchers Wilbur Wood of the Chicago White Sox, who won 24 games; Gaylord Perry of Cleveland, who also won 24 games; Mickey Lolich of Detroit, who won 25 games; Joe Coleman of Detroit, who struck out 14 Oakland batters in a play-off game; and Steve Carlton of the Phillies, who won 27 games. All these guys were in their street clothes or their pajamas when the World Championship was decided. That was partly because the pennant winners nowadays are not decided by the standings in the championship season, but by divisional play-offs that can sometimes be decided by a bad decision, a wild bounce, an injured leg, an upset stomach, or a soggy baseline. Some of the individual champions, of course, just could not drag their clubs first across the finish line. Even so, there were more than two or three minor seers who agreed that the best clubs in the game had not met to decide the championship of the world. Even Vida Blue, who played a large hand in making Oakland best, said he thought the Pirates were better. Charlie Finley would never have agreed with him. Never, never, never.

Indeed, some people had begun to wonder if, now that Finley had proved his genius so flamboyantly, there was going to be any living with the man at all.

Index

About the Author

Robert Smith is an experienced sportswriter, sports storyteller, and author of such best-selling books as *Baseball in America, Baseball's Hall of Fame, Baseball, How the Pros Play Football* (with Bill Dudley), *The Great Teams of Pro Football, Pro Football,* and *Illustrated History of Pro Football.* In addition, he has worked in collaboration with some of baseball's most famous names: Hank Bauer, Willie Mays, Mickey Mantle, and Jim Bunning, and he has maintained close connections with many well-known players, coaches, and sportswriters thoughout the years. In the past, Mr. Smith has coached a prep school baseball team and has managed a semiprofessional baseball team. Born in Boston, he now owns homes in Maine, Massachusetts, and New York, which he shares with his wife, ten cats, and two dogs.